REPORTING AND
PRODUCING FOR
DIGITAL MEDIA

Other Titles in the Media and Technology Series:

REPORTING AND PRODUCING FOR DIGITAL MEDIA

Claudette Guzan Artwick

Media and Technology Series
Alan B. Albarran, Series Editor

Blackwell
Publishing

Media and Technology
A Blackwell Publishing Series

Claudette Guzan Artwick, Ph.D., is Associate Professor of Journalism in the Department of Journalism and Mass Communications at Washington and Lee University in Lexington, Virginia. There she heads the Rockbridge Report, a digital news lab in which students in broadcast, print, and mass communication courses produce a Web site and television news program. In addition to her academic teaching and research experience, she has served numerous television stations in writing, reporting, research, and technical capacities.

©2004 Blackwell Publishing
All rights reserved

Blackwell Publishing Professional
2121 State Avenue, Ames, Iowa 50014, USA

Orders: 1-800-862-6657
Office: 1-515-292-0140
Fax: 1-515-292-3348
Web site: www.blackwellprofessional.com

Blackwell Publishing Ltd
9600 Garsington Road, Oxford OX4 2DQ, UK
Tel.: +44 (0)1865 776868

Blackwell Publishing Asia
550 Swanston Street, Carlton, Victoria 3053, Australia
Tel.: +61 (0)3 8359 1011

Authorization to photocopy items for internal or personal use, or the internal or personal use of specific clients, is granted by Blackwell Publishing, provided that the base fee of $.10 per copy is paid directly to the Copyright Clearance Center, 222 Rosewood Drive, Danvers, MA 01923. For those organizations that have been granted a photocopy license by CCC, a separate system of payments has been arranged. The fee code for users of the Transactional Reporting Service is 0-8138-0628-3/2004 $.10.

∞ Printed on acid-free paper in the United States of America

First edition, 2004

Library of Congress Cataloging-in-Publication Data

Artwick, Claudette Guzan.
    Reporting and producing for digital media / Claudette Guzan Artwick.—1st ed.
        p. cm.—(Media and technology series)
    Includes bibliographical references and index.
    ISBN 0-8138-0628-3 (alk. paper)
    1. Online journalism. 2. Reporters and reporting. 3. Digital media. I. Title. II. Series.

PN4784.O62A78 2004
070.4—dc22

                                                              2004006860

The last digit is the print number: 9 8 7 6 5 4 3 2 1

To Thomas and Spencer

Contents

Foreword

Reporting and Producing for Digital Media explains the challenge of being a journalist in a rapidly changing era of technological development. Claudette Artwick, a journalism professor at Washington and Lee University, sets a foundation by focusing on the importance of journalism in a democracy, and then delves into the core values and ethical considerations needed by journalists working in both an online and offline world.

Focusing primarily on developing news content for the Internet, the author introduces the reader to the fundamentals of digital storytelling by focusing on the five I's: interactivity, involvement, immediacy, integration, and in-depth opportunities, as well as other unique qualities of the Web. Other chapters discuss the importance of "old media" and how to draw upon these techniques when preparing content for the Internet, as well as the way to frame stories on the Web.

Artwick explains the numerous tools for digital storytelling that will provide excellent preparation for tomorrow's journalists. The author addresses new challenges to reporters, working with images in developing online content, and the impact of convergence on newsgathering and reporting.

Designed primarily as a textbook for online journalism courses, *Reporting and Producing for Digital Media* will no doubt be a useful text for many courses dealing with reporting, editing, news management, and ethics. Students will find the book engaging because the material is presented in a clear and concise manner. Professors will appreciate the use of learning objectives at the beginning of each chapter and activities that conclude each of the chapters. Working journalists will benefit from new ideas on newsgathering and reporting in a digital media environment.

Alan B. Albarran, Ph.D.
The University of North Texas
Series Editor, Media and Technology

Preface

This book began, in concept, with a motorcycle ride down a dusty road in the Upper Amazon of Peru. It was before the days of digital newsgathering—even before Tim Berners-Lee invented the World Wide Web. There, in the remote village of Moyobamba, I used the tools of a multimedia journalist to research the sights, sounds, and stories of the people who cleared the jungle to grow crops. After gathering a mountain of information I returned to the states to report my findings in a multimedia, interactive presentation. It was carefully planned and executed, replete with color slides, black and white photos, maps, cassette recordings, a human translator, personal narration, and Q&A. Despite its success, I wished I could communicate in this way to a larger audience through a mass medium. While I recognized that separate stories could be produced for print and broadcast using the appropriate material, at the time there was no way to replicate that personal, multimedia, interactive presentation as a cohesive whole. The experience stayed with me and fueled my interest in online reporting and producing.

Today, the Web facilitates multimedia, interactive storytelling, setting it apart from the traditional forms of print and broadcast news. My goal for *Reporting and Producing for Digital Media* is to prepare you for your journey into online journalism, discovering the richness and depth of this medium and its storytelling possibilities.

Acknowledgments

I extend my warmest thanks to all the people who have helped make this book a reality. My sincere appreciation goes to Mark Barrett at Blackwell Publishing and series editor Alan Albarran, for their interest in this project. Colleagues in the Department of Journalism and Mass Communications at Washington and Lee University sparked ideas, shared insight, and gave support. A special thanks to my third-floor partners, Bob de Maria and Michael Todd, for their camaraderie and expertise; to Lou Hodges for feedback and inspiration; and to Ham Smith, for making Reid Hall digital. Thanks to all the wonderful people who allowed me to photograph them for this book. I extend my gratitude to students, past and present, who have motivated and enriched my work, to my teachers and mentors throughout the years, and to the many industry professionals who shared with me their time and insight. Thanks to Andrew Nachison at the American Press Institute for the inspiring Digital Story Master Class. I truly appreciate the support of the Washington and Lee University Glenn Grant and the Charles E. Culpeper Foundation Grant. And I give heartfelt thanks to my family, for love and patience.

REPORTING AND PRODUCING FOR DIGITAL MEDIA

CHAPTER 1

Journalism in a Digital Age

Chapter Objectives

Imagine transporting today's journalists back in time, technology in tow, to cover events of the early 20th century. We might witness live broadcast images of the "unsinkable" Titanic submerging, or link to the Internet for interviews with survivors. A reporter covering the 19th Amendment would likely write an in-depth newspaper story on women's right to vote, and go online for a chat with Web site users. Or crews covering the 1906 San Francisco earthquake could report live via helicopter and later compose a story for the Web, complete with links to seismology sites and an interactive world map featuring earthquakes over time.

While contemporary journalists must approach each story with the same respect for truth and fairness as their predecessors, additional rigors guided by a new skill set must also be navigated. A pervasive online and cross-media presence defines journalism today. More than 4,000 newspapers in the United States alone have online sites (newslink.org 2003) and nearly sixty convergence relationships operate nationwide (API 2003). Today's digital news professional requires sound journalistic perspective and the skills to research, report, write, and present news in a world of digital and converging media. At the core of that perspective is an understanding of the role of news media in society and journalism's importance to our freedom as individuals and as a nation. This chapter examines that role in a digital age.

What are Digital Media?

Digital media—the term is becoming part of our everyday vocabularies. Definitions range from the latest technological gadgets, such as the BlackBerry handheld device and camera phones, to storage and distribution media, such as DVDs and CDs, to the information industries that generate news and entertainment content. At the crux of digital media we find the bit, that colorless, odorless state of binary being, which is on or off, one or zero (Negroponte 1995). A string of eight bits makes a byte, a unit of code which can be read by a computer. News media are digital when they use these bits and bytes to gather, process, and disseminate information. Today's newspapers, television, radio, and magazines all are digital to some degree, from basic computer text processing to satellite broadcasting. And while the bits make it all possible at the most basic level, looking at the bigger picture, the Internet has been a powerful force, facilitating a communion of reporting on the news Web site. These online news sites not only provide an additional vehicle for print and broadcast companies to disseminate traditional forms of news, but are emerging as a venue for distinct forms of communication. In most cases, they are related in some way to a legacy news medium—the traditional media forms of newspaper, radio, television, or news magazine. That connection may be ownership, partnership, operating agreement or other arrangement. For today's journalist, reporting and producing for digital media means being adept at online newsgathering and storytelling within the framework of the legacy news media.

The Role of Digital Journalism in Society

Excitement turns to horror as fire sweeps through The Station, a crowded night club in Rhode Island. One hundred people die after Great White's pyrotechnics ignite the club's foam soundproofing, burning out of control in minutes (projo.com 2003). *The Providence Journal* has been reporting The Station fire story on its Web site ever since that fatal night (Figure 1.1). The breadth and depth of the coverage is unmatched, helping the community to heal. It offers:

- Profiles on the people who died
- An online guest book to post condolences
- Graphics on the club and safety issues

Figure 1.1 *The Providence Journal* covered The Station fire in depth on its Web site, projo.com, helping the community in its time of crisis. Reprinted with permission of Belo Interactive, Inc.

- Series on the dangers of foam
- Series on a burn victim's survival
- Legislation related to the tragedy
- An archive of stories since the first report

What journalists do matters.

A man is crushed to death while he repairs a conveyor belt at a manufacturing plant in Tyler, Texas. Federal law requires that such belts be shut down when they're being maintained. But the man who died had been trained to work on the belt while it was still running (Barstow and Bergman 2003). This was not a single event to be reported and forgotten. An investigation by *The New York Times on the Web*, Frontline, and the Canadian Broadcasting Corporation exposed the conditions at McWane Foundries, where nine workers have been killed and 4,600 hurt since 1995 (Barstow and Bergman 2003).

What journalists do matters.

An in-depth report on washingtonpost.com (2001) revealed that fatal shootings by police in Prince George's County are among the highest in the country. Many of the people shot were unarmed, many had committed no crime. The interactive story provided online documents, 911 audio, victim stories, discussions, and the findings of reporters' research on fifty police departments and more than 2,100 fatal shootings.

What journalists do matters. They report the events and issues of our time, helping us make sense of our world. They expose wrongdoing. And through their work, they help ensure the freedom of our country and its people. In today's digital society, where information flow is fast, far-reaching, and sometimes ferocious, the journalist's role may be more crucial than ever before.

Lasswell's Functions Plus Two

More than a half-century ago, Harold Lasswell (1948) identified three functions of communication in society:

1. Surveillance of the environment
2. Correlation of the components of society
3. Transmission of the social inheritance

Much of what we do as journalists falls within the *surveillance function*—reporting what's going on in the world around us, or, in Lasswell's words, "disclosing threats and opportunities..." (p. 51). The preponderance of online news sites offers users instant access to news from cities worldwide. They can go online at any time, day or night, no longer having to wait for regular broadcasts or publications. And while they're on the run, users can receive headlines and updates on their cell phones or PDAs. They can also explore beyond news sites almost any type of information that interests them. But opening ourselves up to the cyber universe can bring spam and scams, which can annoy and even frighten us. For some, the sheer amount of information available online today can be daunting. But the digital journalist can help sift through it to alert the public to what's important and why. And that's where Lasswell's *correlation function* comes in, because it involves responding to the environment. Digital reporters and producers help news consumers make sense of the world by providing context, depth, and interpretation. Web interactivity can also contribute to this function, giving citizens the means to respond to issues and communicate with journalists.

The stories digital journalists choose to investigate and how they report them on the Web play a role in *transmitting the social inheritance*. They communicate society's values and ideology online through multimedia, interactive presentations. Devoting extensive online coverage to issues tells readers, "This is important." But in the digital realm the audience can also contribute to the transmission function through user interaction. Online chats and discussion boards give users the power to communicate with one another as well as with news leaders. And citizen-based projects reach out to people for important feedback on their communities.

The *entertainment* (Wright 1960) and *economic* (Bagdikian 2000) functions of media also deserve mention here. While we recognize that news is not produced as entertainment, news can entertain. It can also entertain while informing. Numerous news Web sites have incorporated games into their storytelling, and with great success. At MSNBC.com (2003), for example, users learn how difficult it is to check baggage for weapons and explosives in an interactive game, "You be the airport baggage screener" (Figure 1.2). The nature of the news also can dictate its treatment, and digital journalists can identify lighter stories and present them in an entertaining way, giving users a bright spot in their day.

While not often included in a typology of media functions, every discussion of them should include the bottom line. That is, that U.S. media exist to make money, and they do so by selling advertising. The larger their audiences, the more companies can charge for ads in their papers, in their broadcasts, and on their Web sites. "The dirty part of journalism is that this is a business," says Dan Bradley, Vice President of News for Media General Broadcast Division. (2003) "We take journalism-based content, we package

Figure 1.2 Interactive games, such as MSNBC.com's "You be the airport baggage screener," engage online users through interactivity. Reproduced with permission of MSNBC.com.

it, and present it with a profit motive," says Bradley. "If we were unable to sell advertising in newspapers or in newscasts would this company continue? I can tell you that the answer is no." This is especially important to consider for online media because many news Web sites have existed for years without turning a profit, supported by a parent organization, group, or network. Those who haven't fully embraced the online operation may be limited by small budgets, small staffs, and a secondary emphasis on the Web site. Others fear losing viewers or readers by giving away content on the Web. Approaches toward advertising on news Web sites are in some cases pushing the envelope of invasiveness; for example, the ad that's embedded into news text or those that pop up over news stories. These issues have only begun to surface, so economics should be viewed as a moving force when considering digital media function in society.

Another business issue involves media ownership, conglomeration, and convergence. Digital media can facilitate the sharing of news content, which has major implications for the news industry. Areas of potential impact include competition; employment issues, such as numbers of news workers and redefinition of their jobs; and the effect of convergence on news content. Results will depend on each organization and how it handles its desire to make a profit measured against its news operation's commitment to serve the community.

Free Press, Free Society

Imagine living near the site of a nuclear power plant explosion, and not knowing something had gone terribly wrong. The 1986 Chernobyl accident killed 31 people almost instantly, and exposed to radiation an estimated 5 million people in Russia, Belarus, and Ukraine. But Moscow's first report on the incident came a full two days after it happened, and gave no indication of its severity (BBC 2000):

> An accident has occurred at Chernobyl nuclear power station. One of the atomic reactors has been damaged. Measures are being taken to eliminate the consequences of the accident. Aid is being given to the victims. A government commission has been set up.

The Soviet government had reacted by trying to hide it from the world (Lemonick 1989). And in those critical first days, the government-run media gave the people nothing but silence.

In some parts of the world, reporters suffer harassment, imprisonment, and even death because of their attempts to tell the truth. The editor of a business journal in Kazakhstan received a funeral wreath and later a decapitated dog to dissuade her from investigating government financial corruption (Cooper 2002). And in the sub-Saharan African country Togo, the press code dictates that journalists can be jailed for up to five years and fined $8,000 for "insulting the Head of State" (World's worst places to be a journalist 2003). Elsewhere, legislation *protects* journalists and press freedom. The U.S. Constitution's First Amendment allows American journalists the freedom to write truthfully about corruption and wrongdoing.

> Congress shall make no law respecting an establishment of religion, or prohibiting the free exercise thereof; or abridging the freedom of speech, or of the press; or the right of the people peaceably to assemble, and to petition the Government for a redress of grievances.

The primary role of the press in a free society is to protect its freedom. As Thomas Jefferson (1786) wrote, "Our liberty cannot be guarded but by the freedom of the press, nor that be limited without danger of losing it." Despite this precious right, many Americans feel the U.S. press has excessive freedom. A recent study by the First Amendment Center showed that 46 percent of respondents felt the press in America has "too much freedom to do what it wants" (State of the First Amendment 2003). With freedom comes responsibility, for an irresponsible press can harm reputations and ruin lives.

Press Freedom and Social Responsibility

More than a half-century ago, the Commission on Freedom of the Press released its report, *A Free and Responsible Press,* often referred to as the Hutchins Commission Report (1947). This document became the foundation for a press theory of social responsibility, which argues that a free press must also be a responsible press. It cited the following as faults in the press:

> . . . sensationalism, news selected for its entertainment value, "lying" by newspapers, cover-ups of the press's own scandals, the hunger for scoops, reliance on unidentified sources, reinforcement of group stereotypes, advertisements disguised as news, and, especially, concentrated ownership (Bates 1995).

Many of those concerns drive a public discontent with the media today. Recommendations presented more than fifty years ago (Commission on Freedom of the Press 1947) offer guidance for a more socially responsible press, to meet the needs of a free society. Digital media, when used to their potential, offer exciting opportunities to meet the requirements for social responsibility.

1. *A truthful, comprehensive, and intelligent account of the day's events in a context which gives them meaning* (p. 21)

Digital media can make news coverage more comprehensive than ever before, providing rich context limited only by the time a user is willing to spend with the issue. Stories can be told in many different ways, from straight text to highly interactive audiovisual presentations. The words "complete coverage" and "full coverage" now appear as hyperlinks on numerous online news sites. On *The New York Times on the Web* (2003), for example, one can click on "Complete Coverage: Targeting Terror," from a top story about the capture of a suspect in the Indonesia terrorist bombings. Once there, one can link to more than twenty related stories, video, a slide show, graphics, government documents, and discussion opportunities, as well as another complete coverage page, "After the War." Readers can also search archives quickly and easily for greater background if they desire. The context the Internet news site can provide is unmatched by other media.

2. *A forum for the exchange of comment and criticism* (p. 23)

For years, readers have relied on letters to the editor for making their opinions public. Today, digital media can go beyond this forum with moderated online discussions and question/answer sessions with newsmakers and journalists. Small, local market media as well as national and international online news sites offer discussion boards or chats where readers can respond to stories or post opinions. After reading a story, users can react, or simply observe what others are saying by clicking on a link to a discussion forum.

For example, after the biggest power outage in history, washingtonpost .com (2003) added the topic to its forum page, along with discussions on the Mideast, and other issues. Other interactive features can also provide a forum for comment and criticism. Web polls give users instant feedback, and civic journalism projects, such as budget balancers, ask users to solve problems in their communities. From Seattle to Tampa, online news providers are reaching out to citizens for their opinions. The online edition of *The Seattle Times* (2003) invited readers to help solve some of the area's transportation problems and plan its policy. The interactive exercise called "You Build It" attracted more than 1,500 readers, giving them the chance to choose the projects they favored before the community voted on the issues (Pryne 2003). Tampa's project on TBO.com (2002) asked users to compare their views on issues with the candidates who were running for governor. While online civic projects can't guarantee the results are representative of the entire community, they can give voice to the people, which is the foundation of democracy.

3. *The projection of a representative picture of the constituent groups in the society* (p. 26)

In the digital arena, constituent groups can now pursue new avenues to represent themselves. The public can access reporters directly and immediately through e-mail rather than being screened by a telephone switchboard. These contacts can serve to inform and expand the journalist's source possibilities. Online discussions can also provide a forum for groups to present themselves and their views. The Internet's interactivity can give the public a voice that had few options to be heard in the past.

4. *The presentation and clarification of the goals and values of society* (p. 27)

In 1947, when the commission presented its report, media choices were far more limited than they are today. Today, myriad news sites on the Internet offer greater choice to the public, opening the way for fuller presentation and clarification of the goals and values of society. But the sheer volume of information can be overwhelming, making it difficult to discern what is important. News sources that can help people determine what's salient and why have become increasingly valuable. Major news Web sites, such as *The New York Times on the Web,* MSNBC.com, and USATODAY.com, limit the number of major stories they showcase on their front pages to five or six. When these Web sites open on users' computer screens, the presentation signals that these are salient stories. MSNBC.com featured five main stories on its October 22, 2003, cover page: the war on terrorism, the D.C. sniper trial, North Korea and nuclear weapons, wildfires, and the stock market dropping. Considered together, these stories convey our collective value of safety and security.

The days of the one-way flow of information from media organization to the public are numbered as digital media now offer instant feedback. CNN's "America Rocks the Vote" forum invited viewers to respond to Democratic candidates by sending messages from their mobile phones. And while news media still help clarify the goals and values of society by what they cover and how it's treated, the public's response and comment can now help shape that coverage. Interactivity, information access, organization, and presentation, can all have an impact on this element of social responsibility.

5. *Full access to the day's intelligence* (p. 28)

Never before has more information been as readily available and easily accessible. Some argue that this deluge on the Internet overwhelms citizens, who require guidance in sifting through the thousands of Google hits and hundreds of headlines on their favorite news sites. Even in 1947, the commission realized that not all citizens will actually use all the information available to them at all times; that many turn to leaders, both formal and informal, to analyze issues and help guide their decisions. One person's leader may today be a neighbor, or tomorrow a discussant from an online news forum. Journalists who report and produce for digital media will sometimes fill that leadership role, but they will also turn to experts to help make sense of issues. The unfettered flow of information on the Internet is essential to a free society.

Defining News on the 'Net

Does a digital universe change the meaning of news, and consequently, have an impact on journalists and their work? Over the years, definitions of news have ranged from "man bites dog" to "whatever news organizations say it is." Some journalists struggle to define news, saying, "I know it when I see it." Such a nebulous sense of news can lead to ambulance chasing and sensationalism that titillates rather than informs. Instead, a citizens-based approach can help us better serve the public and fulfill our responsibilities as journalists. In their book, *The News About the News,* Len Downie, Jr. and Bob Kaiser of *The Washington Post* write that good journalism "...enriches Americans by giving them both useful information for their daily lives and a sense of participation in the wider world." (Downie and Kaiser 2002, p. 6). Online reporting can deliver both through its breadth, depth and interactivity. Links and layers allow online coverage to extend beyond the limitations of a 30-minute newscast or fixed news hole. Consumer, health, science, and other specialized reporting can coexist with civic journalism rather than competing with it for time and space. And the Internet's interactivity allows the public to voice its opinion through polls, discussion boards, and live chats with journalists and community leaders. This moves the *sense* of participation into the *realm* of participation. Jan Schaffer, executive director for J-Lab: The Institute for Interactive Journalism (2002), says, "Future news will be more about story making than story telling." What this means is that people are taking charge of the information they receive and constructing their own narratives from various sources. Digital journalists can facilitate this process through interactivity on the Internet. Interactive tools such as clickable maps, tax calculators, and simulations can give citizens what they need to make sense of their world.

It Looks Like a News Site, But Is It?

Critics of the online venue argue that users won't be able to identify "real" journalism on the Web. They fear that Web pages advocating a point of view will pose as news, and that truth and accuracy will go the way of the dinosaur because anyone with an Internet account can post a Web site. As digital journalists, must we be concerned with this argument? Those of us who rely on the Web edition of a major news organization may not see the validity in this concern. But the line between news and opinion on the Internet may not be as clear as we would like it to be. For example, running a search on news.google.com (2003) for the latest news on Arnold Schwarzenegger turned up more than 20,000 hits in online publications. One would assume that because this was a news search, the results would be culled from news sites. And while the bulk of the entries were from bona fide news organizations, some were not. For example, *The Hill*, a publication by the U.S. Congress and *The Spoof,* a U.K. news satire publication, were both included in the results. Neither exactly qualifies as news. Even the savvy news consumer may be misled. After all, displayed prominently under the news.google.com (2003) search box are the words, "Search and browse 4,500 news sources updated continuously." The results become more complex if the user runs a search for Arnold Schwarzenegger on the entire Web. Nearly 1.9 million hits will be returned, with joinarnold.com (2003) at the top of the results list. Click on the link and you'll find a Web page that looks just like a news site (Figure 1.3). It actually has "lead story" above its featured headline, and "top stories" above linkable text. But is that journalism? Looks can be deceiving. Our commitment to truth and accuracy as journalists is more important than ever in this digital arena.

And, what about Weblogs, or blogs—the frequently-updated sites with postings in reverse-chronological order on just about any topic imaginable? Just because some are written by journalists, are they journalism? At least one newspaper doesn't think so—it fired one of its reporters for writing a blog under the pseudonym of Banjo Jones. Some say the blogger crossed ethical lines because he criticized the newspaper and could have

Figure 1.3 The Web site for Arnold Schwarzenegger's gubernatorial campaign resembles a news site.

compromised his ability to report for the paper (Mintz 2002). But what about blogs as an information form? Blogs can act as catalysts to expand sourcing beyond government and corporate walls (Andrews 2003). They can flag ideas that news media can cover in greater depth (Lennon 2003). And they can shape coverage by giving readers input and story ideas (Gillmor 2003). But blogs are distinct from news, and information posted to a blog cannot necessarily be considered reliable. Journalists can use blogs as a starting point for a story, and confirm information elsewhere through a reputable source.

Newsworthiness in Cyberspace

Who decides what events and issues deserve coverage online, and how do they make those choices? In some newsrooms, the computer chooses, through an automated program that grabs stories from the Associated Press news service and posts them to the Web site. But, in most cases, editors and producers make those decisions, using news judgment to guide their choices. Many factors can contribute to what journalists deem as newsworthy. But, to make solid, informed choices, the newsperson must keep the audience at the heart of each choice. And with the audience in mind, the journalist can then judge newsworthiness by considering the story's *significance* and *interest* (Fuller 1996).

While an issue or event is often significant *and* interesting, it need not be both to qualify as newsworthy. The challenge is to balance the two, and not to rely heavily on interest over significance to drive our news decisions. A key factor in this process is a focus on the community. While the whole world may have access to a news site, the news organization will most likely define its audience locally. In Maryland and Washington, D.C., for example, the sniper trial had great significance and interest to the people who lived in fear during the 2002 killing spree. Recognizing this, online editors and producers featured news of the trial prominently on news Web sites in D.C., Baltimore, and eastern Virginia. And while the New York Yankees and Florida Marlins were battling it out for the 2003 World Series title, news sites in their respective states provided ample coverage of the games. Elsewhere, the significance of those stories was not as great. For example, Minneapolis Web site startribune.com (2003) carried them, but not as top stories. Instead, a fatal blast at an ethanol plant had more significance to that community, and topped the site during those events.

The struggle between interest and significance can be difficult for traditional media, but may be especially tough online because of the cost factor in online news operations. We've seen sensationalized reporting on local television news during ratings sweeps periods. Often interesting, but perhaps not significant, stories are put on the air to gain viewers, but not necessarily to inform a community. A similar approach may drive online producers and editors to choose interesting over significant stories. Making the commitment to serve readers as citizens rather than simply customers can help guide journalists to make well-informed news coverage decisions, balancing interest and significance.

Another factor in judging a story's newsworthiness concerns the number of people the event or issue will affect. The power outage in fall 2003 left millions in the dark, and was considered highly newsworthy not only in the midst of the blackout, but nationwide, because it affected so many people. News organizations also call this the story's impact.

The nature of the medium also influences news judgment. Because the Internet offers instant access and continuous updates, the focus on what is *new* will influence coverage. The relationship to a legacy medium will also have an impact. For example, a television station connected to a Web site may focus heavily on spot news, such as crashes, fires, and crime, and as a result, what goes online may reflect that broadcast news focus.

Producers may decide to take a pass on issues-based stories because they may be perceived as difficult to report for television, even though they would be ideal online. And a newspaper's Web site may post stories that some consider old, because they're reported online only after publication in the newspaper. But, these medium-specific news philosophies should not constrain the appropriate use of the Internet news site. Revisiting news philosophies to include specific online attributes can make judgments of newsworthiness more appropriate for online news Web sites.

Online Gatekeeping

Information flows through a series of gates and gatekeepers before reaching the public as news (White 1950). A reporter seeking information could run into a roadblock if police or a private individual won't release it. In this case, the authority closes the gate. But a reporter can just as easily stop the information flow when she abandons a story idea to develop another. And a producer can shut a gate when he drops a story from his newscast because he's running out of air time. These examples can apply among traditional media as well as online, but new considerations are emerging because of the nature of the Internet. The gates are rattling, new gatekeepers are gaining power, and the roles of others are shifting.

One of the most profound examples of this change took place on September 11, 1998. Not to be confused with 2001, when terrorists turned commercial airliners into missiles, but three years earlier, when the U.S. House of Representatives posted the Starr Report on several government Web sites. Independent Council Kenneth Starr's investigation of President Clinton got more than 15 million hits on the four sites over a three-day period (Jackson 1998). Posting the 450-page report online marked a major change in the way the public could get information to govern itself. Instead of waiting for journalists to sift through the report, interview experts for quotes and sound bites, and craft stories that may or may not have included the testimony of Monica Lewinsky about sexual encounters with Mr. Clinton, the public could go to http://thomas.loc.gov/icreport (1998) and read it for themselves. The news media gate had been unhinged. Granted, journalists informed the public that the government would make the report available to them online, but access to that full report was unprecedented.

Technological Determinism

Most college students were born into the digital age and have never known life before computers. Their world is experienced in bits and bytes. Proponents of technological determinism would argue that "...technology is the principal if not only cause of historical change" (Grossberg, Wartella, and Whitney 1998, p. 47). To what extent are digital media shaping this generation's history? Before the digital age, in the 1960s, communications scholar Marshall McLuhan argued that the media do more than provide information. "Societies have always been shaped more by the nature of the media by which men communicate than by the content of the communication" (1967, p. 8). McLuhan contrasted the print culture, with its lines of text defining a linear mode of thinking, with the electronic culture of the television age, fostering unification through a shared experience. Is today's digital technology shifting our culture and its ways of knowing? Evidence of a change may be seen in the recent, seemingly "unexplainable," drop in television viewing by 18- to 24-year-old males. In one year, television viewership in this age group had dropped 20 percent. Poynter Institute Senior Editor Steve Outing argues that these young men have grown up knowing interactivity through computer games and the Internet as the norm. "I suspect that this is the first generation for which interactivity is expected in the media it consumes," says Outing (2003). Digital media's interactivity may have an impact on our ways of receiving information and using it. And today's news professionals should be aware of the potential digital technology holds for shaping our culture.

It's an exciting time to be a journalist!

Activities for Further Learning

1. Find a top story on a major news site such as CNN.com or washingtonpost.com. Discuss the social responsibility of that story and its coverage.

2. Compare the front page of a television and newspaper Web site from your home town. Identify the news values that drove the coverage of stories on each of the sites.

3. Find a story on a U.S. news Web site that might not be reported in a country with restricted press freedoms. How does reporting that story contribute to your freedom as an individual and to our country's freedom?

References

Andrews, P. Fall 2003. Is blogging journalism? A blogger and journalist finds no easy answer; but he discovers connections. *Nieman Reports.* http://www.nieman.harvard.edu/reports/contents.html

API. U.S. convergence tracker. http://americanpressinstitute.org/convergencetracker/

Bagdikian, B. H. 2000. *The Media Monopoly.* Boston: Beacon Press.

Barstow, D. and L. Bergman. 2003. Dangerous business. http://www.nytimes.com/ref/national/DANGEROUS_BUSINESS.html?pagewanted=all&position=top

Bates, S. 1995. *Realigning Journalism with Democracy: The Hutchins Commission, Its Times, and Ours.* http://www.annenberg.nwu.edu/pubs/hutchins/hutch01.htm

BBC News. June 5, 2000. The Chernobyl accident: What happened. http://news.bbc.co.uk/2/hi/europe/778477.stm

Bradley, D. Oct. 17, 2003. Telephone interview.

Commission on Freedom of the Press. 1947. *A Free and Responsible Press; A General Report on Mass Communication: Newspapers, Radio, Motion Pictures, Magazines, and Books.* Chicago: The University of Chicago Press.

Cooper, A. 2002. Attacks on the Press in 2002. Committee to Protect Journalists. http://www.cpj.org/attacks02/introduction.html

Downie, L., Jr. and R.G. Kaiser. 2002. *The News About the News: American Journalism in Peril.* New York: A. A. Knopf.

Fuller, J. 1996. *News Values: Ideas for an Information Age.* Chicago: University of Chicago Press.

Gillmor, D. Fall 2003. Moving toward participatory journalism: 'If contemporary American journalism is a lecture, what it is evolving into is something that incorporates a conversation and seminar.' *Nieman Reports.* http://www.nieman.harvard.edu/reports/contents.html

google.com. Oct. 23, 2003.

Grossberg, L., E. Wartella, and D.C. Whitney. 1998. *Media Making: Mass Media in a Popular Culture.* Thousand Oaks: Sage Publications.

Jackson, W. Sept. 21, 1998. Government Computer News, v. 17 n31, p.3. Millions hit, Millions miss Starr report on Web. Retrieved online from Expanded Academic Index.

Jefferson, T. 1786. *Thomas Jefferson on Politics & Government.* http://etext.lib.virginia.edu/jefferson/quotations/jeff1600.htm

joinarnold.com. 2003.

Lasswell, H. D. 1948. The structure and function of communication in society. In Bryson, L. (Ed)., *The Communication of Ideas.* New York: Institute for Religious and Social Studies, Harper & Brothers.

Lemonick, M. D. Nov. 13, 1989. The Chernobyl cover-up: Are Soviet officials still concealing the truth about the disaster? Time. http://www.time.com/ time/daily/chernobyl/891113.coverup.html

Lennon, S. Fall 2003. Blogging journalists invite outsiders' reporting in: 'To be interesting, the blog must have a discernible human voice: A blog with just links is a portal.' *Nieman Reports*. http://www.nieman.harvard.edu/ reports/contents.html

McLuhan, M. and Q. Fiore. 1967. *The Medium is the Massage*. New York: Bantam Books.

Mintz, Y. July 26, 2002. Web site targeting local politics shut down. *The Facts*. http://thefacts.com/story.lasso?wcd=4266

msnbc.com. 2003. You be the airport baggage screener. http://msnbc.com/ modules/airport_security/airsecurity_front.asp?0cb=-31-135833

Negroponte, N. 1995. *Being Digital*. New York: Knopf.

news.google.com. Oct. 23, 2003.

newslink.org. 2003.

nytimes.com Aug. 14, 2003.

Outing, S. Oct. 23, 2003. TV execs don't understand drop; Here's a hint. http:// www.poynter.org/column.asp?id=31&aid=52445

projo.com. 2003. The Station fire. http://www.projo.com/extra/2003/stationfire/

Pryne, E. 2003. http://www.j-lab.org/ericp.html

Schaffer, J. Aug. 8, 2002. Building zones of connectivity. http://www.pewcenter. org/doingcj/speeches/s_aejmczones.html

Seattle Times. March 30, 2003. http://seattletimes.nwsource.com/news/local/ links/transportationgame/calculator/

startribune.com. Oct. 22, 2003. 1 killed in blast at ethanol plant. http://www. startribune.com/

State of the First Amendment. 2003. http://www.firstamendmentcenter.org/ PDF/SOFA.2003.pdf

tbo.com. 2002.

thomas.loc.gov. 1998.

washingtonpost.com. 2001. A blue wall of silence. http://www.washingtonpost. com/wp-dyn/metro/md/princegeorges/government/police/shootings/

washingtonpost.com. Aug. 14, 2003.

White, D.M. 1950. The gatekeeper: A case study in the selection of news. Journalism Quarterly, 27, p. 383-390.

World's worst places to be a journalist. 2003. http://www.cpj.org/enemies/ worst_places_03/worst_places_03.html

Wright, C. R. 1960. Functional analysis and mass communication. *Public Opinion Quarterly*, 24, 606-620.

CHAPTER 2

Core Values Online

Chapter Objectives

Mary-Kate and Ashley—the Olsen twins—coming to a university near you. E-mails blanketed the nation in January 2003 announcing the twins had made their college choice. Perhaps you received one. You might have even clicked on the link to the "CNN" story that reported their school of choice as Texas A&M. Or perhaps the site you saw reported that it was the University of Dayton...or Penn State...or the University of Miami. The sites looked authentic, and included CNN's logos and format. But they were phony! Scammers used a Web site called the Fake CNN News Generator to create them, spoofing thousands of students who linked to the site and a number of journalists who reported the information as if it were true. Although the teens who created the site apparently built it to play a practical joke on their friends, it swiftly became a widespread Internet hoax (Kahney 2003).

With print and broadcast media, the chances of someone duping the public with faked news are far less likely. Access to the technology is much tighter, so that generally, only people inside the organization could make it happen. Nonetheless, untruths have slipped through to the public over the years through newspaper stories and broadcasts. In May 2003, 27-year-old Jayson Blair resigned as reporter for *The New York Times* after leaving what the newspaper called "a long trail of deception." According to the *Times*, "He fabricated comments. He concocted scenes. He lifted material from other newspapers and wire services. He selected details from photographs to create the impression he had been somewhere or

Figure 2.1 An Internet hoax tricked thousands of students into thinking Mary-Kate and Ashley Olsen were enrolling at their university.

seen someone, when he had not." (Barry, Barstow, Glater, Liptak and Steinberg 2003).

More than twenty years earlier, Janet Cooke, a reporter for *The Washington Post,* returned a Pulitzer Prize when the organization discovered she created an eight-year-old heroin addict in her story "Jimmy's World." And, in the early days of radio, millions of people panicked when they heard a report about Martians invading the United States. Orson Welle's radio drama, "War of the Worlds," began with an announcement that sounded very much like a news report. But, these examples are the exceptions, because the gatekeepers in print and broadcast organizations keep fairly tight control of what flows out to the public. For the Internet, however, many gates are open, or there simply are no gates. At the time of this writing, people with Web access could go to fakednews.com to create stories on a page similar to CNN, C-Net or MTV, and then send an e-mail link to the phony page. While extreme, this example illustrates how people can make lies look like news online. And that goes against one of the major tenets of western journalism, to "seek truth and report it" (Society of Professional Journalists 1996).

Pursuing truth is one of five core journalistic values presented in this chapter. The others are accuracy, fairness, independence, and serving citizens. These values guide journalists in all media, and don't vary because of the technology. However, digital media do present new challenges and special considerations, which we will recognize and address here.

Seeking Truth

On its face, reporting the truth seems fairly straightforward. Journalists should not lie. If we know something is false, we don't report it as truth. That's understood among journalists, and expected by the public. But truth *seeking* is not quite as simple, and in our digital age has become even more complex. While philosophers debate the existence of absolute truth, many journalists operate on the assumption that there are many interpretations of the truth. This section draws from guidelines on truth set forth by the Radio-Television News Directors Association (RTNDA) and the Society of Professional Journalists (SPJ) codes of ethics. It discusses this core value as related to digital journalism and in more general terms. Find the full text of the codes in Appendix 1 at the back of the book.

Sources and Truth

The people we choose to interview, what we ask them, and how we handle that information in our stories has a direct impact on reporting truth. For a story on college student housing, a reporter asks a landlord about noise complaints for the houses he rents to undergraduates. It's known among students as a real party haven. He says there really haven't been any problems, just a call or two over many years. But, his perspective offers only one side of the story. Neighbors may call the police frequently, but the landlord may not know about every call. They may also complain among themselves, feeling uncomfortable confronting the students or the landlord. So, while the landlord tells the reporter what he feels to be true, his interview, when used alone, would not necessarily tell the truth. Going to police records would be a more reliable method of verifying noise complaints, and by talking with neighbors, the reporter could also move closer to the truth. So, consider what sources know and who would be best able to provide the information you're looking for.

In many cases reporters first turn to official sources when pursuing a story. School administrators, heads of government offices, company spokespersons from public relations departments, and the like fill newspapers with quotes and broadcasts with sound bites. Their official points of view appear online as well. These sources are usually persons of authority who often have experience talking with reporters. They're most likely available during the reporter's workday, and can often be reached fairly easily. Unofficial sources, however, often lack status or authority, may have never spoken to a reporter, and are likely difficult to reach and hesitant to be interviewed. According to SPJ (1996), each "can be equally valid." Beat reporters often find themselves relying on official sources alone to help them tell their stories. The best use both to seek truth.

In 2003, reporter Diana Sugg of *The Baltimore Sun* won a Pulitzer Prize in Beat Reporting for what the judges called "her absorbing, often poignant stories that illuminated complex medical issues through the lives of people." (Pulitzer.org 2003) Her story about allowing families into emergency rooms and critical care units during a loved one's resuscitation is a case in point. While Sugg used an official trauma physician and cited survey data in the story, the voices of unofficial sources added something beyond the pros and cons of the issue. A mother who was allowed to stay with her 11-year-old son as emergency workers resuscitated him conveyed the emotion and impact of the experience. Sugg also quoted a nurse who had a personal experience with the issue—staying in the ER with her great-aunt who had suffered a fatal heart attack (Sugg 2002). Using unofficial sources gives "voice to the voiceless," according to SPJ (1996). Sugg describes her search for sources in the following sidebar.

Diana Sugg

The Search for Sources

Figure 2.2 Diana Sugg of *The Baltimore Sun*. Photo courtesy of *The Baltimore Sun*.

I always want to get the people who actually experienced the moment, the trend, the subject, in the story. I actually knew of this trend and searched for a family for eight months, calling every single emergency room in the state. I talked with nurse managers, ER docs, asking them to try to remember cases, begging that they give my name to a family. I was working on other stories at the same time, and actually had the bulk of this story written. I considered running it without a local family for a while, but since it wasn't breaking news, I held off.

I believed if I waited and worked long enough, I would find someone. Too often, reporters give up too quickly.

I finally hit on a nurse who remembered the King case at Hopkins. I drove out to their home on a cold, dark Friday night. I did feel badly that I was asking them about the most painful moment of their lives. But I explained what I was doing, and we talked for four hours. At the end of the night, they took me up to his room, which was still set up, with his toys and medical equipment.

It was a privilege to be with them and hear Ryan's story. And without him, my article would not have had nearly as much impact. (Sugg 2003)

Davis (Buzz) Merritt, Jr. of *The Wichita Eagle* finds too many stories in the media pitting one extreme view against another. He encourages journalists to find a middle ground, where most people sit on issues, as a means to finding and presenting truth (1998). As an example, a logger who also hunts, hikes, and fishes can offer a point of view that represents the conflict many of us feel on the issue of logging national forests. He wants the cutting to be managed to preserve the wildlife's environment while allowing him to make a living.

Sources have a great impact on the truth of a story. Finding sources who represent both the official and unofficial points of view, and taking care to avoid polar extremes, can help digital journalists find and present the truth to their audiences.

Visuals and Truth

With Photoshop 7.0, we can now use our computers to "heal images," removing blemishes and wrinkles with the click of a mouse. For the portrait photographer, this feature might please clients and boost business. But for the photojournalist, using the "healing brush" could mean the end of her job. Digital video editors can use Avid Xpress DV 3.5 to flip over images if they want to change the direction of movement in a shot, or use an image stabilization tool to control shaky shots. But if they do this for a broadcast news story, are they telling a visual lie?

RTNDA guidelines say "Professional electronic journalists should not manipulate images or sounds in any way that is misleading." The SPJ code of ethics (1996) says, "Journalists should never distort the content of news photos or video. Image enhancement for technical clarity is always permissible." While these guidelines offer a good starting point for telling the truth with images, much of the language is open for interpretation. For example, what is considered manipulation? How does one determine what is misleading? What is distortion? And how does one define technical clarity? Let's consider each of these items individually.

Visual manipulation

During the second Gulf War, the *Los Angeles Times* fired photojournalist Brian Walski for violating the newspaper's policy that "forbids altering the content of news photographs." (Sherer and Long 2003) In an editor's note the paper's online edition explained that Walski used his computer to improve the composition of an image by combining elements of two photographs taken within seconds of each other (latimes.com 2003). The National Press Photographers Association condemned the image fabrication, saying, "Any visual lie, big or small, is a lie. We all must take a strong stand against such conduct, as the *LA Times* did by firing him." (Sherer and Long 2003)

The *Times'* policy states with conviction the rules its journalists must follow. Walski broke the rule and suffered the consequence. Many news organizations have policies governing digital image editing, but many do not. And some are outdated or unclear. So, one of your first responsibilities when hired by a news organization is to find out if there is a policy, and to clarify what that policy means. Media ethicist Louis Hodges says, "*Times'* policy did dictate Walski's firing, but should it have?" (Hodges 2003) He says the first question of ethics in such cases should ask, "What should our policy be?" Hodges argues that the intent to deceive and purposefully changing the meaning of an image determine unethical conduct, not simply editing with digital tools. Begin by asking yourself, "Am I trying to mislead the viewer by making this change?" and "Could this edit change the meaning of the image?" If the answer to either question could possibly be yes, then don't make the change.

Images can also be manipulated in the field. During the mid-'90s, state budget cuts threatened services, jobs, and entire programs at a large state university. Students and faculty organized a number of marches and rallies to protest the cuts, and the local media covered them. At one of the rallies a videographer asked protesters to hold up their signs. It was noon, under a blistering sun, and participants were beginning to wilt, consequently laying their signs on the ground. But upon his request, signs went up with renewed enthusiasm. In this case, the videographer orchestrated the action rather than recorded it. That's the job of a movie director, not a photojournalist. We can assess this action by applying Hodges' criteria. Did the photographer intend to deceive the public? Most likely, not. He probably assumed the protesters were marching and holding signs earlier, so his intent wasn't likely deceitful. Could his request change the meaning of the image? It moved the people from inaction to action, which may have changed the meaning. So, in this case, the visual manipulation could be considered unethical.

Seeking and presenting truth visually requires a clear understanding of and adherence to the news organization's digital image policy. It also calls for a willingness to call on superiors to revisit and revise the policy if need be. When working with images, remember to check yourself by asking if you intend to mislead the viewer through your actions. Also, ask if your action changes the meaning of the image. Purposefully misleading the audience and changing an image's meaning quash the truth and must not be tolerated.

Misleading through images

An undercover narcotics agent simulated a drug buy for a television news story on street drug dealing. He and a plain-clothes police officer exchanged marijuana for cash while a videographer captured the reenactment on camera. And they repeated the action so the videographer could shoot close-ups of the drugs and the money. A microphone picked up the agent saying, "This is really good weed." If the reporter used these images and sound in her report, she might be misleading the public. That's because viewers could construe the scene as real if it were not identified as a reenactment. RTNDA guidelines state that journalists must inform the public when using reenacted sounds or images in their reports.

Using stereotypical images can also mislead. Publishing a photo of a flamboyant cross-dresser at a gay rights parade where most of the participants were wearing everyday attire would be one example. Another might be choosing to picture an Asian person in a high-tech environment even though most there are Caucasian. Or, featuring a woman athlete in tears after losing a game, rather than seeing her in fierce competition. We must ask ourselves, "Does this picture tell the truth about this event or person?"

Distorting visual content

Photojournalists often shoot five, ten, or even twenty times more video-tape than they will use in a final edited story. Utmost care must be taken in selecting shots that will maintain a true visual context. Omitting visuals or making bad editing choices may result in distortion. For example, omission of a single scene led to a lawsuit against CBS. A hunter named Uhl sued CBS for its depiction of him in a documentary called *The Guns of Autumn*. He argued that the film made it appear that he had shot a goose on the ground, which among hunters, is considered unethical and unsportsmanlike. The sequence of visuals in question began with a scene that showed geese walking on the ground in a cleared area of a cornfield. The next visual showed Uhl and other hunters rising and shooting horizontally. It was followed by a shot of Uhl picking up a dead goose in the cornfield. The court said the portrayal was inaccurate, supporting a "reckless falsehood" (Kim and Paddon 1999). To avoid distortion, editors must carefully consider shot sequences to ensure they truthfully represent events. For this story, a missing picture of the geese in flight was key to the context of the event.

Technical clarity

Before computers, photographers used darkroom techniques such as dodging and burning to lighten or darken areas of their prints. Today, with a digital imaging program, an editor can do even more to adjust the technical quality of a photograph, including focus, texture, brightness, tint, contrast, and correcting red eye. Recall that the SPJ ethics code does allow enhancing images for technical clarity. But using these techniques can sometimes alter the meaning of photographs. When police arrested O.J. Simpson and charged him with murder, they released a mug shot to the media, which appeared on the covers of *Time* and *Newsweek* magazines. But the image on the *Time* cover appeared to have been altered. Simpson's skin tone looked very dark, which some say, made him look sinister, or guilty. One might argue that the photo's technical quality was enhanced, falling within the parameters of the SPJ ethics code. However, the National Press Photographers Association found the *Time* cover unacceptable. "Our credibility is damaged every time a reputable news organization is caught lying to the public and one of the most blatant and widely recognized cases was the computer enhancement of the *Time* Magazine cover photo of O. J. Simpson." (Ethics in the age of digital photography 2000)

These examples illustrate some of the problems and issues concerning digital images and truth. Recognizing that changes made before and after the shutter clicks can have an impact on the meaning of a photograph is the beginning to truth telling with images.

Special Considerations on Reporting Truth on the Internet

Print and broadcast storytelling is linear, with a beginning, middle, and end. Online journalism can also be linear, with a streaming video report or straight text story. But interactive options allow for new storytelling formats, often giving the user a choice of what to read, see, and hear, and in what order. And those decisions can have an impact on the story meaning, in essence, its truth.

Multimedia journalist Joe Weiss encountered this challenge when producing his online story, "Touching Hearts," about a team of international heart specialists on a medical mission to Nicaragua. Weiss recognized that people would come to the site with different interests. Some might want to focus on the medical team's experience, while others would have a patient or general interest orientation. While Weiss wanted to give the user a choice in interacting with the story, presenting it in several vignettes, he recognized that approach might be taking something away from the larger story. "It really aggravated me that some of the best parts of telling the story, which are the transitions, and the relationships between one vignette and another are missing in that form," said Weiss (2002). To address the issue, Weiss used programming language within Flash software to create different story paths dependent on choices made by the user. "Behind the scenes, it's changing the stories in reaction to how you're looking at it," said Weiss. "If you come into the stories and it's obvious that you're only clicking things that deal with the medical personnel, it will sort of drive you to some of the other stories, because you should see those too. That project was as interactive as I've ever done." (2002) Weiss won the 2001 Online Journalism Award for Creative Use of the Medium for "Touching Hearts." The judges said, "It uses an innovative combination of interactivity, letting the reader click through it, and TV-style presentation where a reader can simply sit back and absorb." (Online News Association 2001)

Giving the user control without giving away story context is an important consideration when chunking material online. Context is integral to reporting truth.

Accuracy Online

A television reporter I know doesn't always feel comfortable when her stories are edited for the station's online edition. She said that on more than one occasion the Web editor made mistakes when changing the broadcast script to a print story. One might argue this could only happen in a small market where journalists are just learning the ropes, but even major online news organizations make errors. When ABC News was testing a system for automatically posting election results on its Web site, some of the fake test pages went public. ABC fired the person who had sent them out (Weber, Bodipo-Memba, and Peterson 1998). A search on nytimes.com using the key word "correction" yielded 135 story corrections for a 30-day period (2003). Errors included a wrong: job title, location, date, source, school name, and number. There was a misspelled name, dead people named as survivors in an obituary, and a correction to a quote. *The New York Times on the Web* makes its errors public by posting corrections. So do *The Washington Post* and the *Chicago Tribune*. Being accountable for errors is an essential component of a news organization's credibility. Nearly two out of three people polled say they feel better about the newspaper after seeing corrections (Bressers 2001). But they really do dislike the mistakes. Some blame the nature of the Internet and online publishing for the errors. In 2002, MSNBC.com ombudsman Dan Fisher said speed contributed to some site errors. "A lot of what I come across are small, inadvertent slips due to the speed involved in getting things onto the site," he said (Fisher 2002).

A commitment to accuracy can reduce errors. At the *Chicago Tribune*, accuracy is a major priority. Its unwritten policy, "It is better to be last than wrong," has its roots in a headline "Dewey Defeats Truman," which marked the newspaper for many years (Fuller 1996, p. 4). Today, rigorous procedures help ensure accuracy in print and online. The *Tribune's* error policy, adopted in 1996, requires staff to complete correction forms to help track and identify patterns of mistakes (*Chicago Tribune* Error Policy 2002). Recent findings show that about half the mistakes are made during the newsgathering process, with editing accounting for the next largest number of errors (Holt 2003). Journalists often make mistakes when they fail to confirm information or make assumptions. Of course, there are those times when a journalist has a bad day, resulting in mistakes. One *Tribune* journalist explained, "I do not mean to make excuses and am not trying to be funny, but insomnia caused me to get a mere 4 hours sleep the night before and my left eye felt like a hot needle sticking in it. I was really fading when I wrote this story." (Examples of Errors)

The following checklist can help digital journalists strive for accuracy. It is guided by *Chicago Tribune* error examples and explanations, and a "protocol of fact checking" used by the *Atlanta Journal-Constitution* (Holt 2003). My own illustrations embellish some of the points.

1. Confirm information. Even if you have a story clip or news release that contains a name, address, title, or organization, double check to make sure it's right.
2. Review notes to avoid confusion. Sometimes we skip something or write illegibly. Going over notes right after an event or interview may help catch the problem.
3. Do not assume anything. At a recent George Clinton and the P-Funk Allstars performance, a musician clad in a towel came onstage early in the show. Some in the audience assumed he was Clinton, but they were wrong. As journalists, if we're not sure, we've got to ask a reliable source.
4. Look for red flags. If something doesn't look right, it's probably not. A reporter writes an acronym for a local organization as RATS. However, the editor recalls seeing R.A.T.S. painted on its vans. Which is right? Call the organization to confirm.
5. Read the hard copy. Working from a computer screen for hours can play tricks on the eye. Print out a copy of the story to read and correct.
6. Check all numbers and addresses. This goes for phone numbers and Web addresses. Call the telephone number to be sure it's right. Visit the Web address to make sure it works. And get out your calculator to do the math.

When an occasional error does slip through, a correction should be posted online. But the online corrections page appears to be the exception rather than the rule in a digital news world where an error can be changed almost as quickly as it is made. Some online newsrooms promptly correct errors when discovered, and move on (Palser 2001). Why call attention to mistakes that can be fixed? What's really at stake here is credibility. More than two-thirds of Americans say news organizations try to cover up their mistakes (News media's improved image proves short lived 2002). Our role in a democratic society is weakened when the public doesn't trust journalists to report accurately.

Clarity

You may recall reading or seeing a story online and then asking, "Huh?" afterward. Something about it didn't make sense, or needed clarification. Perhaps it happened in the reshaping from broadcast or print to an Internet story.

Or maybe the added pressure of writing a story for an earlier deadline forced the reporter to post a first draft or a work in progress. It could even be that the reporter didn't fully understand what he was writing about, transferring the murkiness to the reader. None of these explanations excuse the digital journalist from shirking on clarity. Avoiding these common traps can help make news on the Internet more understandable.

Clarity and repurposed stories

Reshaping—often called repurposing—news, from an organization's main medium to the Web, requires changing the original story to make it more Internet friendly. For a broadcast script, this might mean expanding the piece by adding greater detail. It also requires clarifying dates, because broadcast scripts often use today and yesterday, rather than Monday or Sunday. Another challenge broadcast editors face is making sense of a script that has incues and outcues for sound bites, rather than their full text. These are the first and last few words of the sound bite. If the editor doesn't see the video story, then it's impossible to know what the sources said. Broadcast reporters sometimes get testy when asked to transcribe sound bites. It takes extra time, and that can mean missing a deadline. Another issue involves the visuals. Often, a visual will carry meaning that is not referred to in the script. For example, a broadcast reporter may show an exterior picture of city hall and not mention in the script the meeting location. But, the online version must make the reference in the text. So, it's important to look out for such instances. Newsrooms could help avert these types of problems by making sure editors have access to a videotape of the newscast. In a fully digital newsroom, the video story would be available for viewing on the desktop. Reporters also can adopt the attitude that the more exposure their story gets, the better. They can help Internet editors by providing them transcribed sound bites, locations, and even notes with details they may not have been able to include in their on-air version.

Repurposing a print story for the Web might mean updating the lead with more current information, cutting its length, making the writing a bit more conversational, and adding headings and subheadings to help guide the reader. Links could also be added to related stories or Web sites. During this process, not losing essential detail and attending to the flow and meaning are key. If the first reference to a source is cut, be sure that person's title isn't lost in the subsequent mention.

Work on improving clarity when reshaping stories for the Web by keeping in mind the medium for which you are writing. Print- or broadcast-specific storytelling may have to be adjusted to achieve clarity online.

Clarity and the developing story

The rush to publish online can influence the clarity of the developing story. Working to post a story as quickly as possible, writers may place a first draft online without taking time to edit. They may do so thinking they can continue refining the piece as the story develops. However, the initial posting should always be carefully edited, no matter how rushed the reporter may be.

Avoiding murkiness by addressing semantic problems

A friend of mine has worked in medical billing for years, and when we get into conversations about health insurance, she often uses language I just don't understand. She'll discuss medical procedures, patient conditions, and drugs I've never heard of. And if I don't probe her for detail and clarification, she won't offer it, because she's so immersed in her job that it probably doesn't occur to her that I'm in the dark. Journalists face similar situations when covering the news. They often talk to specialists who possess an entire vocabulary particular to their disciplines. Without asking them to explain, or to help you understand what they just told you, you're going to have to write about something that may not be perfectly clear to you. And that can lead to semantic problems.

Shannon and Weaver introduced this idea in their book, *The Mathematical Theory of Communication* (1964). They identify semantic problems as those that pertain to the receiver's interpretation of meaning rather than the sender's intended meaning. So, while a specialized technical term may be perfectly clear to the scientific expert, the news consumer who reads it may not understand.

To communicate clearly with the audience, digital journalists must assess the potential for semantic problems. Avoid using terms unfamiliar to the general public, or if used, be sure to explain them fully. Ask for clarification so that you will understand and tell an accurate and meaningful story to your readers.

Fairness

Reporters sometimes find themselves writing and producing unfair stories. In most cases, it's not because of intentional bias, but because they didn't get the interviews needed to make the story fair. They often try, but aren't able to reach a source vital to the story's completeness. For example, consider a manufacturing plant under investigation for dumping industrial waste into an adjacent river where hundreds of fish are found dead. Reporters quoted the agency investigating the incident, but included nothing from the company in question. In this case, it turned out the reporters had called the plant, but couldn't get through to anyone who would talk to them. The message they left was not returned before deadline. I find this problem common among student and beginning reporters who are reluctant to call more than once so as not to "bother" a source. But a reporter should make every effort possible to give subjects of stories the opportunity to comment. And the public deserves to know that effort was made. When a reporter makes a concerted effort to contact a source, and the calls and e-mails are not returned, that should be noted in the story.

The RTNDA ethics code encourages journalists to present diverse opinions and expressions, and to put ideas into context. Reporters who go only to official sources, ignoring the people affected by government agencies and public programs, aren't always telling the story fairly. How would you feel after reading a story about your university's proposal to eliminate the communication major, if it excluded the student point of view? Or a report on tearing down public housing to make room for an upscale shopping center, if it included the developer and city planner, but nothing from the people who live there or their representative? The stories would be incomplete and unfair. Pressing deadlines and lack of resourcefulness might explain why these stories make it on air, in print, and online. But if laziness and bias are the real culprits, then reporters and editors who let these stories pass through the gates should revisit their commitment to fairness.

Their choice of quotes or sound bites can also get journalists into trouble when it comes to story fairness. On-camera interviews with sources sometimes yield lengthy trains of thought that take minutes to tell. And when the reporter has to keep the story length to ninety seconds or two minutes at most, it's challenging to choose the representative piece of that thought. Reporters must keep comments in context and retain their true gist when making edits. One reporter puts editing to the Mom test. If you can edit the interview and say, "It was okay, Mom, I swear I was fair," then your sound bite passes the test (Westin p. 37).

Unidentified Sources and Fairness

News consumers tell us they don't like it when the media use unidentified sources. More than three-fourths of people in a study by the American Society of Newspaper Editors said they were concerned about the credibility of stories that used anonymous sources (Accuracy matters 1999). This concern came to the forefront after the Clinton-Lewinsky scandal in the late 1990s, when many media relied freely on anonymous sources in reporting the unfolding story of the relationship between former President Clinton and the then-22-year-old White House intern. A Freedom Forum study reflected this concern, with 70 percent of survey participants saying they disagreed that it was appropriate to use anonymous sources in reporting what took place inside a grand jury room (Haiman). If it erodes trust, why do it? One television reporter told the Freedom Forum it was sexy. Others argue that journalists couldn't do their jobs without the help of unnamed sources, citing the Watergate story as a prime example. But some media are committed to using on-record sources. *USA Today* developed a strict policy when it was founded in the early '80s because editors felt untrue or misleading rumors and attacks were being fed to reporters who would publish the information and not name its source. (Haiman). The Associated Press, a news service that provides stories to media around the world, requires anonymous material to pass three tests. First, it must be information, not opinion or speculation, that is essential to the story. Second, it's only available if the source is kept anonymous. And, third, the source must be reliable and the reporter must know how the source knows the material to be true (Haiman).

Digital journalists should follow the lead of these major news organizations when faced with not naming sources. Insist on using sources who can be identified. And when there is absolutely no other way to attain the information, discuss the situation with a high-level editor before going with the story.

Avoiding Sensationalism and Extremes

A parody of the worst example of television news might read, "And now, the tragic story of an innocent victim and how senseless violence led to a lifetime of pain and suffering." Both the story topic and presentation are sensational, which by a basic dictionary definition means, "arousing or tending to arouse (as by lurid details) a quick, intense, and usually superficial interest, curiosity, or emotional reaction." (Merriam-Webster's 1999, p. 1066). Sensational story topics usually include crime, violence, celebrity, scandal, sex, disaster, and accidents (Slattery, Doremus, and Marcus 2001; Grabe, Zhou, and Barnett 2001). Presentation involves the language used in telling the story and elements of form. Words that titillate, or that tell a viewer what to feel, are often sensational. *Shocking, horrible, harrowing, terrible*—these are just a few of the sensational adjectives news writers slip into their stories. But using these words to call attention to the story can sometimes cheapen it. Allow the audience to decide what to think, rather than manipulating with subjective language.

Production techniques can also cross the line from serious to sensational reporting. Maria Elizabeth Grabe and her colleagues examined the television magazine programs *Hard Copy* and *60 Minutes* for their presentation forms, such as editing effects and pace, sound effects and music, camera techniques, and voice tone. They concluded, "The bells and whistles that mark a flamboyant production style are clearly associated with *Hard Copy* and are sparingly used on *60 Minutes*." (Grabe, Zhou, and Barnett 2001). Examples of the techniques used more often by *Hard Copy* than *60 Minutes* include slow-motion video, camera zooms, music, and a faster editing pace.

So, again, choice of language and production techniques can have an impact on a story's level of sensationalism. A sensational story can be told straight-forwardly. And our goal as digital journalists should be telling stories responsibly. Much of the news is sensational by nature. Simply choosing not to cover it is often not an option. But we can ask ourselves how we are serving the community by covering a particular story. If the answer is, "It's not really relevant, but we're highlighting it on our Web page because it's so extreme," then we should reconsider our judgment. If you're a Web producer in Michigan and a woman in Texas calls 911 to report she's just killed two of her children, do you include the story prominently on your Web page? Her mug shot and a vivid description including several mentions of blood are available. Just because you have it doesn't mean you should run it. At this point, the story does not serve your community. If there had been a similar case in Michigan, the rationale for including it might be more sound. But sordid detail of a bizarre crime for pure shock value does not meet the conditions for coverage. One might argue that the nature of this crime was so bizarre that it merits inclusion on the Web site.

Placing the story in a less prominent location through a headline link would be preferable to showcasing it with photo and high placement.

Before deciding to run a sensational story on our Web sites, we should ask ourselves two questions. First, does the story serve the public, or are we attracted to it for its shock value? Remember to put the public first. And second, how can I tell the story responsibly? Avoiding charged adjectives and audiovisual editing effects can help digital journalists tell the story that's sensational by nature in a responsible way.

Special Fairness Considerations Online

The ability to link to material outside a news Web site can offer greater depth to a story. But it can also contribute to bias. Take a story on the low-carbohydrate diet controversy. If it offers a link to atkinscenter.com, the Web site for the Atkins companies, but doesn't include a link to *The Journal of the American Medical Association* or another source for studies on such diets, that story treatment could be considered unfair. Additional information should provide balanced points of view, not an endorsement of only one side.

Independence

When a young television news reporter investigated used car dealers who were breaking the law and cheating customers, the station's general manager came down to the newsroom to see her about the story. But instead of praising her for alerting the community to the wrongdoing, he warned her to never again do another story like that. It just so happened that more than one of the dealers ran commercials on the station, and threatened to pull their ads because of the story. After the warning, the reporter kept her distance from the dealerships or risked losing her job.

When advertisers influence news coverage, they undermine the freedom of the press to inform the public. Pressuring journalists to avoid stories, such as the car dealers did, or leaning on them to put a positive spin on coverage, compromises journalistic integrity. But threats to independence aren't limited to advertisers. Political figures and other powerful individuals and groups may also exert influence. Attempts to control content may be obvious or subtle, but as SPJ professes, "Journalists should be free of obligation to any interest other than the public's right to know." (1996)

Serving Citizens

For whom does an artist work? Ask one, and she might tell you she is ultimately responsible to herself; that while others enjoy her music or her paintings, she creates for herself. What about white-collar workers? Most would probably say they're responsible to the company that provides their paycheck. While a journalist uses his own talent to report and produce stories and works for an organization that pays his salary, his first commitment should lie elsewhere. The Project for Excellence in Journalism posts a "Citizens Bill of Journalism Rights" (2003) on its Web site at journalism.org, wherein it states, "We should expect proof that the journalists' first loyalty is to citizens." The bill of rights says this means that stories should meet the needs of the people, not just insiders or the political or business systems. This commitment should hold steady whether the medium is print, broadcast, or Web.

In the early post-Watergate era of the mid-1970s and into the early '80s, journalism attracted many idealistic young people who felt they could truly make a difference by exposing wrongdoing. Serving the public stood as a clear driving force behind their work. Fast forward to the new millennium where the social, economic, and technological landscapes have changed dramatically, and the journalistic value of serving the public may be more important than ever before. Public perception of the news media is alarmingly low. Nearly six out of ten Americans say the news media get in the way of society in solving its problems (News media's improved image proves short lived 2002). Fewer companies now own and control media, which critics such as Robert McChesney (1999) argue threaten democracy. Instead of treating readers as citizens, critics fear media instead view them only as customers. Today's technology is transforming news into an information business in which people can get what they want, when they want it, and how they want it. If readers don't ask for news about their schools or government, how will they ever know about key issues in their communities? Competing pressures on journalists to serve many masters can lead them astray from their commitment to the public.

The reason you're studying journalism may be similar to that of the early post-Watergate student. You recognize that journalists provide information people need to make informed decisions about their lives. You can be a check on government and business. You can make a difference. Perhaps your reasons differ. You write well, like working with people, enjoy integrating words, sounds, and images to tell a story. You're adept at working with digital technology. You like gathering and presenting information. You've always been hungry for news. And in an immediate, visual medium, you may feel at ease in front of a camera, and think well on your feet under pressure. These are all good reasons for pursuing a career in digital journalism. But keeping sight of the citizen as your first commitment can bring deeper satisfaction and meaning to what you do.

Activities for Further Learning

1. Whom would you interview for a story on your student health center distributing "the morning-after" pill? Keep in mind truth and fairness in your choice of sources.

2. In the following sentences, what needs to be checked for accuracy, and how would you go about it? Correct any errors.

   a. Monica Lewinsky was 21 years old when she had an affair with former President Bill Clinton.

   b. The full text of President Bush's radio address may be found at www.whitehouse.com.

   c. Property taxes will go up 50 percent. That means if you now pay $2,000, next year you'll pay $4,000.

3. Tampa Bay's Fox 13 ran the following top stories on its Web site: "Jackass copycat hurt," "Teen mom kidnapped at gunpoint," "Trial begins for cop-killer's girlfriend," and "Explosive debate over nudity ban" (2003). Assess the headlines for sensationalism in story topic and presentation.

4. Evaluate front-page online news photos for stereotyping. Go to newslink.org and choose at least two newspaper sites and two television sites from major metropolitan areas. Do the same for smaller city newspaper and television sites. Do you find any racial, ethnic, gender, age, sexual orientation, or other stereotypes? If so, suggest an alternate, more representative photo.

References

Accuracy matters. Aug. 10, 1999. American Society of Newspaper Editors. http://www.asne.org/kiosk/reports/99reports/1999examiningourcredibility/p7-10_Accuracy.html

Barry, D., D. Barstow, J.D. Glater, A. Liptak, and J. Steinberg. May 11, 2003. Correcting the record; Times reporter who resigned leaves long trail of deception. *The New York Times*. Section 1, Page 1, Column 1. Retrieved from LexisNexis database.

Bressers, B. Aug. 16, 2001. Credibility; Getting a fix on online corrections [Electronic version]. *The American Editor.* http://www.asne.org/kiosk/editor/01.march/bressers1.htm

Chicago Tribune Error Policy. September 2002.

Citizens Bill of Journalism Rights. 2003. Project for Excellence in Journalism. http://www.journalism.org/resources/guidelines/rights.asp

Code of ethics and professional conduct. Radio-Television News Directors Association. http://rtnda.org/ethics/coe.shtml

Ethics in the age of digital photography. 2002. http://www.nppa.org/services/bizpract/eadp/eadp2.html

Examples of Errors. Undated. Chicago Tribune internal document provided by e-mail.

Fisher, D. April 2, 2002. Cited in Lasica, J. D.; Cyberspace's first ombudsman. *Online Journalism Review*. http://www.ojr.org/ojr/workplace/1017775737.php

Fox 13. 2003. http://www.wtvt.com/

Fuller, J. 1996. *News Values: Ideas for an Information Age*. Chicago: University of Chicago Press.

Grabe, M. E., S. Zhou, and B. Barnett, B. 2001. Explicating sensationalism in television news: content and the bells and whistles of form. *Journal of Broadcasting and Electronic Media*. 45(4) 635-656.

Haiman, R. J. Undated. *Best Practices for Newspaper Journalists*. The Freedom Forum.

Hodges, L. Aug. 4, 2003. E-mail discussion.

Holt, M. May 2, 2003. Accuracy update: 1st quarter 2003. *Chicago Tribune* internal document provided by e-mail.

Kahney, L. Feb. 3, 2003. Fake CNN Web site taken offline. *Wired News*. http://www.wired.com/news/culture/0,1284,57506,00.html

Kim, G. H. and A.R. Paddon 1999. Digital manipulation as new form of evidence of actual malice in libel and false light cases. *Communications and the Law*, 21, 57. Retrieved from Expanded Academic Index ASAP database.

latimes.com. 2003. Editor's note. http://www.latimes.com

McChesney, R. W. 1999. *Rich Media, Poor Democracy: Communication Politics in Dubious Times*. Urbana: University of Illinois Press.

Merriam-Webster's Collegiate Dictionary, Tenth Edition. 1999. Springfield, Massachusetts: Merriam-Webster, Incorporated.

Merritt, Jr., Davis (Buzz) Jr. September 1998. Lecture to students at Washington and Lee University.

News media's improved image proves short lived; The sagging stock market's big audience. Aug. 4, 2002. The Pew Research Center for the People and the Press. http://people-press.org/reports/display.php3?ReportID=159

nytimes.com. April 25, 2003. Site search using keyword "correction."

Online News Association online journalism awards. 2001. http://www.journalists. org/awards/winners/winners%202001/index.html

Palser, B. May 2001. Virtual wite-out [Electronic version]. *American Journalism Review.* Retrieved from http://ajr.org/article.asp?id=187

pulitzer.org. 2003. The Pulitzer Prize winners 2003. http://pulitzer.org/year/2003/ beat-reporting/

Shannon, C. E. and W. Weaver. 1964. *The Mathematical Theory of Communication.* Urbana: The University of Illinois Press.

Sherer, M. and J. Long. 2003. Digitally altered photo from Iraq violates NPPA ethics. http://nppa.org/default.cfm

Slattery, K., M. Doremus, and L. Marcus. 2001. Shifts in public affairs reporting on the network evening news: A move toward the sensational [Electronic version]. *Journal of Broadcasting and Electronic Media.* 45(2) 290.

Society of Professional Journalists Code of Ethics 1996. http://spj.org/ethics_ code.asp

Sugg, D. K. Feb. 24, 2002. Present at loved one's last moments; some hospitals let families stay at CPR. http://www.pulitzer.org/year/2003/beat-reporting/ works/sugg3.html

Sugg, D. K. Sept. 4, 2003. E-mail correspondence.

Weber, T. E., A. Bodipo-Memba, and A. Petersen. Nov. 6, 1998. Online: Oops; in cyberspace, news often jumps the gun. *Wall Street Journal.* Retrieved from ProQuest database.

Weiss, J. Aug. 27, 2002. Personal interview.

Westin, A. Undated. *Best Practices for Television Journalists.* The Freedom Forum.

CHAPTER 3

Legal and Ethical Considerations

Chapter Objectives

Teenagers equipped with 3G video mobile phones are going under-cover in bars and clubs to report on juvenile alcohol consumption. The phones produce sounds and images that can be broadcast on the air or streamed on the Web—but should news media use the devices in this way?

Students reporting for an online newspaper want to post a photo of a professor who was arrested at an adult bookstore. They've found his pic-ture on the university Web site—but should they use it?

An Internet news site includes a forum for public discussion of com-munity issues. Some of the postings are vulgar and attack individuals by name. Should the news organization censor those comments?

These questions illustrate some of the legal and ethical issues presented by emerging digital technologies and the Internet's accessibility and in-teractivity. This chapter addresses challenges digital journalists are grap-pling with, and offers guidance for reporting and producing in cyberspace.

Legal Issues and Journalism

Good journalists must sometimes do difficult things, such as talking to the parents of a dying child, or reporting from the scene of a violent crime. Their stories can expose wrongdoing, and may anger people. And, be-cause of the nature of this work, the question, "Can I be sued for this?"

sometimes emerges. The answer isn't always clear, especially online, where the issues are still evolving. In many cases, it's advisable to consult newsroom management or the company's attorney for guidance. But, it's also wise to become familiar with the law as it pertains to everyday news-gathering and presentation. This section offers an overview of libel, privacy, copyright, reporter's privilege, and free press/fair trial.

Libel

Pulitzer Prize-winning journalist Walt Bogdanich spent a year researching and documenting the story "Smoke Screen" for the ABC News program *Day One*. After poring over tobacco industry literature, examining documents, and interviewing an army of sources, he felt confident tobacco companies were manipulating nicotine levels in cigarettes. After the report aired in 1994, Philip Morris sued ABC for $10 billion, the largest libel suit in history. Bogdanich and on-air correspondent John Martin insisted on the story's accuracy, and ABC stood behind it, spending 16 months and millions of dollars defending it in court. A victory for the news organization appeared certain, but ABC eventually settled the case. Critics contend a business deal forced the action—media giant Disney announced plans to buy ABC at about the same time of the settlement. The legal battle ended with an on-air apology to Philip Morris and payment of the tobacco company's court costs, amounting to approximately $15 million. But Bogdanich refused to sign the settlement, standing behind the story's accuracy (Weinberg 1995, Altman 1996, Collins 2000).

Journalists who perform their duty to seek truth and report it can and do get sued—even those at the highest levels. People who feel they and their companies have been harmed by news reports sometimes bring suit for libel to vindicate their names. They assert a story included false information, damaging their reputation. Libel is among the most complex areas of law, so it makes sense for journalists to be familiar with its key components. It is defined as a "false and defamatory attack in written form on a person's reputation or character." (Gillmor, Barron, Simon, and Terry 1990, p. 172) Broadcast defamation is generally considered libel because a written script is usually made. While the First Amendment protects press freedom, libel law protects the people against abuses by the press.

The plaintiff who sues for libel must establish that the statement:

1. Was defamatory. In other words, that it damaged the plaintiff's reputation.
2. Concerned the plaintiff.

3. Was published (this includes broadcast, for the most part).
4. Is false.

Public figures must also prove that the defendant acted with *actual malice*, or in other words, knowing it was false, or with "reckless disregard for the truth." (*Gertz v. Robert Welch, Inc.* 1974).

Private individuals must establish *negligence* of the defendant. And to receive punitive damages in a media case, they must also prove *actual malice*.

Fear of a libel suit can drive journalists away from pursuing difficult stories that may expose individual wrongdoing. The authors of *Mass Communication Law: Cases and Comment* recommend that reporters find more than one source for allegations that may be libelous. They also suggest talking to the person to whom charges are being directed and documenting controversial statements (Gillmor et al. 1990).

Libel online

The Internet is presenting new libel issues for journalists. One involves the treatment of online errors. Let's say your Internet news site posts a story at 5 p.m. that contains a mistake. Instead of writing, *Mr. Jones said he DID NOT download and distribute music from his office computer,* the reporter wrote, *Mr. Jones said he DID download and distribute music from his office computer.* The error goes unnoticed by the news staff until the next day, when Jones' boss calls to complain. At this point, the story's no longer on the news Web page—it's already gone to the archive. What should you do? Simply changing the error or leaving a false statement in the archived story could prove problematic. Instead, legal experts suggest posting corrections at the top of the archived copy, to ensure the reader knows the error has been corrected (Hart 2003). Doing so provides a clear record of what was published and how it was changed.

Another online libel issue concerns place of publication. Before the advent of the Internet, newspapers published where their presses were located and television and radio stations broadcast from their studio locations. U.S. and state law was applied based on a story's place of publication. However, the concept of publication is shifting following a recent international case involving an online news story. An Australian citizen sued Dow Jones & Co. Inc., asserting that an article in *Barron's Online*, "Unholy Gains," defamed him. Dow Jones argued that the story was published in New Jersey, where the Web site's servers were located. But, Australia's highest court ruled that the U.S. publisher must defend the suit in

Australia (Libel suit against Dow Jones to proceed in Australia 2003). "You don't know as a journalist with any certainty what law will apply to you," said Stuart D. Karle, Associate General Counsel for Dow Jones. "Basically, if it's on the Web, you can get sued wherever somebody can read it." (2003) That uncertainty could result in a chilling effect for journalists on the Web. Because they do not know who, in what part of the world, might perceive a story as defamatory, news organizations could censor difficult stories to protect themselves against potential lawsuits from abroad.

Online bulletin boards and discussion forums present another muddy area for news Web sites. Are news organizations responsible for the content posted to them? Section 230 of the Communications Decency Act has created immunity for Web publishers who post content from a third party. Courts have applied this protection broadly, according to online legal expert Jonathan Hart (2003, p. 136):

...the operator of a website may choose to exercise control over the content of its site by removing or editing content provided by third parties without becoming liable as the "publisher" of the third-party statements.

Many online news sites choose to edit comments posted to their forums, because indecent language and remarks that don't address the issues at hand may turn off readers to the site. A news organization's standards of decency would, in most cases, carry over to its Web site.

Privacy

What does privacy mean to you? Turning off your cell phone? Closing the door to your room? Logging off of your e-mail? More than a century ago, Judge Thomas Cooley defined privacy as "the right to be let alone." (1888, p. 29) Today, his words continue to ring true. At what point does reporting what the public needs and wants to know infringe on a person's right to privacy? As a journalist, knowing about the legal aspects of privacy can help us do our jobs more responsibly. Two major areas confront us when it comes to privacy and the media—the gathering of information and its presentation.

Privacy and newsgathering

When does the work of journalists intrude on the privacy of the people involved in their stories? In general, the news media are not intruding when gathering news in a public place. Courts have ruled that journalists who shot videotape of a home or business from a public street did not intrude (*Mark v. Seattle Times* 1982, *Wehling v. CBS* 1983). But this has not been the case on private property. In the late 1970s, a reporter and camera crew in New York visited a number of restaurants cited for health code violations. They entered Le Mistral unannounced, with lights on and the camera rolling, "catching the occupants by surprise." The restaurant sued CBS for trespassing, and won. The New York Supreme Court judge who wrote the opinion noted, as other intrusion cases had in the past, that the First Amendment does not provide the news media the right to trespass (*Le Mistral* 1978). While one may think restaurants or malls are public places because they are open to people to enter and exit as they please, legally, such locations are considered private. Journalists must seek permission to photograph in these and other private locations. While there have been exceptions, as a general rule, journalists should not trespass to report a story.

Another newsgathering privacy issue involves audio recordings. In some states, it is legal to record a personal conversation or telephone call without telling the other party he or she is being taped. However, that's not the case for broadcasting a recording. Section 73.1206 of the Federal Communication Commission's rules requires a licensee to advise the person being recorded of the intent to broadcast the conversation. The commission fined a Tempe, Arizona radio station $4,000 for broadcasting a conversation between one of its on-air personalities and the widow of St. Louis Cardinals' baseball pitcher Darryl Kile. According to the commission's report, the radio personality telephoned Ms. Kile while she was visiting Phoenix, told her she was "hot," and asked her if she had a date to the Cardinal's-Diamondbacks playoff game—without telling her the conversation was being aired (FCC Tempe 2003). Even broadcasting an answering machine message can violate the rule if the person whose voice is on the tape has not been advised of intent to broadcast (FCC AMFM 2002).

It would be wise to follow the FCC guidelines before streaming an audio recording online. Tell the person being recorded of your intent to post the audio to the Web.

Privacy and news presentation

When can news organizations publish or broadcast a person's image, and when is that a violation of privacy? It's illegal if the name or likeness is used without consent for commercial gain. This is called misappropriation, and in media cases it generally concerns using a person's image in advertisements without his or her consent. A defense against misappropriation is newsworthiness. But even the concept of newsworthiness has limits, as a case involving a human cannonball act illustrates. Hugo Zacchini performed his act at a county fair in Ohio, where he was shot from a cannon into a net, approximately 200 feet away. A free-lance reporter videotaped the spectacle for a local television station, which aired the 15-second clip, even though the performer told the reporter not to tape it. Zacchini sued, and won when the case went before the U.S. Supreme Court. Justice White wrote the Court's opinion (*Zacchini v. Scripps-Howard* 1977):

> The broadcast of a film of petitioner's entire act poses a substantial threat to the economic value of that performance. As the Ohio court recognized, this act is the product of petitioner's own talents and energy, the end result of much time, effort, and expense. Much of its economic value lies in the "right of exclusive control over the publicity given to his performance"; if the public can see the act free on television, it will be less willing to pay to see it at the fair.

The entertainer has a right to control his or her "property," which may be an act, or simply a likeness of that person's image.

Broadcasting or publishing private information that is true, but embarrassing, can be grounds for an invasion of privacy suit. And while newsworthiness is a strong defense against embarrassing facts cases, the media have lost when the courts found that they had gone too far. A case in which a newspaper published a photograph of a woman whose skirt had blown over her head, exposing her legs and underwear, and another in which a magazine article referred to a woman as "the starving glutton," both garnered awards for those who brought suit (Creech 2003). Information acquired from public record, such as police or court documents, can be published (*Cox Broadcasting Corp. v. Cohn* 1975).

Privacy online

Lawmakers at the state and federal levels are taking steps to secure the privacy of citizens on the Internet. The 108th Congress introduced at least fifty bills that involved some aspect of online privacy (Thomas .loc.gov 2003). And some states have adopted Internet privacy legislation.

The conflict between the privacy of citizens and freedom of information challenges journalists when doing their jobs. Numerous resources are available to assist reporters and producers in working with information online. Some are free, others charge a fee. On Columbia Journalism Review's Power Reporting Web site, journalists can find links to thousands of free research tools (http://powerreporting.com). Duff Wilson of *The Seattle Times* has a page on the Investigative Reporters and Editors' Web site called "Who is John Doe—and where to get the paper on him" (http://www.reporter.org/desktop/tips/johndoe.htm, 2003). The page provides links to sites that journalists can use to find specific information on individuals, from phone numbers to criminal records.

Privacy online and children. The Children's Online Privacy Protection Act of 1998 governs the collection of information online from children under the age of 13. It specifically deals with Web sites or online services that collect information from minors. The act sets forth requirements, including obtaining parental consent, to collect, use, or disclose personal information about children. A news site that contains a kid's section may be subject to this act if it collects information from the children who visit the site. The full text of the act may be found on the FTC's Web site at http://www.ftc.gov/ogc/coppa1.htm.

Seeking permission from a parent or guardian is advisable when interviewing or photographing children for an online news story.

Copyright

Myriad sources of information fill today's newsroom. The Associated Press news wire, CNN Newsource, and other network services and news feeds pump text, photos, video and audio into the newsroom 'round the clock. In addition, the readily-available information stream online makes access just a few keystrokes away—from a competitor's news site, to research and creative works. Perhaps this free-flowing availability of information confuses some journalists into believing that they have a right to use anything available online in whatever way they wish. But they are sadly mistaken. Your news organization's contracts with media services dictate the parameters of the material's use. And much of the information found online is protected by copyright. Copyright law protects original works of authorship (Copyright Section 102), including:

1. Literary works
2. Musical works, including any accompanying words
3. Dramatic works, including any accompanying music
4. Pantomimes and choreographic works

5. Pictorial, graphic, and sculptural works
6. Motion pictures and other audiovisual works
7. Sound recordings
8. Architectural works

This means that such material belongs to the owner of the copyright, and those who wish to use it must obtain permission to do so. The Digital Millennium Copyright Act of 1998 extends protection to works produced in digital media (Hart 2003). Legally, we can't just grab a photo off a Web site, reproduce a story reported by a competing newspaper, or enhance a television news piece by downloading a favorite riff. Clarify with your supervisor what materials your newsroom subscribes to and the parameters for their use.

Fair use

A provision of copyright law allows for "fair use" of material for the purposes of "criticism, comment, news reporting, teaching (including multiple copies for classroom use), scholarship, or research." (Copyright Section 107) The following factors (Copyright Section 107) would be used to determine fair use of copyrighted material:

1. The purpose and character of the use, including whether such use is of a commercial nature or is for nonprofit educational purposes
2. The nature of the copyrighted work
3. The amount and substantiality of the portion used in relation to the copyrighted work as a whole
4. The effect of the use upon the potential market for or value of the copyrighted work

Often, the fourth point weighs heavily in determining copyright infraction. But the copyright office warns that, "The distinction between 'fair use' and infringement may be unclear and not easily defined. There is no specific number of words, lines, or notes that may safely be taken without permission. Acknowledging the source of the copyrighted material does not substitute for obtaining permission." (Copyright, Fair Use 1999)

Public domain

Materials whose copyright has expired, and those produced by the federal government, are considered to be in the public domain and may be used without infringement of copyright (Lutzker 2003). Works funded by public tax dollars may include government films, images from space, federal reports, and other materials. But one cannot assume that an image or text available on a government Web site is free from copyright restrictions. An independent contractor who is not an employee of the government may have created the work in question, and may own the copyright. Check to see if a copyright notice is posted along with the work (Lutzker 2003). If you cannot determine that it is in the public domain, seek permission before using it.

Copyright online

Some special considerations involving copyright are evolving with the Web.

Linking is at the heart of the Internet, allowing the user to navigate many levels through cyberspace. Jonathan Hart, one of the nation's leading experts on the law and Web publishing, wrote, "Without more, a simple link to a website is generally not understood to implicate the copyrights of the site being linked to." (2003, p. 96) But journalists should be aware that deep linking to specific material on the internal pages of a Web site has led to a number of lawsuits. In one of the more prominent cases, Ticketmaster Corp. sued tickets.com for linking to its deep interior Web pages, but the court eliminated the copyright claims from the action (2003). The content, its presentation, and the way tickets.com accessed the internal pages had an impact on the court's decision. Nonetheless, the case calls attention to the act of deep linking as an area of potential problems.

Framing has also prompted copyright disputes. This is the practice of displaying another's Web site in a smaller box, or frame, within one's own site. By framing, the user stays within the original Web site instead of being directed away, to the site linked to. Photographer Leslie Kelly sued Arriba Soft Corporation for copyright infringement involving unauthorized display of photographs from his Web site. Arriba's site displayed Kelly's work as thumbnail images on its site. When the user clicked on a thumbnail, it linked to Kelly's full-frame photo and displayed it within Arriba's site. This practice of in-line linking allows Web sites to incorporate works into their Web sites without actually copying them there. The court found the thumbnails fair use, but in 2003 remanded for further proceedings display of the full-frame photos (*Kelly v. Arriba* 2003). As with deep linking, framing can be a problematic area for news sites.

Another issue on the Web involves free-lance writers and reuse of their work in online databases or CD-ROMs. In The *New York Times Company,*

Inc. v. Tasini, the U.S. Supreme Court ruled that reproducing free-lance authors' magazine and newspaper articles in computer databases, without the authors' permission, infringed on the authors' copyrights (2001). In its opinion, the court cited the potential harm of the database on the value of the freelancers' work:

> In years past, books compiling stories by journalists such as Janet Flanner and Ernie Pyle might have sold less well had the individual articles been freely and permanently available online. In the present, print collections of reviews, commentaries, and reportage may prove less popular because of the Databases.

But, instead of compensating independent writers for including their articles in the electronic forms, publishers reacted by posting notices that they would pull the work from the databases if the writers did not sign a release from compensation. This included some 115,000 articles for the *New York Times* alone (Freelance Writer Who Did Not Allege Personal Injury Had No Standing 2002). Tasini sued the *Times*, asserting that the release agreement is unlawful and unenforceable, but the court dismissed the claim.

So, while the court recognized the rights of free-lance journalists who own the copyright to their works, the industry can control the use of those works through release agreements.

Reporter's Privilege

If a source says she will give you information only if you promise to keep her name confidential, would you be able to keep that promise? What if it came down to revealing the source's name or going to jail? A writer investigating a Houston murder served nearly six months in a federal detention center for refusing to turn over her notes and reveal her sources to a grand jury. Vanessa Leggett was released after that grand jury ended its investigation (Lipton 2003). In many states, the reporter's privilege gives journalists the right to refuse to testify, allowing them to maintain the confidentiality of their sources (The Reporter's Privilege 2002). But this was not the case for Leggett in the Fifth Circuit federal court in Texas, where the judge found no reporter's privilege. This issue was further complicated because Leggett was an unpublished author, and not recognized by the U.S. Department of Justice as a journalist. While shield laws in thirty-one states and the District of Columbia afford some protection to journalists against revealing confidential information, the conditions vary. The Reporters Committee for Freedom of the Press publishes an online guide to The Reporter's Privilege, which provides a searchable database and state-by-state and federal circuit guides (http://www.rcfp.org/privilege/index. html). Digital journalists can use this resource to familiarize themselves with the conditions in their reporting area before making confidentiality agreements.

While confidential sources have led to some of the most powerful reporting in journalism history, such as Deep Throat and Woodward and Bernstein's investigation of Watergate, professional news organizations encourage identifying sources whenever possible (SPJ 2002, RTNDA 2003).

Free Press, Fair Trial

Journalists can sometimes get caught up in the excitement of an arrest in a big local crime case. After weeks, months, or even years, the community may view the arrest as closure—even though our criminal justice system assumes the person charged with a crime is innocent until proven guilty. Sometimes prejudicial information not allowed in a trial appears in newspapers, online, or on the air. Add to that, negative story tone and heavy coverage, and it can be difficult to find jurors who have not formed an opinion about the guilt or innocence of the defendant. And, so, we have the conflict between the First Amendment's free expression guarantees, and the right to a fair trial, afforded by the Sixth Amendment.

Free press, fair trial online

In November 2001, the U.S. military captured a 20-year-old American, John Phillip Walker Lindh, among Taliban fighters in Afghanistan. Newspapers, broadcasts, and online media worldwide covered the story, including a CNN interview with Walker Lindh. When his case came before the U.S. District Court in Alexandria, Virginia, Walker Lindh asked the court to dismiss the indictment due to prejudicial media attention that he argued would impair his Sixth Amendment right to a fair trial. The court (2002) referred to the Internet's role in the publicity, but denied the request:

> No doubt the publicity in this case also includes some expressions of opinions on newspaper editorial pages or the Internet that were specifically designed to inflame or persuade readers. Yet, on the whole, the record does

not warrant a conclusion that prejudicial pre-trial publicity has been so "inherently prejudicial that trial proceedings must be presumed to be tainted" or that Lindh cannot receive a fair trial.

Walker Lindh later pled guilty to supplying services to the Taliban and is serving a twenty-year sentence (2002).

Another case with an Internet component concerns basketball star Kobe Bryant, and the identity of his accuser in a rape case. In late July 2003, online searches for Bryant, his accuser, and his wife were fifteen times more popular than any other topic on the Internet (Special report: Kobe Bryant 2003). Online publicity surrounding the case and the posting of his accuser's name and photograph have raised concerns about her privacy and the fairness of his trial. Rape shield laws exist to limit testimony about an accuser's psychological and sexual history. But stories about Bryant's accuser are easily accessible, even on reputable news sites. A search on news.google.com for Kobe Bryant produced thousands of hits, including a bounty of stories about his accuser. Top headlines included:

- Accuser of Kobe Bryant treated at Arizona facility (Henson 2003)
- Kobe Bryant's Colorado accuser in medical center (Reuters 2003)
- Report: Kobe's accuser had checked into treatment center (thedenverchannel.com 2003)

At the time of this writing, the trial had not begun. However, experts are predicting the publicity online will have an impact on the case.

Ethics and Digital Media

This chapter's examination of legal issues and news media should give digital journalists a better idea of what the law suggests we can and cannot do. The next question is, what *should* we do? The answers are seldom easy. Knowing that an action is legal doesn't always mean it's the path we should follow. But how do we make ethical decisions? Often, we rely on our gut to guide us. But, ethicists warn, that's not enough. Bob Steele of the Poynter Institute (2002) advises that, "The best ethical decisions are a blend of influence from gut, head, and heart." This section presents a practical approach to ethical decision making, laying out steps journalists can take to prepare themselves for ethical problem solving.

Also, see Appendix 1 and Chapter 2. Appendix 1 includes codes of ethics from two major news organizations, SPJ and RTNDA. Chapter 2 addresses ethics through its focus on core values and digital media, which include truth, accuracy, fairness, independence, and serving citizens.

George Bailey and the Poison Pills

In the classic movie, "It's a Wonderful Life," young George Bailey faces a monumental decision. As a counter and delivery boy for a small-town drug store, he witnesses Mr. Gower, the pharmacist, accidentally grab a bottle of poison while filling a prescription. Gower is despondent after learning his son has died, and George can't bring himself to tell his beloved boss about the poison in the pills. After packaging the tainted prescription, Gower hands it to George and instructs him to make the delivery. Faced with the dilemma of disrespecting Mr. Gower or delivering a possibly lethal medicine, he immediately seeks out his father for advice. But the senior Bailey is tied up at the office—so George must make the decision on his own. He chooses against delivering the poison pills, and returns to the drug store to face Gower and the consequences of disobeying him.

While director Frank Capra (1946) doesn't let the viewer inside George's head to witness his decision making, George may have followed a process, similar to the one below, to guide his action (adapted from Hodges 2001, Steele 2002). George:

1. Defined his problem: the poison.
2. Gathered the facts of the situation: Gower made a mistake, it was an accident, the poison could kill the recipient.
3. Identified the stakeholders—those with an interest in the situation: George, Mr. Gower, the sick family.
4. Considered the rules: obey your elders, do not kill, do as you're told.
5. Considered the possible courses of action: deliver the pills, don't deliver the pills.
6. Considered the potential outcomes: the recipient could die, George could be punished, George could lose his job.
7. Sought advice: tried to ask his father, but had to make the decision on his own.

When George returns to the drug store, Gower is on the phone with the person expecting the medicine. He hangs up and proceeds to bat George about the head for his disobedience. George cries and shouts that there was poison in those pills. Gower stops, in shock and wonder, and embraces

George for his life-saving decision. At this point the viewer pulls out the tissue box (OK—some viewers—even though they've seen the movie fourteen times) and prepares for the next dilemma.

The seven-step process

Some of the ethical issues facing journalists are fairly straightforward, such as young George Bailey's dilemma. Others are exceedingly more complex. But, in either case, the seven-step process outlined above can help us in our ethical decision making. Applied to the question posed at the beginning of this chapter, here's how it might work. Recall the scenario: Teenagers equipped with 3G video mobile phones are going undercover in bars and clubs to report on juvenile alcohol consumption. The phones produce sounds and images that can be broadcast on the air or streamed on the Web—but should the news media use the devices in this way?

1. *Define the problem*
   Should your newsroom give video mobile phones to teens to report undercover in bars and clubs?

2. *Gather facts*
   Answers to the following questions should provide a factual framework for the issue.
   Are bartenders carding?
   Are teens using fake IDs?
   How prevalent is the sale of alcohol to minors?
   Are the teens driving after drinking?
   Is there any danger to the teen reporters?

3. *Identify stakeholders—those with an interest in the situation*
   Teenage reporters, bar owners, bartenders, teen drinkers, parents of teen drinkers, authorities that oversee underage drinking, liquor companies, police, reporter, the news organization.

4. *Consider the rules*
   What's the legal age to be allowed in bars?
   Are the bars and clubs private places?
   Is audio recording legal?
   Are cell phones allowed in bars?
   Who is responsible for the teen reporters? Are they employees?

5. *Consider the possible courses of action*
   The teens order drinks and consume them while their phones are recording the action.

The teens record with their phones while other teens (who know they are being recorded) are ordering and consuming alcohol.

The teens record with their phones while other teens (who don't know they are being recorded) are ordering and consuming alcohol.

A reporter who is of legal age records with the video phone.

A reporter who is of legal age observes but does not record any video.

6. *Consider the potential outcomes (including harm)*

The video may reveal that bars all over the city are selling alcohol to minors. This could lead to an official investigation that closes down a number of clubs. The story gets heavy traffic online and the news organization is lauded for its efforts.

Phones could be collected at the club's door because they're not allowed inside. Or, technical difficulties could make the recorded video unusable.

A bartender discovers the teens videotaping with their phones. She confiscates them and calls police.

A bar patron discovers the teens videotaping with their phones. He fights with them to destroy the phones.

The teen reporters are arrested for underage drinking.

Bars sue the news organization and the teen reporters for invasion of privacy.

Parents of teens consuming alcohol sue the news organization and teen reporters.

Bar patrons sue the news organization and teen reporters.

Reputations of teens who consumed alcohol could be damaged.

Bartenders who served alcohol to the minors could be fired, even though the bar owners may have encouraged them not to card. They could have a hard time finding a job if their faces appear in the video.

7. *Seek advice*

Editors, news directors, and senior reporters can be helpful in discussing difficult decisions.

At this point in the process, review all your information and reassess the situation. Use your head, heart, and gut to find the answer.

Moral philosophy lies at the core of the seven-step process. From the virtue-based teachings of Aristotle, to the results-based theory of Mill, moral judgment has challenged philosophers for centuries. Digital journalists can explore these ethical traditions by reading the original writings of moral philosophers, or an overview put into the context of journalism in an ethics textbook. Suggested readings are listed below.

Activities for Further Learning

1. Return to the three scenarios posed at the beginning of the chapter. Discuss the relevant legal and ethical issues for each of them, and reach a conclusion for action in each case.

For Further Reading

Black, J., B. Steele, and R. Barney, R. 1997. *Doing Ethics in Journalism: A Handbook with Case Studies*. Boston: Allyn and Bacon.
The Institute for Learning Technologies at Columbia University offers full text of many philosophical works online, including Aristotle, Kant, Locke, and others. http://www.ilt.columbia.edu/publications/digitext.html.
The full text of Mill's *Utilitarianism* is online at The University of Adelaide. http://etext.library.adelaide.edu.au/m/m645u/index.html.

References

Altman, H. June 20 to 27, 1996. "Smoke damage." *Philadelphia citypaper.net*. http://citypaper.net/articles/062096/article038.shtml
Capra, F. 1946. It's a Wonderful Life.
Children's Online Privacy Protection Act of 1998. 1998. http://www.ftc.gov/ogc/coppa1.htm
Collins, W. Spring 2000. From behind the scenes, UW grads bring forth the stories of the century. *On Wisconsin*. http://www.uwalumni.com/onwisconsin/Spring00/breaking1.html
Cooley, T. M.1888. *A Treatise on the Law of Torts*. Chicago: Callaghan and Co.
Copyright, Fair Use. 1999. http://www.copyright.gov/fls/fl102.html
Copyright Law of the United States of America, Section 107. http://www.copyright.gov/title17/92chap1.html#107
Cox Broadcasting Corp. et al. v. Cohn. 1975. 420 U.S. 469.
Creech, K. C. 2003. *Electronic Media Law and Regulation*. Oxford: Focal Press.
FCC, AMFM Radio Licenses. March 19, 2002. File Nos. EB-01-IH-0682.
FCC, Tempe Radio, Inc. Oct. 7, 2003. File No. EB-02-IH-0812.
Freelance Writer Who Did Not Allege Personal Injury Had No Standing. *Tasini v. New York Times Company, Inc.* 2002. *New York Law Journal*. Retrieved from LexisNexis.
Gertz v. Robert Welch, Inc. 1974. 418 U.S. 323.
Gillmor, D. M., J.A. Barron, T.F. Simon, and H.A. Terry. 1990. *Mass Communication Law: Cases and Comment*. St. Paul: West Publishing Company.

Hart, J. Nov. 13, 2003a. What's law got to do with it? Panel presentation to the Online News Association conference.

Hart, J. 2003b. *Law of the Web: A Field Guide to Internet Publishing.* Denver: Bradford Publishing Company.

Henson, S. Nov. 28, 2003. Accuser of Kobe Bryant treated at Arizona facility. http://www.azcentral.com/news/articles/1128bryant28.html

Hodges, L. Nov. 9, 2001. The Essential Questions. Presentation at The 32nd Annual Institute on the Ethics of Journalism. Washington and Lee University.

Karle, S. D. Nov. 13, 2003. What's law got to do with it? Panel presentation to the Online News Association conference.

Kelly v. Arriba Soft Corporation. 2003. U.S. App. LEXIS 13557.

Le Mistral, Inc. v. Columbia Broadcasting System. 1978. 61 A.D.2d 491.

Libel suit against Dow Jones to proceed in Australia. February 2003. *E-Business Law Bulletin.* Retrieved from LexisNexis.

Lipton, J. March/April 2002. Vanessa Leggett: Why she wouldn't give up her notes. *Columbia Journalism Review.* http://www.cjr.org/issues/2002/2/qa-leggett.asp

Lutzker, A. P. 2003. *Content Rights for Creative Professionals: Copyrights and Trademarks in a Digital Age.* Oxford: Focal Press.

Mark v. Seattle Times. 1982. 457 U.S. 1124.

New York Times Company, Inc., et al. v. Jonathan Tasini, et al. 2001. 533 U.S. 483.

Power Reporting. 2003. *Columbia Journalism Review* Web site at http://powerreporting.com.

The Reporters Committee for Freedom of the Press. Searchable database on The Reporter's Privilege. http://www.rcfp.org/privilege/index.html

The Reporter's Privilege. 2002. The Reporter's Privilege Compendium: An Introduction. http://www.rcfp.org/privilege/item.cgi?i=intro

Reuters. Nov. 26, 2003. Kobe Bryant's Colorado accuser in medical center. http://www.cnn.com/2003/LAW/11/26/crime.bryant.reut/

RTNDA. 2003. Code of Ethics and Professional Conduct. Radio-Television News Directors Association. http://rtnda.org/ethics/coe.shtml

Special Report: Kobe Bryant. July 24 to 27, 2003. http://50.lycos.com/072403.asp

SPJ. 2002. Society of Professional Journalists Code of Ethics. http://spj.org/ethics_code.asp

Steele, B. Sept. 26, 2002. Be Prepared: Deal with Ethical Issues Before they Become Problems. *Poynteronline.* http://poynter.org/column.asp?id=36&aid=7130

thedenverchannel.com. Nov. 26, 2003. http://www.thedenverchannel.com/news/2666912/detail.html

thomas.loc.gov. 2003.

Ticketmaster Corp. v. Tickets.Com, Inc. 2003. U.S. Dist. LEXIS 6483.

United States of America v. John Phillip Walker Lindh. 2002. 212 F. Supp. 2d 541.

Wehling v. Columbia Broadcasting System. 1983. 721 F.2d 506.

Weinberg, S. November/December 1995. Smoking guns: ABC, Philip Morris and the infamous apology. *Columbia Journalism Review.* http://archives.cjr.org/year/95/6/smoking.asp

Wilson, D. 2003. Who is John Doe—and where to get the paper on him. http://www.reporter.org/desktop/tips/johndoe.htm

Zacchini v. Scripps-Howard Broadcasting Co. 1977. 433 U.S. 562.

CHAPTER 4

Digital Storytelling: Its Own Genre

Chapter Objectives

At first glance, online storytelling may look very much like print and broadcast news. You've seen stories from the morning paper posted verbatim on its online edition, and local television Web sites streaming video reports that aired on their newscasts. Isn't news on the Internet much the same as broadcast and print?

This chapter will show you that good digital storytelling is different from other forms of news, and explains what makes this genre distinct. The Internet's qualities of interactivity, involvement, immediacy, integration, and in-depth opportunities set online journalism apart from its traditional media counterparts.

The New Online Storyteller

A new breed of storyteller now sets the standard for online news. These journalists know that the Internet is more than just another delivery system for the newspaper or television, and avoid posting broadcast scripts and print pieces directly on the Web site. They find ways to interact with the audience through non-linear presentations. And they embrace the immediacy of the medium, responding to developments by updating, when need be, on a minute-by-minute basis. Their work often facilitates user involvement with the issues on which they report. It's integrative, comfortably bringing together multimedia, or contributing to synergy among media. And it's often in-depth, linking to background within their own sites or to relevant locations elsewhere.

Online storytellers often bring to the digital realm an expertise in another medium. And by adapting that strength and enhancing it through new skills, they bring energy to their stories on the Internet. Others are coming to the Web first. So, whether you are just starting out in journalism with plans to produce or report for the Internet, or have already established a specialty in print or broadcast, examining and understanding the distinctive characteristics of this medium serves as a universal starting point to online storytelling.

The Five I's: Interactivity, Involvement, Immediacy, Integration, and In-Depth Opportunities

More than 50 years ago, television gave birth to nightly newscasts through the Camel News Caravan on NBC and the CBS Television News with Douglas Edwards. The announcers (the term anchor hadn't yet been invented) for both programs came to television from radio, as did the early presentation format. These men read the news, much as they would have done for radio. For the occasional visual, the news readers held up still photographs which the camera homed in on, or turned to limited film footage and sometimes crude illustrations. The aural medium had moved into another dimension, but with little change, at first. That was 1948.

Today, a large number of news organizations treat their Web sites in much the same way early network television treated its newscasts, by simply transferring their legacy content and techniques to the new medium. But as news leaders came to recognize the visual strength of television they molded broadcast journalism to capitalize on that strength. In some ways, digital journalism is still nascent, as television news was in 1948. But a number of news organizations recognize the qualities of the Internet and have begun to use them to their fullest, moving online news beyond just another delivery system for the newspaper or television.

Interaction and Involvement

When people visit Internet news sites, they don't expect to put up their feet up and place their brains on automatic pilot. They actively enter the Web and are poised to do something at their computers. They're ready to interact. For some, that interaction is very basic, and is limited to clicking on a link to read a story or to advance the photos in a slide show. For others, it engenders making decisions at greater levels of complexity. This is the basis of the interaction/involvement continuum, which runs from the simplest relationship with site elements to true involvement with stories and issues.

Two reasons underlie the importance of interaction and involvement on the Web. The first represents a major shift in the flow of mass communication, from one-way transmission toward a multi-directional flow. This has an impact on how news is defined, the way it is presented, and how journalists do their jobs. The second concerns what people learn from news. Elements of both of these areas fall within the continuum, and are represented in Figure 4.1.

The physical act of clicking icons or links is basic to navigating a news site, but the behavior itself doesn't contribute to what a user learns from online news. While some scholars hypothesized that the greater user control afforded by the Internet would enhance learning from online news, their findings did not support that theory (Eveland, Jr. and Dunwoody 2002). Research does suggest, however, a relationship between increased

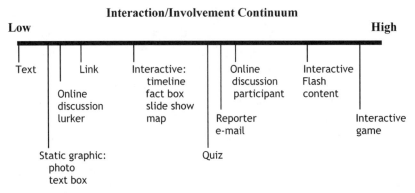

Figure 4.1 Interaction/Involvement Continuum

learning and the cognitive activity that takes place when a person goes on-line. As Professor Richard Mayer (2001) argues in his book, *Multimedia Learning*, meaningful learning depends on cognitive activity rather than behavioral activity. In other words, the thinking appears to have a greater impact than the doing. And the process seems related to the structural nature of the Internet, which resembles the complex interconnections of the human mind (Eveland, Jr. and Dunwoody, 2002). In this environment rich in links and related content, these associations can spur cognitive activity, which, in turn, may facilitate learning (Eveland, Jr. and Dunwoody 2002).

Therefore, interaction and involvement that help users make mental connections appear to be more important to learning news content than the physical manipulation of a Web site. Of course, we can't discount the importance of hyperlinks to online navigation. Those basic Web site interactions are necessary as a means of access, akin to turning a newspaper page to continue a story on page A11. The user simply clicks on a link to call up the full text or to listen to an audio clip. This physical behavior would be found on the lower end of our continuum. As the interaction becomes more complex, the level of involvement increases. Responding to a poll requires slightly greater involvement, because the user must form an opinion to participate. At the next level of involvement the user might open a multimedia presentation that provides numerous choices or paths a user may follow. And a program that gives users the opportunity to make choices and receive feedback on those choices can offer the greatest level of involvement and interactivity.

The day police arrested two men in connection with the 2002 D.C. area sniper shootings, *The New York Times on the Web* (2002) offered 26 choices on its "Complete Coverage: End of a Hunt" page. This included numerous stories, from details on the capture to the "Duck in a Noose" folk tale reference. But, the coverage didn't end there. An interactive map showed the locations of each shooting, which, when clicked, brought up a photo of each victim and related details. A slide show revealed events of the day as they unfolded. And many choices led to even more material, including streaming video stories and a discussion forum. These offerings gave users the opportunity to interact with the story on many levels.

Involvement also encompasses multi-directional communication among the news organization and the community. An e-mail link from a story to its reporter makes it easy for the reader to comment or question. Or, reporters can seek story sources by asking people to contact them. *Washington Post* reporter Lyndsey Layton posted a reporter's query online adjacent to the main story about the 13th sniper victim (2002). It read:

Caught in Traffic?

Did you get caught in gridlock this morning and have an unusually tough trip? Reporter Lyndsey Layton wants to hear from you. E-mail **laytonl@washpost.com** and include a daytime telephone number and a brief description of what happened.

She received at least three dozen responses, which provided rich detail to her story on police dragnets and their effect on the people caught in them. Layton tells more about using the reporter's query in the following sidebar (2002).

The discussion board is another means of encouraging the community to communicate with the news organization as well as among themselves. Generally, these forums accompany a story or issue of importance. Users send their messages to the Web site, which may automatically be posted directly on the site, or may first be reviewed by someone on staff as a check against offensive material.

Lyndsey Layton

Using the Online Reporter's Query

Washington Post reporter Lyndsey Layton talks about sourcing through the Internet:

I've posted other queries on our site and, generally speaking, they've been quite helpful in terms of connecting me to sources. It's a fast way to find very specific sources, who have already indicated some willingness to talk with you. To find people stuck in gridlock the old-fashioned way, I would have had to go to the gridlocked area and hunted for people who were stuck—typically I'd go to a gas station near the highway and ask motorists filling their cars to ask if they had come off the highway or away from a checkpoint. It's time-consuming and, even if you do find someone who fits, you have to hope they're willing to be quoted.

But, Layton also recognizes the disadvantages in using the Internet for sourcing.

You're mining a select group—people who have access to the Internet and read your Web site. That's not the general public, and to rely on a subset is to miss a lot of other people. It's also somewhat antiseptic—you don't get the color you'd get if you were on the scene, saw the people you're interviewing.

Taking care to recognize these potential drawbacks, the reporter's query can be a valuable form of interaction and serve as an important reporting tool.

Interactive maps can also engage the reader and present information in an easily accessible manner. They can be used in the most straightforward way, to tie a location to an incident, or more abstractly, to tap into rich information depositories. When the 2000 U.S. census figures became available, *USA Today* used the Excel database files provided by the government to create dynamic maps for displaying those data. (Figure 4.2) Web site users began by clicking on a state in the map of the United States. That state map would then pop up, offering numerous choices for viewing the census data within that state, from graphs and percentages to color-coded regional indicators. Users could easily see where the population increased or decreased, racial and ethnic composition by area, and where the children were clustered. Not only were the interactive maps helpful to the public, reporters used them to enterprise stories to make further sense of the numbers. A collaborative effort among writers, designers, producers, editors, and database editors made the project possible. This approach requires expertise with technological tools including the Excel database, ArcView mapping software, and Flash (Thomassie 2002).

Another interactive option many online sites now offer is a question of the day. These are usually yes/no questions related to a featured story or current issue, and with immediate feedback, let respondents gauge their answers against others who have participated. They range from the highly newsworthy, such as, "Bush's address: Is the economy more important than Iraq?" (MSNBC.com 2003), to the fluffier, entertainment realm "Will $1 million help or hurt the chances of Joe Millionaire's Evan and Zora staying together?" (azcentral.com 2003) Of 8,652 responses to the Bush question, 64% voted yes and 36% voted no. And more than half of all responses to the million-dollar-question said it won't make a difference.

Because these are unscientific polls, some journalists warn against using them for sensitive topics, fearing misrepresenting public opinion. The results should always include a disclaimer to advise that the findings are not scientifically valid.

Online sites can also post quizzes to involve audiences in stories. Again, good judgment must be exercised with this approach. For example, including a few questions about countries and capitals in a story about poor geography performance in high school students would be perfectly appropriate. On the other hand, a quiz on best diets in a story about weight loss may be misleading, because controversial findings regarding a number of popular diets have recently surfaced.

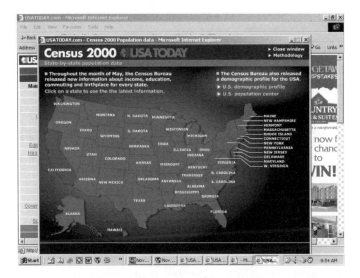

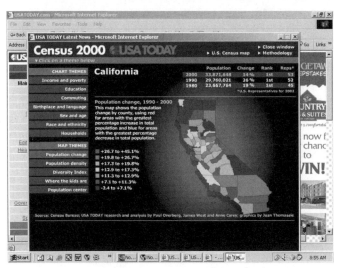

Figure 4.2 *USA Today* used interactive maps to display census information in easy-to-use graphics.

Involvement and civic journalism

Moving along the interactive/involvement continuum, a number of on-line civic journalism projects would be ranked as high involvement. They include interactive tools and games to encourage citizen participation in

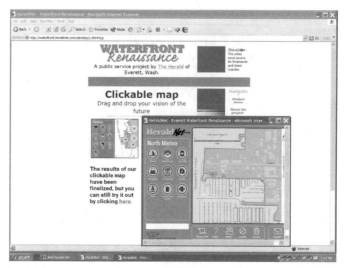

Figure 4.3 This interactive feature gave people in Everett, Washington, a voice in developing the city's waterfront. Reproduced with permission of *The Herald*.

their community issues. For example, heraldnet.com (2002), the online edition of *The Herald* of Everett, Washington, posted a Sim City-type activity for citizen input on the city's waterfront development (Figure 4.3)

Users shared their ideas about developing the area by using interactive maps, placing icons that represented parks, restaurants, condos, and other elements of development. And, with a mouse click, users sent their plans to herald.net. More than 1,000 people used the maps to submit their ideas to *The Herald*. Through interactives like this, Web sites elicit citizen feedback on important community issues.

Another project came about when *The Tampa Tribune* and WFLA-TV combined forces on their Web site, TBO.com, to bring voters a new interactive tool to help them decide for whom to vote for governor. This Candidate Selector used a list of questions to measure an individual's stance on thirteen issues, from gun control, to gay adoption. It then compared the user's answers to the candidates' stand on the issues. After receiving the data, the tool displayed the user's scores, which showed the level of agreement with each candidate's views. It also provided links to the candidates' Web sites. Jim Riley, a TBO.com senior manager, said the selector is "another good example of something you can't do with a broadsheet newspaper." (2002)

But tools like the selector must be carefully crafted to be reliable and effective. And Riley says TBO.com took the proper steps to ensure the tool's credibility. "We were very careful to make sure we talked to the expert reporters, the people who are most in tune with those beats," said Riley. "We didn't just sit here and wing it"(2002). And voters who didn't want to wing it on election day turned to the selector to help them sort out the candidates and issues. TBO.com registered more than 9,100 selector responses, indicating a respectable level of interest in and involvement with this tool (Candidates nearly tied on TBO.com 2002).

The power of involvement via interactivity ranks among the most important qualities of digital news. For the user, the benefits include enhanced learning and story understanding through increased cognitive activity. Citizens can also contribute to community problem solving and provide feedback to reporters on issues of importance. For journalists, communication with the audience can augment newsgathering and presentation through opportunities for sourcing and by keeping a pulse on the community. Moving away from one-way to multi-directional communication is among the most prominent changes digital journalism brings to mass media.

Even small-market and student journalists can incorporate interactivity and involvement in their online news coverage. Providing a link to reporter e-mail with each story takes little technical expertise, and gives users a means of immediate feedback. Other approaches that can be taken without an army of staff and a major investment in technology include questions of the day, quizzes, and discussion boards.

Immediacy

Another distinctive feature of journalism on the Web is its ability to bring news to the public as it happens. For newspapers, this has required major adjustments from their once-a-day publications. And for most television and radio news operations, being available to the public 24/7 has created new challenges. While few online news sites have realized the full potential of the Internet's immediacy, many are moving in that direction. Speed is indeed a reality on the Web. Journalists have actually gotten feedback on their writings while still out in the field covering events. Dan Gillmor (2003), a columnist for *The San Jose Mercury News*, is a case in point. While at a technology conference he used a wireless network link to update his Web log (blog), noting the lamentations of a telecom executive who was onstage at the time. Gillmor soon received messages from a reader who had something to share about the speaker, including links to a credible Web site. The site showed how the speaker had sold more than $200 million in stock during difficult times for his company. Gillmor posted that information immediately, and says, "Some in the audience were soon reading our blogs, and the mood toward the CEO seemed to chill. Talk about real-time feedback." (Gillmor 2003)

While the real-time response may not be as tangible for most online journalists, working with frequent updates is. In addition to rewriting text, online editors often provide other story elements as they become available. For example, TBO.com draws content from WFLA-TV and *The Tampa Tribune*, and as a big story develops this can mean updating as often as every two minutes. "We start out with words," says TBO.com senior manager Jim Riley. "But pretty quickly we add pictures, video clips, photo galleries. We just keep building the layers on" (2002). So, in addition to contending with deadlines that just keep coming, managing content that goes beyond the comfort of the printed word sometimes makes the job of an online editor a Herculean task. Handling each element in the right way is key to serving the public well.

But under deadline pressure, the chosen "extras" may not enhance the coverage. This happened on a major online news site in September 2002. As protesters demonstrated against the International Monetary Fund in Washington, D.C., the site featured a video link as part of its coverage. But instead of viewing a video of the street protests, the user got to see a reporter in the newsroom describing what he had seen. That story treatment was misleading to the user, who expected to see the event unfolding. While the reporter video may have been useful before a full text story was available, its usefulness waned after the text was posted. At that point, images from the street, whether photos or video, needed to appear on the site. But contending with multiple media forms under pressure adds to the demands of online immediacy.

Wire service on the Web

The Associated Press (AP) calls itself "the backbone of the world's information system" (2003). This news service provides story content for more than 15,000 newspapers and broadcast organizations worldwide, boasting an audience in excess of 1 billion people a day. It cranks out a steady stream of news—about 20 million words daily—24/7 through its global bureaus and domestic members (Associated Press 2003). A large chunk of these stories find themselves on national and international news Web sites. On an average news day, about one-fourth of top stories on major U.S. metropolitan newspapers' Web sites are AP stories (Artwick 2002). That figure more than tripled the day police captured D.C. sniper suspects John Allen Muhammad and John Lee Malvo (Artwick 2002).

For breaking news such as the sniper story, AP may be the most immediate source for chunks of story copy. Web sites can cut and paste full stories with no editing, allowing for quick updates and reasonably current information. What can be troubling, however, is overuse of the AP wire on the broadcast or newspaper Web site; for example, when a paper has its own reporter working on a local issue but runs AP coverage of the story on its Web site. The reporter's version is often held for the next day's newspaper. Plus, the AP story may be more general, not tailored to the local angle. And, it's likely written as newspaper copy, rather than as a Web piece. Viewing the Web site as a wire service hybrid may contribute to this syndrome.

AP, itself, is moving away from providing strictly wire copy. Plans to transform the service are under way, with "eAP," or "the electronic AP," an interactive database and news network. Merging news operations would allow the company to provide a "multimedia product." (Humbert 2003)

Online television news sites and immediacy

Contending with frequent deadlines is nothing new for television and radio. They've been operating as immediate media, in a broad sense, since their inceptions, and, with further refinement, since the advent of satellite broadcasting. Some radio and television news conventions carry over to the Web well. Others don't, especially the linear model of information delivery. Broadcast producers shape news programs to be viewed in their entirety, from beginning to end. Producers determine the shows' flow. And in the early days of broadcast Web sites, this is how broadcasters thought the Web should work for them—as simply another platform to deliver the entire newscast. Some persist in this approach, streaming entire shows. Others post full program scripts on their sites. One of the early innovators of an alternative to linearity of broadcast news online is Jon Klein, CEO and founder of The FeedRoom. Klein's organization streams video news stories from major providers, including NBC and Tribune stations, allowing users to choose which stories to watch in what order. It's one of the largest streaming news providers on the Web. Klein says his idea for The FeedRoom came to him while he was producing during the Gulf War, while he watched banks of video monitors. "...one monitor had troops surrendering, one had Colin Powell, another had burning oil fields...and I thought, I'm only letting a trickle of this out to the American public. It would be so cool if the viewers could actually come in here and pick what was interesting to them." (2003) And that's basically what The FeedRoom allows viewers to do, by providing a menu of news stories from which to choose.

But live video feeds aren't limited to broadcast Internet sites. They are becoming increasingly prominent on newspaper Web sites through partnerships with television stations and Associated Press video. Some of the technical hurdles include the small screen size of the streaming content and being able to keep up with heavy user traffic. These problems were evident to people who went online to see President Bush's State of the Union Address in January 2003. Even those with a high-speed connection likely gave up and turned on the radio or television after encountering numerous episodes of "net congestion." But these problems should eventually be resolved as the technology advances.

Both print and broadcast news organizations have had to make adjustments to handle the immediacy of the Web. Making frequent updates that incorporate multimedia elements can sometimes pose a daunting challenge.

Integration

Two basic levels of media integration exist on the Internet—integration among media, and integration within media.

Among-media integration

With more than 4,000 U.S. newspapers publishing online editions (Newslink.org 2003) and an abundance of broadcast sites on the Web, among-media integration has become a daily occurrence, at least between the traditional media forms and their own Web sites. This involves a newspaper placing its reporters' stories in the online edition, or a television station streaming a piece of video from the evening news directly onto its Web site. The practice is often referred to as "shovelware," meaning the news organization shovels its content onto its own Web site, unchanged. But, even with this model, integration exists between the existing medium and its Web site, albeit minimal.

Another form of among-media integration involves print and broadcast content coming together on a news Web site. Some organizations, such as *The Washington Post,* have developed units to create their own broadcast content. But this approach is more the exception than the rule. Instead, "convergence" is attained through a formal partnership between newspaper and broadcaster (*The Washington Post* also partners with numerous media). Through this approach, the media are integrated on the Web site, but essentially remain separate. For example, coverage of a fatal head-on collision in the *St. Petersburg Times* online edition integrates a brief print story and a broadcast piece that aired on WTSP on a morning newscast (sptimes.com 2002). For many such stories, each organization's reporters cover the story separately, but their reports appear online as an integrated piece.

Yet another level of converged integration involves print reporters creating broadcast pieces for the Web and broadcast reporters writing stories to be read. This integration of resources requires cross-training, or at least a knowledgeable team leader who can guide the reporter through the essentials.

Producing stories for more than one medium takes time and expertise, without which the end products suffer. One of the premiere converged news operations in the nation houses *The Tampa Tribune,* WFLA-TV, and TBO.com in one complex. Although some of the organization's reporters work across platforms, each medium has its own mission and separate operations. TBO.com's Riley says, "I think that the great fear was that we were all going to turn into three-headed monsters and do three times as much work in eight hours, and you just can't. And furthermore, you probably won't do it that well; particularly in a market this size you can't afford to have a mediocre person on TV or a mediocre news writer." (2002) But a familiarity with media outside a particular expertise and a willingness to venture there are critical. "You're expected to," says Riley. "You can't just exist in your own silo anymore; you have to help the others" (2002).

Within-media integration

This is where the Internet has created a venue for new forms of storytelling, which involves combining media within online reporting. Many in the field refer to this format as multimedia, because it merges distinct media to create a new gestalt.

What does it take to tell a compelling digital story? For multimedia journalist Joe Weiss, it's meant making a 47-hour bus trip to Mexico along with an illegal migrant worker returning home to his family. It's also meant witnessing the grief of a parent whose child has died in a Nicaraguan hospital. But great digital storytelling doesn't necessarily require chasing stories outside U.S. borders. What sets Weiss's stories apart from the shovelware found on many news Web sites is the *multimedia experience.* At Durham, North Carolina's heraldsun.com, Weiss brings his stories to life through words, sounds, pictures, and interactivity. He's an innovator who merges media to yield a hybrid in storytelling, who believes the total effect is greater than the sum of the parts. For example, by pairing photographs with an audio interview, Weiss believes the end result is distinct from viewing the visual or hearing the sound independently. "The goal in my mind isn't to explain the still photo with the audio, it's to have the audio and the photograph work together," says Weiss. "And you see this moment in time and the audio can help you understand how universal that moment is." Weiss says that multimedia helps the user focus on photos for longer than they might normally, "And, so, you can see the nuances, you can see relationships in those photographs, the complex imagery." (2002)

The inspiration for this "NPR meets still documentary photojournalism" came from Corbis executive Brian Storm, who was at MSNBC at the time. Weiss heard Storm's ideas at a seminar in the late 1990s. See the following sidebar for the details on how Weiss got started as a digital storyteller.

Joe Weiss

Digital Storytelling

Multimedia journalist Joe Weiss discusses his early interest in digital storytelling. A photo feature on a home for boys sparked the fire while he was working at The Herald-Sun *in Durham, North Carolina.*

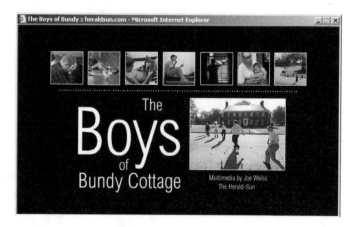

Multimedia journalist Joe Weiss admires his Online News Association award for most innovative use of the medium.

I was working on this long-term picture story, probably spent eight months up there, once a week, getting to know these twelve or thirteen kids. And it really dawned on me that the thing that I would get upset about on the drive home, or the thing that I would burst in the door and tell my wife, were the stories these kids were telling about their past, or about their worries about the future. And I really love still photojournalism, but its power is in the moment, in the here and now. They've yet invented a camera that can go back in time. But through audio you can pair a photograph in the moment with audio that sort of reflects on the past, and you get this third effect between the two of them. That really fascinated me. Visually you had this sense that time was frozen in this moment, but through the audio you could hear things in the future, you could discuss how they relate with that moment in time, and you've got this really great internal communication between these two media. I was really just blown away by that. Hearing a child talk about how his dad told him it was OK to cry if he was sad—that plays in with these photographs I took. And it really upset me when it ran in the paper and it seemed empty without these kids' voices. So I was really driven to go up there and interview them and drag the mikes up there and sit down with them.

Judith Siviglia describes herself as a "big old NPR geek." The *Raleigh News & Observer* interactive news producer loves National Public Radio storytelling, and has always been intrigued by the idea of taking pictures for the radio. She first got the chance to marry photographs with sound when a North Carolina couple came to the newspaper with a story to tell. Their unborn baby had spina bifida, a severe spinal abnormality, and the couple decided to proceed with fetal surgery, a new and controversial option to ending the pregnancy or seeing their child die from the deformity. Siviglia shot roll after roll of film to document the couple's experience, not realizing at the time that the story would go onto the paper's Web site. But as "A Chance for Anna" progressed, she decided to produce a Flash presentation, and during the editing process, she thought, "Oh man, I wish I had been recording audio!" But all was not lost. A fellow photographer suggested she take the pictures to the family so they could comment on them. "And it just couldn't have been better," said Siviglia. In the following sidebar, Siviglia discusses multimedia storytelling (2002).

Judith Siviglia

Online Storytelling

The basics are still the same, which is what they've always been. Every step along the way, the mantra is always, we're doing the same job, the rules still apply, we're still telling stories. We still need to be accurate and fair, but what's interesting is that your approach changes. You may think of things a little differently when you're shooting for the Web—more detailed pictures, or more sequence pictures, and thinking in terms of audio. You have more options.

Media integration sparked by the Internet is having a major impact on newsgathering and presentation. From among-media relationships where content is shared, to changing the storytelling format through an integration within media, the options for online news are still being discovered.

In-Depth Coverage

A five-minute top-of-the-hour radio newscast doesn't allow much time for story depth. And while newspapers can provide greater depth than the daily broadcast news programs, it's unlikely they can regularly find the space to include full court documents, and impossible to include an interactive database for readers to calculate potential taxes under various scenarios. Nor do the "legacy media" provide immediate access to story archives. The virtual space on the Internet allows Web sites to exceed the limitations imposed on print and broadcast news by time and space. But this doesn't mean it's appropriate to provide links to five sidebars on a front-page story. Nor does it give journalists carte blanche to run a 45-minute unedited interview as streaming video. Here's why: attractive, user-friendly design, and cost. Steve Yelvington of Morris Communications says, "Every word, every link we add takes away from the prominence of the other. When everything's important, nothing's important." (2001) Cluttering pages with too many links can be overwhelming to the user, and counterproductive to the Web site.

One way of getting away from clutter is through a clean, attractive design that incorporates story elements creatively. PBS.org Frontline/World (2002) won a first place Online Journalism Award in 2002 for its global issue coverage. Figure 4.4 shows a piece of that coverage that focuses on

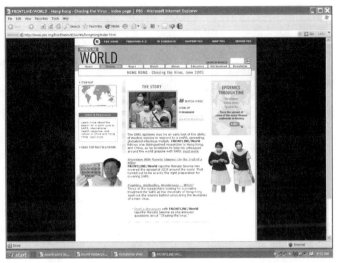

Figure 4.4 A clean, uncluttered design, such as this PBS.org Frontline/World Web site, helps organize content for online users.

Nigeria. Notice how uncluttered the page is, even though it offers numerous elements that link to depth on subsequent pages. Organizing content in such a way, especially on in-depth stories, helps the user navigate what might otherwise seem a daunting data dump. Limiting the major categories to seven choices makes it manageable and inviting.

Another in-depth report that offers many pieces is MSNBC.com's airport security investigation (2002). As you can see in Figure 4.5, the material is organized as a five-week series, and each segment contains extras that help tell the story. MSNBC.com also features three multimedia elements on the story's front page. Again, keeping initial choices down to a manageable level, usually about seven or eight, makes it easier for the user to navigate and explore stories to their fullest. Highlighting multimedia features on the story's home page showcases them for easy access.

Cost concerns also dictate a site's level of depth, organization, and presentation. It takes time and expertise to create a user-friendly database interface or to build game-like simulations to give users hands-on experience with a story. And the cost of storing and streaming video has a realistic impact on how much a Web site can do. Even large organizations such as MSNBC.com seek alternatives to streaming large amounts of video. Hence, the adoption of Flash presentations, whose file sizes are

Figure 4.5 Clear choices make this in-depth MSNBC.com airport security story easy to navigate.

measurably smaller. Nonetheless, devoting resources to projects that deserve them, and striving for clearly organized presentations, can make the volumes of information more manageable and useful.

Activities for Further Learning

1. Consider the following story idea and plan its online coverage. How would you make the most of the "Five I's"
    a) facing a tight deadline with limited resources?
    b) in a more flexible time frame with a staff of artists, programmers, and multimedia journalists?
  The story: A student who attends your university is killed on the interstate as he returns to school after the Thanksgiving holiday. A tractor trailer was involved in the crash just a few miles before the exit that leads to your school. The stretch of highway that runs through the area has become increasingly dangerous, with six fatalities so far this year, five of which involved trucks. Traffic has doubled in twenty years. And while the road was designed to carry 15 percent truck traffic, 40 percent of the vehicles that travel the two-lane highway today are trucks.

2. Visit the online site of your hometown newspaper or television news station and evaluate the content and presentation vis-à-vis the "5 I's." Is it legacy content, simply plunked down online, or is the site handling news by making the best of the medium? Make suggestions to improve online coverage, including specific examples.

References

Artwick, C. G. 2002. Agenda setting on the Web. Work in progress.

Associated Press. 2003. http://www.ap.org/

azcentral.com. Feb. 18, 2003. Will $1 million help or hurt the chances of Joe Millionaire's Evan and Zora staying together? Online quiz. http://azcentral.com

Block, M. 1994. *Broadcast Newswriting: The RTNDA Reference Guide*. Chicago: Bonus Books.

Candidates nearly tied on TBO.com. Nov. 5, 2002. www.tbo.com

Eveland, W.P. Jr. and S. Dunwoody 2002. An investigation of elaboration and selective scanning as mediators of learning from the Web versus print. *Journal of Broadcasting and Electronic Media*. 46, 34-53.

Gillmor, D. January/February 2003. Here comes 'we media.' Tech-savvy readers want in on the conversation [online version]. *Columbia Journalism Review*. http://cjr.org/year/03/1/gillmor.asp

heraldnet.com. 2002. Waterfront renaissance. www.heraldnet.com/waterfront

Humbert, M. 2003. AP chief promises to transform news service. http://www.ap.org/pages/whatsnew/eap.html

Klein, J. 2003. The FeedRoom Web site. http://www.feedroom.com

Layton, L. Nov. 1 and 5, 2002. Personal e-mail correspondence.

Layton, L. 2002. Reporter's query. washingtonpost.com

Mayer, R.E. 2001. *Multimedia Learning*. Cambridge, New York: Cambridge University Press.

MSNBC.com. 2003. Bush's address: Is the economy more important than Iraq? Jan. 28, 2003. Online quiz. http://MSNBC.com

MSNBC.com. 2002. Soft target; How our airports became the first line of defense. http://www.msnbc.com/modules/airport_security/airsecurity_front.asp

newslink.org. 2003. http://newslink.org/news.html

PBS.org Frontline/World. 2002. Nigeria, the road north. http://www.pbs.org/frontlineworld/stories/nigeria/index.html

Riley, J. Jr. Nov. 13, 2002. Personal interview.

Siviglia, J. Aug. 26, 2002. Personal interview.

sptimes.com. 2002.

The New York Times on the Web. Oct. 25, 2002. http://nytimes.com/

Thomassie, J. May 21, 2001. Presentation at *USA Today* headquarters.

Weiss, J. Aug. 27, 2002. Personal interview.

Yelvington, S. Dec. 1, 2001. Home pages from hell: Is there an editor in the house? *NewsFuture.* American Press Institute. http://americanpressinstitute. org/content/1540.cfm

CHAPTER 5

Learning from the "Old" Media

Chapter Objectives

When Benjamin Harris wrote about a smallpox epidemic in 1690, little did he know that his Boston newspaper would mark the beginning of print journalism in the United States. In the three centuries since *Publick Occurrences, Both Foreign and Domestick,* appeared, U.S. newspapers have been informing readers across the nation. And while radio and television have had shorter life spans, their immediacy and ability to bring the sights and sounds of history into our homes have made them integral to our daily lives. Over the years journalistic conventions have evolved for reporting and presenting the news. Some of the steadfast strategies of the legacy media carry over appropriately to the Internet, whereas others just don't transfer well. This chapter introduces what we can learn from the "old" media—approaches that work just as well in the digital realm as they do in analog, and those that must be adjusted for an online, interactive audience.

The Developing Story

As stories develop, the immediacy of the digital environment allows Web users worldwide to access the latest news. But before the days of bytes and LCDs, radio and wire service reporters turned around stories against unending deadlines, giving listeners and readers new information as it became available. Digital journalists can learn from the experience of their colleagues.

Radio's Changing Leads

It's 9 a.m. and Nathan Hager is getting ready to call it a day. His shift as writer/editor at WTOP radio in Washington, D.C. is ending, and people all over the city have awakened to the stories he crafted. Others drank their first cup of coffee listening to later versions of that news. And thousands heard the reports while commuting to work. As news breaks, Hager and writers in radio newsrooms nationwide, update stories throughout morning and evening drive times to bring listeners the latest developments.

As they acquire new information it's incorporated up high in the story, most often changing the lead. "In an all-news radio environment, leads are very fluid, and can change drastically as events develop," says Hager (2003). In the sidebar on the next page, Hager discusses the changing lead.

The quick-paced, developing story requires constant vigilance, whether it happens in Washington, D.C., or a small town in the Midwest. Here's how a radio story might evolve in central Illinois, or anywhere, for that matter.

At 7 a.m., lightning hits a tree that knocks a power line into a busy intersection. No one is hurt, but the live electric wire poses a danger. The 7:10 a.m. lead might read:

> Police are warning commuters to avoid the intersection of Maple and Vine. This morning's storm knocked a tree into a power line, which crashed into the intersection.

Shortly after the broadcast, the power company arrives on the scene, and begins working on the lines. Traffic is backing up. The 7:40 a.m. lead might read:

> Illinois Power crews are on the scene at Maple and Vine, where a live wire in the intersection has traffic backed up for miles.

Soon after, a worker suffers a shock and heads for the hospital. At 8:10 a.m., the lead reads:

> A downed power line on Maple and Vine has sent a power company worker to the hospital, and continues to back up traffic.

You get the idea. As new information comes in, the lead changes to inform listeners of the latest. The same principle applies to news on the Internet, but it may be executed differently. With radio, unless the story preempts regular programming, the updates are made for scheduled news deadlines. For the Internet you could update more frequently, or less often, depending on the story, the staff, and the organization.

Nathan Hager

The Changing Lead

Nathan Hager, WTOP Radio Writer/Editor

At WTOP we keep a constant eye on the wire services, and we also have an affiliation with CBS Radio News, which provides us with live feeds of national news as it breaks. So if the president makes a speech or some other important news conference is held, we can record it directly from the satellite feed, using Cool Edit digital audio software, isolate sound bites, and incorporate them into the stories we broadcast. And obviously, the very act of news breaking forces you to change a lead. Where at first, the lead might be, "President Bush is headed to Africa for a five-nation trip where he's expected to announce millions in HIV/AIDS and education aid," the lead might change to, "President Bush has promised to send 15-million dollars in humanitarian aid to Namibia—his first stop in a five-nation trip to Africa." Cue the sound bite, add a tag-out line, and you're home free.

The process is similar in our coverage of local news, except that our reporters cover the stories directly and feed the writers and editors freshly-updated leads on an hourly, or sometimes half-hourly basis. One of our most recent ongoing stories of a serial arsonist in the D.C. area is a good example. This morning two fires were set in the same Southwest D.C. apartment building, and investigators were looking to determine whether they were connected to a string of twenty-two arsons that appear similar, and five that are positively linked to the same criminal. Early in the morning it was just one fire. Hours later, the second fire broke out, changing the lead. Then, late in the day, investigators determined the fires weren't linked, which again changed the story completely.

All-news radio stations have an advantage over newspapers, and even TV stations. Our stories are never static. Because we are constantly on the air and someone is always on duty watching the wires and manning the phones, we can always stay on top of a breaking story in some capacity, whether it's at the scene or getting the information from a source over the phone, or by fax or e-mail.

The Wires and Updating

Radio isn't the only "old" medium used to continuous updates. Organizations such as the Associated Press provide news to the world, and for these wire services updating is a way of life. After Delta Flight 1141 crashed on takeoff at the Dallas-Fort Worth Airport in 1988, the Associated Press reported 15 stories within 90 minutes (Fensch 1990). The first story, reported eleven minutes after the crash, contained only thirty-seven words (Fensch 1990, p. 3).

A jet described as a 727 plowed into the dirt on a north-south runway at Dallas-Fort Worth Airport and burst into flames shortly before 9 a.m. today.

A witness said the plane exploded in flames.

Seventeen minutes later, AP filed its first full story. The first three paragraphs follow. Note how the lead now includes the airline. A mistake also went uncorrected (plowed exploded) (p. 4).

A Delta 727 plowed exploded during takeoff shortly before 9 a.m. at Dallas-Forth Worth International Airport today.

"We are working on an alert three. That is a crash," said DFW Airport spokeswoman Marilyn Beauvais.

Eyewitnesses said the plane exploded in flames and plowed into the dirt of a north-south runway. There were no immediate reports of injuries or fatalities. Ms. Beauvais did not say where the plane was bound.

In an online news environment, urgent stories like the Delta plane crash also require continual updates. What we can learn from the wire services is that the updates require reshaping the presentation into a new story. We want to avoid what MSNBC.com technology editor Jonathan Dube (2003) calls "pile-on," in which the writer just adds new information to the bottom of the story. At this point in the Delta plane crash coverage, the missing piece of information that deserves placement in the lead is the number of dead—and are there any survivors? While most people would assume no one survived the crash (even reporters on the scene initially thought this was the case), 94 lived and 13 died (Fensch 1990). So, when this information is acquired, it must go in the lead, rather than down at the bottom of the piece.

The wire service will also begin compiling related information for "sidebar" stories. For the Delta Flight 1141 story, the early sidebars included a history of plane crashes and a piece on a Delta airliner that crashed in 1985. The reporter on the scene also described what he saw at the location. These sights, sounds, and smells can be used as a separate story. Online, we can also use sidebars, which would be linked to the main story. But the online producer can go beyond straight text through other possibilities. For example, an interactive timeline could present the history of plane crashes in which the user clicks on the date to reveal a pop-up window with the details. The reporter's description could be recorded on video or audio at the scene and streamed online. Or, the sights and sounds could be recorded and made into a slide show.

Adapting Broadcast and Print Writing Styles

Much of the content on Internet news sites comes directly from print or broadcast stories. While repackaging news from print and broadcast may not be the optimal use of the Internet news medium, this form of online storytelling, sometimes called print-plus, can be found on most major news sites (Dube 2003). Print and broadcast news operations take an existing story and adapt it for the Web, sometimes adding links and other "extras" to enhance the piece. These stories are not always changed for readability on the Web. But by making some adjustments to each writing style, text stories on the Web could be much improved.

Using What Works from Broadcast News on the Web

Writing for the ear requires clarity because broadcasters have only one chance to get their message through to the listener. One of the best ways radio and television newswriters accomplish this is to limit themselves to one idea per sentence. The approach also works online, because even though online users read text, the screen interface can make text processing more difficult. This MTV.com lead uses one idea: "Britney Spears won't be ripping off her flesh-colored pants ever again." (Vineyard and Robinson 2003). So does this MSNBC.com lead: "Viewing 'The Matrix Reloaded' is like being eaten alive—slowly—by a machine" (Elliott 2003). And, on a more serious note, this lead from USATODAY.com: "Employees who earn more than their colleagues may be especially vulnerable to layoffs in this sluggish economy." (Armour 2003). While it's not always easy to contain ideas to one per sentence, meeting the challenge can improve clarity and readability.

Another approach to clear Web writing is to catch yourself when you write long sentences replete with clauses. This confusing sentence does not belong on air nor on the Web: *Councilman John Walker's vote, which angered some parents who say they will picket City Hall, allows the Anytown library to keep* Harry Potter and the Chamber of Secrets *on its shelves.* Instead, rework by splitting the text into two, or, better yet, three sentences: *Anytown library will keep* Harry Potter and the Chamber of Secrets *on its shelves. Councilman John Walker's vote decided the issue. But it angered some parents, who say they will picket City Hall because of the vote.*

Broadcast writing also uses an active style, avoiding the verb form *to be* as much as possible. If you're always writing, *is, are,* and *was,* find a more active verb. Instead of writing that a boy was instrumental in saving his baby sister from drowning, tell how he grabbed her arm as the current pulled her under. Rather than saying that the concert attendance was disappointing, write *only eleven people showed up to hear the high school jazz band concert.* But beware of eliminating *to be* altogether. Former CBS and CNN network correspondent Deborah Potter (2000, 2003) warns that purging scripts of verbs can be stilted, if not laughable.

Another technique for writing in an active style encourages avoiding passive voice. For example, *Police arrested the woman*, rather than, *The woman was arrested by police*. Think of it as who does what to whom. *Eminem dangled a doll over a railing*, rather than *A doll was dangled over a railing by Eminem*. Remember to keep the person or entity who did something in the first part of the sentence, and you'll have no trouble writing in active voice.

Adjectives and adverbs can enhance our writing when chosen with care, but can be overused in broadcast and online. An "amazing" person, a "horrible" accident, a "wonderful" experience, can be "offensive" clichés in online news. Let the reader decide a person is amazing by showing, not telling. Describe the person's actions to demonstrate that which is amazing: *Mary Jones volunteers every weekend at the hospital neonatal ward. For five years, she's spent Friday and Saturday nights holding and rocking crack cocaine babies, hoping it will ease their pain.* Choosing our adjectives and adverbs sparingly can improve our writing's effectiveness.

Broadcast news veteran Mervin Block says two rules guide writing news for broadcast. "Rule 1: Write the way you talk—or should talk. Rule 2: Never forget Rule 1." (1994, p. 2). Following this advice can help make online writing more personal and lively. But first, let's put some boundaries around this conversational writing style. Conversations vary, from the laid-back slang floating about among teens hanging out at a mall, to an engaging classroom exchange among students and professor. The style we're striving for requires thoughtful choice of words that clearly communicate a message. That, for the most part, eliminates the slang and stream-of-consciousness approach. Conversational style garners attention. It does not overwhelm with excessive verbiage that can't be processed. And its rhythm and flow almost carry the listener through the story. Again, it's designed to reach people through the ear. But even though online users process text through the eye, conversational writing can be an effective approach for them. Online audiences employ a scanning mode and must read from a screen (Nielsen 1997). So, it's up to the digital journalist to write in a clear and lively writing style that will overcome the screen barrier to attract and engage the user.

Here's how you can use conversational style in your online writing.

Clear and Succinct

Why write *in order to* when you can say *to*, or *due to the fact that* when *because* will do? Don't burden the online reader with these lazy excesses.

Train yourself to seek and destroy these wasted words that clog your copy.

Destroy:	Replace with:
prior to	before
at this point in time	now
in order to	to
provide assistance to	help
as of this moment	now
due to the fact that	because
for the purpose of	to

Rhythm and Flow

One of the best ways to achieve a flowing story with an interesting rhythm is by reading aloud as you write. Listening to the words can help a writer understand how readers might hear them in their heads. Vary sentence length. A few short sentences interspersed with a longer one can improve the rhythm. Listen for this. Pay attention to the rhythm. Charles Kuralt wrote some of the most rhythmic stories in television news while reporting his *On the Road* series for CBS. Read the following excerpt aloud to hear the beauty.

> It is spring in Vermont, and here is how you can tell: The birds are back; every animal, wild and domestic, is released from the grip of winter; and the ping of the sap of maple sugar trees is heard in tin buckets on every hillside. (Kuralt 1985, p. 298).

Improve flow through conjunctions and transitions. Remember that a conjunction connects words and phrases. *And, but,* and *so* work well and are the most conversational. While more formal, *however* can also be used on the Web. Transitions take the reader from one thought to another, almost like a road map to the story. They also connect, functioning to move the story forward. A story on SARS by National Public Radio's Joe Palca (2003) includes some excellent transitions. He cleverly uses the words *cases* and *case* to carry the story from location and background to detail on a new development. Here's how he wrote it: "Researchers at the University of Hong Kong now suggest that a single extremely ill patient caused many of the cases. Amoy Gardens is a special case." Conjunctions follow to keep the story flowing. "Most people become infected with the virus when someone who is already sick coughs on them. *But* the Amoy resident sick with SARS didn't give people the virus directly. *Instead*, he was excreting the virus into the sewer system." (Palca 2003) Rely on conjunctions and transitions to enhance your online writing flow.

Use Contractions Wisely

Browse the top story on your favorite online news sites, and you'll find a mixed bag when it comes to using contractions. My brief scanning on May 30, 2003 turned up *he'll* twice in the lead paragraph on MSNBC.com's story about President Bush traveling overseas. A USATODAY.com story on mutual funds used *didn't and don't*, and I even found *can't* in an Associated Press story about gambling in Arizona. But CNN.com confined contractions to sports and entertainment stories. Many online editors, even those working in broadcast online newsrooms, come from a print background, where the formal writing style shies away from contractions except within quotes. Nonetheless, this writing convention is slowly finding its way online. Use contractions wisely where they would occur naturally, without forcing them into copy. And don't overdo. Repetitive contractions may indicate you are slipping into that laid-back stream-of-consciousness talk that belongs in the mall, not in your news story.

Converting Sound Bites to Quotes

Broadcasters write in and out of sound bites differently from the way print journalists handle quotes. In the most extreme cases, the speaker isn't even identified in the text, but is on screen, with name and title appearing on its lower third (called a CG, lower-third, or super). Often the script just provides the last few words the person says (outcue), and the length of the sound bite. Translating this for the Web requires viewing the piece to hear what the bite says, and to see the name and title if they're not included in the script.

Broadcasters also use another technique in which they lead in to the sound bite with a complete stand-alone sentence. This has its roots in radio, where the sound bites, called actualities, were recorded onto individual tracks on a large tape cassette called a cart. If, for some reason, a technical mix-up meant the sound bite never made it on air, the story could go on and still make sense. The SARS story by NPR's Joe Palca (2003) uses such a treatment. Compare it to the Web version, that introduces a quote.

Broadcast version:

Andy Chan, one of the Hong Kong University team, says the direction of the air plume matched the apartments where people got sick; at least that's the theory. (Chan's sound bite follows.)

Web version:

The WHO agrees with the conclusion, but it remains preliminary. "Of course, we cannot say this is a complete theory nor can we say this is the only thing that explains everything, but so far it explains all the phenomena that was presented to us," says Andy Chan, part of the University of Hong Kong's investigation team.

The adjustments are slight, but necessary, for proper style and flow. And, of course, without identifying the source, the story would be incomplete and would not make sense.

Using What Works for Print on the Web

Who, what, when, where, why, and how—it's our journalism mantra, as valid today as it was 150-plus years ago. And it's been delivered to the digital age from an era when telegraph wires carried Morse code across the country and carrier pigeons flew news across the English Channel from London to Paris. When it comes to finding facts and putting them into context to give them meaning, newspapers have been king. Digital journalists can model this on the Web without simply dumping the newspaper story there.

The Lead

A well-crafted lead that tells the reader what the story's about is crucial to good Web storytelling. "In this new world, the inverted pyramid is here to stay," says Chip Scanlan of the Poynter Institute (2002). That's a style of writing developed in the early days of the wire services, which kept the key facts at the top of the story, placed less critical information in the middle, and saved the least important for last, so editors could cut where they wished. It's also effective on the Web. Because Web users scan online content (Nielsen 1997), it's important to give them the story gist in the lead to keep them reading. Holding back content too long risks losing them. You can see how major news organizations used the inverted pyramid style to report two of the most devastating events of modern history. The first appeared in a 1945 edition of the *New York Times.* (Lawrence 1945, p. A-1). In the story's first four paragraphs, note how the most salient information comes first, with supporting comment and secondary material following:

> The first atomic bomb wiped out 4.1 square miles of the Japanese city of Hiroshima on Monday, it was announced today. Gen. Carl A. Spaatz, commanding general of the Strategic Air Forces, made the disclosure that 60 per cent of the city had been destroyed.
>
> Hiroshima, on the Inland Sea, had a built-up area 6.9 square miles and a pre-war population of 343,000.
>
> General Spaatz's announcement, based on a careful study of photographs taken a few hours after the bomb had been dropped, made clear the terrific destructive power of this new secret weapon, which has harnessed the power of the universe and turned it against the Japanese.
>
> General Spaatz said that the single bomb "completely destroyed" the area cited, including five major industrial targets. The pictures made it clear that there was other damage in the area of the city that was not completely destroyed.

CNNfn also used the inverted pyramid online when reporting on the September 11, 2001 terrorist attacks (cnn.com 2001). Note how the lead paragraph provides the key facts, with subsequent text offering additional detail on the economic impact.

> NEW YORK (CNNfn)—The worst terrorist attack in U.S. history killed thousands, destroyed the World Trade Center in New York, damaged the Pentagon and shook financial markets and businesses around the world. And the shock waves continued overnight as Asian markets dropped dramatically while the human cost and economic damage were still being assessed.
>
> The crash of four hijacked U.S. airliners led to the unprecedented grounding of all commercial flights in the United States through at least noon Wednesday and led to the closing of U.S. financial markets for a second day Wednesday.

So, for the majority of online text stories, follow newspaper's convention of using the inverted pyramid when crafting your lead. Consider the lead a summary of the most important information to tell your audience. Online news readers want to know what the story is about up front, and with this approach you will provide the essentials in the lead.

Alternatives to the inverted pyramid can also work if headlines and sub-headlines serve as a telegraph to readers, telling what the story is about up top. When using this approach reporters can tell the story chronologically, or by using a short anecdote to represent the larger story.

Adjusting Broadcast and Print Styles for the Web

Some print and broadcast conventions just don't carry over well to the Web. Issues involve: differences in leads, writing too short or too long, working with visual references, using too little or too much detail, and what to do with straight text.

Broadcast to Web

Joe Palca's SARS story discussed earlier in the chapter works well on NPR's Web site because it's crafted differently for each medium. In the broadcast version, there are actually two leads; an anchor lead and a reporter lead. The anchor, or host lead, sets up the story by telling listeners that researchers have learned something new about SARS. This lead does not reveal what researchers actually know, but instead, entices the audience to keep listening to find out more. It ends, as most anchor leads do, by introducing the reporter, "NPR's Joe Palca reports." Then, the reporter's lead takes the listener to the location of the story.

That two-lead approach is different from the Web version. Instead of holding back on what the researchers found, the headline and subheadline reveal the finding, "Faulty Drains Led to Outbreak at Hong Kong Apartment Complex." The lead tells who came to this conclusion, and sets the scene at the apartments where there was a large number of SARS cases. The details flow from there.

With broadcast stories, we capture attention and keep audiences watching or listening with the promise of finding out more. On the Web, we tell them what the story's about right away, and if it's important, compelling, or interesting to them, they will keep reading. If we take too long to tell them what it's about, they'll just move on. MSNBC.com's technology editor Jonathan Dube says, "You can't afford to bury the lead online because if you do, few readers will get to it. When writing online, it's essential to tell the reader quickly what the story is about and why they should keep reading—or else they won't" (2003).

Another way we change broadcast stories to conform to the Web is through expansion. Courtney Cochran (2002), news editor for TheSanDiegoChannel.com, says, "You don't want to just put up a thirty-second blurb, because that ends up being three sentences. You definitely have to expand and you have to give your viewer something to relate to." They may have seen the story on the evening broadcast, and later visited the Web site for more information. So, the online story should provide the detail the brief broadcast piece could not. Cochran advises adding phone numbers and addresses when appropriate, and, to include descriptions to make the story readable. Cochran calls this "being able to imagine the story actually taking place." When you see a television story, the visuals play an integral role in conveying its meaning. Writers weave the words and pictures to tell the story. And if a Web editor simply pulls the text apart from the visuals, the story will unravel; it won't make sense. Jim Riley (2002) of TBO.com says, "I think that just grabbing a script is a really bad idea. Working with TV people to get information is a great idea." To facilitate that interaction, the TBO Web staff sits near the assignment desk, as the photo in Figure 5.1 illustrates, and has access to reporters to get information. So, enhancing broadcast scripts through detail and description are key when reshaping those stories for the Web.

Online news style—that is, presenting numbers, titles, abbreviations, and more—also differs from broadcast in most cases. Print style generally dominates online news sites, with the Associated Press Stylebook providing the guidelines. However, some online newsrooms have their own style, which should be followed consistently on those sites. If your newsroom does not have its own stylebook, use AP. Here are some basics to get you started (AP 2002).

Numerals:	Spell out whole numbers below 10, use figures for 10 and above (p.181).
Ages:	Always use figures (p.8).
Temperature:	Use figures for all except zero. Use a word, not a minus sign, to indicate temperatures below zero (p.245).
Titles:	Capitalize formal titles when they are used immediately before one or more names... (p.251).
Dollars:	Use figures and the $ sign in all except casual references or amounts without a figure... (p.76).
Percentages:	Use figures: 1 percent, 2.5 percent....For amounts less than 1 percent, precede the decimal with a zero (p.192).

Figure 5.1 The converged newsroom at *The Tampa Tribune*, TBO.com, and WFLA facilitates interaction among reporters, editors, and producers.

Print to Web

Thorough issue coverage, detail, depth, and analysis—that's what newspapers are made of. As digital reporters and producers, we want to maintain these qualities online. But that's not likely to happen by simply posting newspaper stories unchanged on news Web sites. Even minor changes can make a print story more suitable to the online medium.

Story Length

Conventional wisdom guiding the perfect length for an online story is still evolving. If we follow Jakob Nielsen's advice, we should cut the conventional word count in half (1997). Nielsen's been studying Web usability for more than a decade, and has been called "the guru of Web page usability" (*The New York Times*), "the reigning guru of Web usability" (*Fortune*), and "eminent Web usability guru" (*CNN*). His research shows that nearly eight out of ten users scan Web pages rather than read word-for-word (Morkes and Nielsen 1997). They're seeking information and want to find it quickly and easily. Another frequently-cited source, Dr. Roy Peter Clark of the Poynter Institute, writes that we can tell most good stories in fewer than 800 words. Generally, our Web stories will be shorter than the conventional newspaper story and longer than the television news counterpart. Online producers and editors who work with breaking news often write shorter and tighter for the Web than they would for print. For example, on June 26, 2003, five out of seven Readers' Choice stories on MSNBC.com ran less than 800 words each. But, compelling content can justify greater length. One Reader's Choice piece exceeded 3,000 words. It's a *Newsweek* story, "We're not in the mood," about dwindling sex among busy married couples. While lengthy pieces online are more the exception than the rule, they can and do garner reader interest when the content draws them in and the writing keeps them there. Using headings, subheadings, and bullets helps guide the reader through these longer enterprise and in-depth pieces. Because guidelines for story length online are still evolving, we can also benefit from another observation from Dr. Clark (2003), who warns that "at times, our short stories are too long, and our long stories are too short!"

The Key Facts

While a story's length can vary, its clarity must not. Identifying key facts can help achieve this goal. Here's how it works. If you're adapting a long newspaper story or rewriting wire copy, list or highlight all the key facts presented. Do the same with your own reporting notes. Now, examine the list and assign the facts an importance level from one to three, with one being most important. You'll most likely want to include all level-one items in your story. Exclude some level-two and most level-three facts. You may also discover that level-three facts don't really fit that well with the main focus, but will group together nicely into a separate story.

The following is a set of key facts derived from several sources on a music downloading lawsuit settlement (Healey and Huffstutter 2003, Miller 2003, Ahrens 2003, Miller and Egan 2003). I've changed the students' names to protect their privacy. Writing this for the Web will mean that we will keep most level-one facts, discard some and include other bits of level-two information, and most likely drop level-three material. Or, the level-three information could be used in another presentation, perhaps an interactive box that uses photos as hyperlinks to information on each of the defendants and the companies involved in the lawsuit.

Level-One Facts

- Four university students who ran music file-sharing on campus networks settled a lawsuit with major record companies.
- Students must pay between $12,000 and $17,500 to the industry's trade group, the Recording Industry Association of America.
- The music industry lawsuit accused the students of music piracy on file-sharing networks.
- The students are from Rensselaer Polytechnic Institute, Princeton University, and Michigan Technological University.
- Students promised not to violate the companies' copyrights, but did not admit to piracy.

Level-Two Facts

- David Gent, an 18-year-old Princeton University sophomore, will pay $15,000.
- Steve Nelson, a Rensselaer student, will pay 17,500.
- Vince Johnson, a 21-year-old Michigan Tech junior, will pay $15,000. He is a computer science student.
- Alan Davis, a 19-year-old Rensselaer freshman, will pay $12,000. His father owns thousands of CDs and records and says he will never again buy anything from those companies.
- The students may pay these settlements in installments over several years.
- The students did not appear to make any money off the file-sharing systems.
- The file sharing systems were sophisticated, Napster-like systems.
- Many in the record industry blame file-sharing networks for sliding CD sales.
- A record industry spokesman says the judgments could have been more than $1 million.

Level-Three Facts

- Johnson's payment amounts to nearly three years' tuition.
- Michigan Tech officials say Johnson took down his site before the music industry filed suit.
- Davis wrote his first computer program at age 9.
- Davis' father is unemployed.
- Gent won a silver medal in an international physics competition.
- The music industry sued and shut down Napster Inc.
- This is the first time the recording industry will receive money from people in the United States accused of pirating music on file-sharing networks.

By identifying and ordering key facts, the writer can quickly see the details, organize, and write the story. This approach can help save you time and improve your writing.

Eliminate Excess Verbiage

You can often rid your copy of unneeded words by giving it a thorough edit after you've let it sit for a few minutes. When deadlines loom, it's not always feasible to leave the story alone, even for a moment. But, in the long run, doing so can pay off. Return to the story with fresh eyes that will seek the superfluous, the unneeded. Here are two quick fixes:

Wordy: *As of right now, unfortunately, the program for enhancing the management skills of women business owners does not reach much farther than the greater Miami area.* (26 words)

Improved: *The management program for women business owners serves mostly the Miami area.* (12 words)

* * *

Wordy: *Here on the campus of the University of Illinois, students majoring in advertising in the school's award-winning department of communication are working with elementary schools in Urbana and Champaign to increase students' awareness of body image in television commercials.* (39 words)

Improved: *Advertising students at the University of Illinois are working with local elementary schools to heighten awareness of body image in television ads.* (22 words)

Capture surplus adjectives and adverbs, rework phrases, simplify, and tighten that copy.

User-Friendly Stories Through Chunking, Section Heads and Bullets

What's the longest piece of text you've ever read from a computer screen—a research paper, or perhaps a technical report? Did you eventually give up and print the piece because you felt your eyeballs might fall out if you continued reading the screen? On the other hand, perhaps you kept with it because it wasn't presented as a deep sea of text. Instead, the writer chunked the material for ease of navigation, including headings to help guide you. Essential details might have been further highlighted by using bullets or boldface type.

MSNBC.com does a nice job of chunking a story on the aftermath of Hurricane Isabel. After summarizing the latest in the lead—twenty-three people killed and 8 million people without power—the story presents a five-paragraph overview and then organizes the bulk of the story into chunks. In boldface type and all caps, the sub-headings include: "Millions without power;" "Capital returns to life;" "Rain, flood reports;" and "Damage less than expected" (Power, 2003). Chunking the material into four major categories helps the reader scan the story and sift through the details.

Before you begin writing your online stories, examine your key facts and parse them into categories where you can chunk supporting material.

Writing Headlines for the Web

Browse online news headlines and you're likely to find a lot of straightforward language. "Martha Pleads Innocent" (cbsnews.com 2003), "Abducted baby returned" (denverpost.com, 2003), "Woman finds, returns, $1,700." (signonsandiego.com 2003) Think again about the Web user, often at the office, scanning sites for information. The straight headline delivers what that user is looking for, telling what the story is about in a few words. It also lends itself to the breaking news story, which often deals with crime and issues that demand a serious tone. But witty, rhythmic headlines should not be abandoned when appropriate. The Minneapolis *Star Tribune* crafted a beauty, "Uncorked: Cubs' slugger Sosa caught with bum bat" (startribune.com, 2003). This works because of three word plays. First, the word *uncorked* sets up the story perfectly. It refers to the cork inside Sosa's bat and paints a picture of controversy spewing out as would a bottle of bubbly that's popped. "Slugger Sosa" describes him succinctly while using alliteration (the words used sound well together). And "bum bat" sounds almost musical while it tells what went awry.

Crafting the perfect headline takes more than playing with puns—which often leads to groaners. Use word associations to find contrast, or to seek the right sound, says *St. Petersburg Times* news editor John Schandler (2000). Rhyming can also work, or finding words that sound like they look. Being able to hear the headline in your head can be essential. Jim Barger of the *Pittsburgh Post-Gazette* calls this the "doo-dah" principle. Most everyone has heard the song, "Camptown Races," and knows the familiar "doo dah, doo dah." Barger says, "The best headlines are the ones after which you can say 'doo dah.' They just sound right. Readers like the way they feel." (2002) Another popular technique online is homing in on a key quote from the story in the headline. "Bush to troops: Mission accomplished" and "Stewart: I am innocent" both ran on *USA Today's* online site (2003).

The bottom line for headlines is to keep them straight for the most part, unless you can devote the time and effort to craft a more memorable one. And watch out for bad puns—your audience won't stand for them.

Using Audio as an "Extra"

The one thing radio news has always done best is bring sounds into stories to make them come alive. Hearing Edward R. Murrow on a London rooftop during a World War II air raid made for a more compelling report than listening to a man in a studio reading about the bombings. And you know the slurping a seven-year-old makes sucking in the last drops of a chocolate shake, because most of us have made that sound. Without that audio enhancement, a story about an ice cream shop would lack texture and interest. Good radio has painted audio pictures for its listeners for more than seven decades. Audio enhancements on the Web should do the same for the online audience. Does a Web user really want to take the time to listen to a reporter sitting in a newsroom talking about a World Bank protest? Not likely. The user wants the protest to come to him. Audio from the scene makes the story real. Let's hear the exchange as police handcuff protesters and load them onto buses. Or at minimum, hear a speaker or even a motorist who can't get to work because the streets are blocked. These real sounds mean more than a reporter simply talking about what he saw. An audio extra should always provide something more than the text does. For example, including audio from a call to a Chicago-area 911 dispatcher enhanced *Tribune Interactive's* coverage of a murder story (2002). The woman, Marilyn Lemak, was sentenced to life in prison for killing her three children. The following is a partial transcript of Marilyn Lemak's call to 911:

> 911 Dispatcher: *What's the problem?*
> Lemak: *My three kids are dead, and I wanted to be there, too, but it didn't work.*
> 911 Dispatcher: *OK, what happened, can you tell me...can you tell me how?*
> Lemak: *I did it.*

Analysis and commentary offer another good option for the audio Web extra. Let's say you're covering a story on human cloning, and you interview a university professor to help understand how the process works. As you're talking, the professor makes an eloquent statement on the bioethics of cloning. You can use the information on the process in your text piece and include the bioethics commentary as an audio extra. Be cautioned that point-of-view pieces must be labeled as such. To avoid bias, pursue myriad voices in commentary.

When to Use Video

Adding video to the story signals the user that this is important, it's something to look at and listen to. So, you had better deliver what you're promising. Streaming video on your Web site can give users an unforgettable visual experience, or it can frustrate and even anger them. Imagine this scenario for a moment: A relentless rain storm threatens your area with flooding. It's already put a nearby town practically under water, and the station's videographer has been out all morning shooting tape. Your television producer eagerly awaits the video for the noon news, but won't share with the Web until after the broadcast. Instead, you stream video of your morning weathercast. At noon, people at their desks check your Web site for the latest on the storm, but find dated material. They promptly turn to another site because you haven't given them anything new. Too bad. This storm has the potential to affect the entire community, so citizens should be able to see it on your Web site.

Alligator Attacks

On the other hand, some stories may not justify the video extra, but some producers appeal to the morbid curiosity of their audience to get them to click on video if it's there for the offering. Numerous Web sites included streaming video for a story on an alligator attack in Florida. The reptile killed a 12-year-old boy who was swimming in a river at dusk, prime feeding time for alligators. Pictures featured the location the following morning as well as dead alligators, hunted down after the boy was killed. In Florida, or other states with alligators, the story may have merited video. But outside those areas, the video is purely sensationalistic. CNN.com covered the story more responsibly, foregoing the video for a link to a related piece with the headline "Gators blamed for some 10 fatalities in 55 years" and the subhead "Statistics show that dogs lead in attacks on people." (cnn.com 2003) Putting the story into context helps inform the audience about the behavior of alligators, rather than prompting an emotional reaction.

Questions to Ask When Deciding to Use Video

Streaming video isn't always appropriate just because you have it to offer. To make an informed decision on whether or not to use it, first identify how the video serves the viewer. Next, answer the following questions. If you answered "yes" to all the questions and established that the video does serve the viewer, then you should most likely run the video. If not, you should reconsider running it.

1. Does the video complement the text? In other words, does it offer more than an audio version of the text with pictures?
2. Is it more than pure sensationalism?
3. Is it within the boundaries of tastefulness?
4. Is it more than simply a reporter in a newsroom?
5. If it's videotape of a live report, is it still timely and relevant?

Focus on the Human Element

The best journalism serves the community. It helps us to make decisions about our daily lives, from what happens inside our homes, to who represents us on Capitol Hill. The critical question a digital journalist must ask, then, is the question good journalists have been asking for years: "What does this story mean to my audience?" If we begin with the Web users in mind, and focus on them throughout the reporting process, our stories will do more than feed the daily beast—that 24/7 monster of a news hole that requires a continuous supply of stories to fill.

When a car crash kills, the reporting may end when the story is posted online—a tragic, singular event that touches family and loved ones. Or, the reporter may learn the driver was drunk, with a suspended license for a repeat offense. By asking what this story means to the audience, journalists can do more than report the crash. Philly.com (2003) went beyond the basics with its series, "Loaded for Trouble," an investigation of drunken driving in Philadelphia. Journalists examined five years of accident data to create an interactive map that readers can use to help them avoid the worst areas for alcohol-related accidents. They took a close look at the system, including law enforcement, repeat offenders, and where Philadelphia stands in the fight against drunken driving. They even provided a tool to help visitors estimate their blood-alcohol level, based on gender, weight, number of drinks, and duration of consumption. Not every story will lend itself to this type of in-depth investigation. Nor will online reporters be given the time and resources needed to accomplish such a feat. But putting the audience first should be a priority for online journalism.

Giving our stories a human face also carries over well to online news from print and broadcast. But the way it's done may need to differ to suit the medium. Recall that online users want to know what the story is about right away, because they're really scanning Web sites. So, when introducing a central character who represents an issue at the top of a story, quickly get to the nut graph that explains the issue. And telegraph the guts of the story in the headline and sub-head.

Activities for Further Learning

1. Find a top story on a local newspaper Web site and rewrite it using the following techniques. First, identify and group key facts into three levels. Order the level-one facts, and draw from some level-two facts to tell your story. Strive for one idea per sentence, eliminate clauses, streamline excess verbiage, make the copy more conversational, change passive to active voice, and use active verbs. Print a copy of the original story to hand in with your rewrite.

2. Write a lead for your Web site based on the following information. It is 7:30 a.m. and the incident happened 30 minutes ago.

   • A 22-year-old man was driving a Honda motorcycle west on Main Street in Ourtown.
   • He crashed into three parked cars at the corner of First Avenue, according to police.

- Sandra Wilmington, owner of the Java Coffee Shop across the street, said, "He went flying over the cars and landed on the sidewalk about 50 feet away."
- Traffic is backed up for miles.
- Police say motorists should avoid the area.
- A rescue crew took the motorcycle driver to City Medical Center.
- The man's name is not being released.

It's now 9 a.m. and you have new information, which is noted below. Update the lead.

- The driver died at 8:03 a.m. of massive head injuries.
- Main Street is now clear and traffic is moving at its usual pace.
- Police say the driver was NOT wearing a helmet.
- Police say the driver may have been speeding.

3. Write a headline for the music downloading story in the "key facts" section of this chapter.

References

Ahrens, F. May 2, 2003. 4 Students to Pay for music File Swapping; Agreement settles suit by recording industry. The Washington Post. Financial; P. E01. Retrieved from Lexis-Nexis.

Associated Press Stylebook and Briefing on Media Law. 2002. Editor Norm Goldstein. Cambridge: Perseus Publishing.

Armour, S. 2003. Retrieved from usatoday.com

Barger, J. April 19, 2002. Rhythm makes your headline sing (Doo dah, doo dah). *Poynter Online* http://poynter.org/content/content_view.asp?id=14273

Block, M. 1994. *Broadcast Newswriting: The RTNDA Reference Guide*. Chicago: Bonus Books.

cbsnews.com. June 4, 2003. http://www.cbsnews.com

Chicago Tribune Online Edition. Aug. 8, 2002. http://www.chicagotribune.com/

Clark, R. P. 2003 *Writing to Length*. http://poynter.org/shop/product_view.asp?id=500

cnn.com. Sept. 11, 2001. http://www.cnn.com

cnn.com. June 19, 2003. http://www.cnn.com/

cnn.com. May 30, 2003.

Cochran, C. August 2002. Personal interview.

denverpost.com. June 4, 2003 http://www.denverpost.com/

Dube, J. 2003. Online storytelling forms. http://www.cyberjournalist.net/storyforms.htm

Dube, J. 2003. Writing news online: A dozen tips. http://www.cyberjournalist.net/features/writingtips.html

Elliott, D. May 15, 2003. http://msnbc.com/

Fensch, T. 1990. *Associated Press Coverage of a Major Disaster: The Crash of Delta Flight 1141.* Hillside, New Jersey: Lawrence Erlbaum Associates, Publishers.

Hager, N. July 7, 2003. E-mail correspondence.

Healey, J. and P. J. Huffstutter. May 2, 2003. 4 Pay Steep Price for Free Music; Students who ran file-sharing systems will each give the recording industry up to $17,500. Los Angeles Times. Main News; Part 1; Page 1; Business Desk. Retrieved from Lexis-Nexis.

Kuralt, C. 1985. *On the Road with Charles Kuralt.* New York: G. P. Putnam's Sons.

Lawrence, W. H. Aug. 8, 1945. Atomic Bomb Wiped Out 60% of Hiroshima; Shock awed fliers; Tokyo cabinet meets; Carrier planes strike near China Coast. Page A1.

Miller, S. A. II. May 2, 2003. Internet music lawsuits are settled; Students must pay fines, dismantle their network. Milwaukee Journal Sentinel. News; Pg. 02A. Retrieved from Lexis-Nexis.

Miller, S. A. II and D. Egan. May 4, 2003. College students bond over file-swapping suit; Record labels grapple with cavalier attitude toward Internet piracy. Milwaukee Journal Sentinel. News; P. 01A. Retrieved from Lexis-Nexis.

Morkes, J. and J. Nielsen. 1997. Concise, scannable, and objective: How to write for the Web. http://www.useit.com/papers/webwriting/writing.html

msnbc.com. May 30, 2003.

msnbc.com. June 26, 2003.

Nielsen, J. 1997 How users read on the Web. *Useit.com: Jakob Nielsen's Website* http://www.useit.com/alertbox/9710a.html

Palca, J. May 16, 2003. Tracing the spread of SARS. http://www.npr.org/display_pages/features/feature_1265956.html

Palca, J. May 16, 2003. Studying how SARS spread through one apartment complex in Hong Kong. *All Things Considered.* Retrieved from LexisNexis database.

philly.com. 2003. http://www.cnn.com/

Potter, D. 2003. New hope for verbs. *NewsLab.* http://newslab.org/

Potter, D. July 2000. I'd like to buy a verb [Electronic version]. *RTNDA Communicator.* http://newslab.org/

Power could be out for a week. Sept. 20, 2003. http://msnbc.com/news/961894.asp?0cv=CA01

Riley, J. Nov. 13, 2002. Personal interview.

Scanlan, C. 2002. The Web and the future of writing. *Poynter Online.* http://poynter.org/content/content_view.asp?id=14501

Schandler, J. June 23, 2000. Stuck for a headline? *Poynter Online.* http://poynter.org/content/content_view.asp?id=4547

signonsandiego.com. June 4, 2002. http://www.signonsandiego.com/

startribune.com. June 4, 2002. http://startribune.com/

usatoday.com. May 30, 2003.

usatoday.com. June 5, 2003. http://usatoday.com/

Vineyard, J. and I. Robinson. May 26, 2003. http://www.mtv.com/

CHAPTER 6

Framing Stories
for the Web

Chapter Objectives

The summer of 1998 was a tense time for Chicago basketball fans. After head coach Phil Jackson left the Bulls, many wondered if the team could maintain its championship status, and if superstar Michael Jordan would continue playing for Chicago. So, when this one-line bulletin moved over the Associated Press wire, journalists in Chicago jumped on the story: "A New Orleans television station is reporting that Iowa State basketball coach Tim Floyd will resign this morning to take the head coaching job with the Chicago Bulls." The news practically turned one television newsroom upside down. Within minutes, a News 2 helicopter took off to track Floyd's arrival in Chicago. Reporters darted out of the station to pursue Michael Jordan's reaction, and the noon producer threw out half his newscast to make room for the breaking news. Bulls fever had taken the newsroom hostage.

That morning, News 2 reframed its presentation of reality for viewers. People who tuned in saw the coach's plane landing at Midway Airport instead of hearing about scams against senior citizens. Speculation about Michael Jordan playing the next season displaced a story on teacher recruitment. And background on Floyd's record moved out a report on the community combating drugs. Those issues didn't disappear in Chicago, but because of the Floyd event, they were absent from News 2. The station, in essence, altered the reality it presented to viewers by framing its newscast around Floyd.

Since then, Floyd has moved on to coach the New Orleans Hornets and Jordan has retired from basketball, but journalists around the world continue to frame reality. They frame it every day when they decide what's news and how it will be covered in print, on air, and online. Frames help journalists process and present information and organize the world (Gitlin 1980). Framing involves packaging and presentation, and is molded by decisions about which elements of a story are emphasized (Price, Tewksbury, and Powers 1997).

This chapter addresses framing news online. Like their counterparts in print and broadcast, digital journalists construct the news, choosing what to cover and what to exclude. And they frame that news through their reporting and presentation decisions and practices. These actions may relate to citizens' perceptions of and beliefs about their world.

Why Frame Matters

Can the pictures in a television news story affect what a viewer remembers about the report? Can the language a reporter uses to craft a story about a battered woman influence what the reader thinks of the attacker? And can presenting war as a high-tech, bloodless battle have an impact on public opinion toward that war? Numerous studies suggest the answer to all of the above is yes. Journalists' choices about what to cover and how to cover it can make a difference in how people make sense of their world. This is not strictly an issue of objectivity and subjectivity. As journalists, we recognize opinion, and strive to keep our own out of the stories we report. But the issue of frame is more complex because of its many variables and the differences among individual readers, viewers, and online users. We don't have control over what the audience brings to the interpretation of a message, such as age, cultural background, or education level. But we do control our choice of stories to cover, sources for information, the questions we ask, what to highlight, and what words, pictures, and sounds we use in our reports. Online journalists must also contend with multimedia and interactive story elements. As journalists, we strive to seek truth and report it. Carefully building our story frames can help us achieve this goal.

Major News Frames

News can be classified into two major frames—the episodic and thematic (Iyengar 1991). Car wrecks, fires, shootings, and on the milder side, parades and ribbon cuttings, are the stuff of episodic news. They're events, single snapshots of time. Studies show that event-oriented news accounts for up to 80 percent of local television stories (Gordon and Artwick 1993). The thematic news frame, on the other hand, is issue-oriented, focusing on more abstract content through in-depth analysis (Iyengar 1991). Let's say police arrest five underage students for drinking at a campus-area bar. Three of those students have dangerously high levels of alcohol in their blood. The thematic story would tackle the issue of alcohol abuse among college students, while the episodic version would simply report the arrests. An episodic story about a drowning at a city pool focuses on who died, when, where, and what took place, and how it happened. The breaking news can be reported fairly quickly by focusing on and gathering facts, and advises the community of the tragedy. A follow-up story reported in a thematic frame might address questions about lifeguard staffing and training and safety regulations at the pool. It goes beyond the isolated event to focus on the broader issue of public safety. Understanding of the event would be different in each treatment. The depth of the issue-oriented coverage would provide the citizen with information to take action and change the community if so desired. However, jumping straight to the thematic coverage without first reporting the event could be insensitive and premature; for example, raising questions about the Space Shuttle Columbia's damaged wing before fully reporting the astronauts' deaths. Of course, not all stories fall neatly into just one of these categories. Nonetheless, the overarching frame for most stories is either episodic or thematic (Iyengar 1991).

If journalists rely exclusively on the episodic frame, they present the world to their audience as a series of disconnected events, possibly depriving the community of depth and context. Nonetheless, some news organizations operate primarily in this realm. Use of the episodic frame can be explained by examining the western definition of news, the surveillance function of the media, and the nature of news media. More than a half century ago, pioneer communication scholar Wilbur Schramm (1949, p. 288) defined news as "an attempt to reconstruct the essential framework of the event." His fully event-oriented focus remains at the crux of many contemporary news definitions. And the basic who, what, when, where, why, and how reporting model taught in most introductory journalism classes today also centers on events. A news-as-instinct approach may also explain the episodic frame. Pamela Shoemaker (1996, p. 35) proposes a theory that addresses the possibility. She argues that humans possess a biological need to survey our environment for survival.

News, and more specifically, episodic news, fulfills this need. Consider our ancestors, the cave dwellers. As Shoemaker explains, "Warning others that the tiger was outside the cave allowed our ancestors to avoid injury or death, and this important function meant that survivors of environmental threats were more likely to pass on their genes to future generations." Today, instead of tigers we're confronted with bombings and drive-by shootings. While not scientifically proven, we can apply Shoemaker's theory to contemporary news media to see why some of them focus on crime, plane crashes, and other threatening events.

In addition to the biological aspects of news decision making are the socioeconomic makings of the newsroom. Time constraints, competition for audience, and the drive to do more with less lead to episodic news coverage.

It's easy. A "shots fired" call on the police scanner can lead to an instant story by simply dispatching a crew to the scene. It may promise dramatic visuals and action and require very little effort. On the other hand, a thematic story about causes and effects of domestic violence would require more enterprise, and, more resources.

It's economical. The newsroom's fax machine spews out a news release on a successful drug task force bust. A photographer or videographer can go to the news conference to bring back visuals of the cache and the sheriff lauding the task force performance. This episodic frame frees up precious time for the news staff.

It's visual. Flames, flashing lights, and screaming red and yellow fire trucks make for some eye-catching pictures. So does the Gravitron at opening night of the county fair. Most often, episodic news provides compelling images, while thematic frames may rely on talking heads, statistics, and documents. Thematic stories require time, energy, and creativity to be told well. So the straightforward episodic visual often wins.

It's immediate. Listen to the promos or introductions for your local news and you'll likely hear the words, "live," or "late breaking," among the hype. Television news, and now the Web, can bring events into our homes as they unfold. A live-from-the-scene report of a five-car pile-up gives viewers up-to-the-minute information on traffic conditions and may also satisfy their morbid curiosity. These breaking news events exemplify the episodic frame.

Often the episodic story becomes thematic, and justifiably so. But in some cases, news media go overboard in their thematic coverage. When John F. Kennedy Jr.'s plane went down off the coast of Martha's Vineyard, killing him, his wife, Carolyn Bessette and her sister Lauren Bessette, saturation coverage on the airwaves had the audience's heads spinning. The major television networks ran live, wall-to-wall coverage, pre-empting commercials to stay with the story. Days later, as the search continued, CNN Headline News was devoting eight minutes to the story every half hour. The coverage began as an episodic frame, with bulletin-like reports providing sketchy details of the occurrence. It soon grew into an enormous thematic octopus, with tentacles reaching into the Kennedy family legacy, John Jr.'s flight experience, his career, his "hunk" reputation, and more. Episodic updates of the search progress also continued.

What drove this near-obsessive coverage? Critics blame television's focus on emotion and quest for viewers (e.g., ratings) for the wall-to-wall reports. Proponents argue Kennedy's notoriety justified the reporting, because he was the son of an assassinated president, a successful magazine publisher, and, according to *People* magazine, "The Sexiest Man Alive." By deciding the story was important enough to merit continuous live coverage, network news executives forced an episodic, event-oriented story into a thematic frame.

Both the episodic and thematic news frames are well suited to an online environment. The Web can deliver news quickly and is rapidly updated, which meshes well with the episodic. And the ability to layer information and present it in interactive formats complements the thematic story. Framing stories appropriately for the Web is a challenge digital journalists must work hard to meet.

Determining Frame

Within the overarching episodic and thematic frames are myriad story frames. They range from the conflict frame—featuring polarized groups or individuals often attacking each other—to the problem frame, which stresses fear and danger. How do journalists determine frame? Three major realms of impact can influence frame: internal, external, and organizational. The internal realm encompasses the values, attitudes, creativity, and other personal attributes journalists bring to their jobs. While we strive for journalistic objectivity, fairness, and balance in our work, our personal history and what's inside our hearts and minds affect news frames. The external realm includes audience, interest groups, public relations organizations, politicians, and any organization trying to get its message out. Other media may also exert influence on coverage and presentation whether knowingly or unknowingly. Organizational routines (Gans 1979) can also have an impact on frame. Each newsroom has its own philosophy and policies that guide and sometimes dictate coverage. And they can make subtle, or even major differences in framing.

Internal Influence on Frame

A young reporter races out of the newsroom to cover a tornado in a nearby town. Her stomach turns as she pulls up to the disaster scene, which brings back vivid memories. As a teen she had lived through a twister that leveled a grocery store and concrete overpass just a block away from her home. Because of her experience she connects with the victims of this storm, and they open up to her with their sadness as well as optimism. Recalling the devastation in her own neighborhood, she's struck by the clear demarcation of the tornado's path. She stands with one foot in rubble and the other on an undisturbed field and walks into the destruction to show viewers the extreme contrast. Her compelling story touches viewers and later wins a broadcast award from United Press International. Personal experience guided her storytelling, as individual differences influence every journalist's news framing. Each of us brings to our work a history of living that includes a mix of personal, cultural, social, economic, political, religious, and other experience. These influences on frame can be positive or negative, fair or unbalanced, and it's up to the journalist to recognize life experience and use it appropriately.

External Influence on Frame

News releases spew out of newsroom fax machines by the minute, announcing book tours, research findings, and government meetings. E-mails to city editors and assignment desks invite reporters to attend open houses and speeches. Disgruntled consumers call "on-your-side" news hotlines to complain about everything from toasters that overheat to scam artists preying on the elderly. Public relations practitioners want free publicity for their clients. Some even produce interactive Flash presentations and other Web content for online news sites to use. Politicians want their voices to be heard. And journalists must sift through all these sources calling for attention. Some certainly have more influence than others. A small group of parents concerned about eliminating recess in the local elementary school may be unable to draw attention to its cause, whereas a grocery chain may easily attract reporters and cameras to its school computer campaign kick-off because it's giving away food and prizes. Choosing to cover an orchestrated public relations event because it's convenient and can fill some space on air, in print, or online isn't enough. Instead, ask yourself, *What does this mean to my audience?* If it's significant, then it merits attention. If interesting, then assess the level of interest. Weigh what's not being covered if you choose to follow the public relations lead. Remember that the decision to cover stories constitutes framing in its largest sense.

Sometimes, a story in one part of the country can have an impact on the way journalists frame news in their own cities. In the early 1990s Los Angeles police pulled over a speeding Hyundai and ordered the driver out of the car. Rodney King complied. The LAPD officers then clubbed and kicked him repeatedly (Tobar and Colvin 1991). Nearby, George Holliday was out on his apartment terrace trying out his new video camera, and captured the beating on tape. A local television station paid Holliday $500 for the tape (Instrument of Justice 1992), and soon the beating was broadcast into the homes of millions of people worldwide. The tape got repeated air play. Four months later, an investigation of the LAPD pointed to racism and possible brutality in the department. Shortly after the beating and ensuing report, many journalists nationwide adopted a heightened awareness of police brutality. The following two examples show journalists using a police brutality frame in their crime stories. In Seattle, a KING-TV reporter and anchorman questioned the action of local police who shot a suspect who was trying to escape. During a live report, the anchorman repeatedly asked whether the man had been shot in the front or the back (KING-TV 1991). And in Chicago, a WLS-TV reporter called into question the action of a federal drug agent who shot to death a suspect who apparently tried to run him over with a pick-up truck. The reporter devoted a large portion of the story to interviews with the suspect's family members and other witnesses who argued the man didn't deal drugs (WLS-TV 1991). While it's a reporter's responsibility to monitor and report nationwide trends, there is a danger in adopting a story frame influenced by a single event.

Other external forces can influence news frames. Free, professionally produced interactive content for your Web site may look very attractive. But before using it, assess its fairness and balance. Would you be advocating a certain product, service, or procedure if you ran the content on your Web site? Let's say a hospital produced a professional-looking interactive quiz on breast cancer awareness. One of the questions asks when women should have their first mammogram. The choices are age 30, 40, or 50. The correct answer according to the quiz is 40—but there's a controversy in the medical community about the optimal age for screening. Some say age 50 is best. By accepting the interactive quiz because it's from a reputable hospital and is professionally produced, rather than scrutinizing the content, you may be advocating a point of view.

Organizational Influence on Frame

In the mid-1990s KVUE television in Austin, Texas, adopted a crime story policy that had a great impact on how it framed crime in the community. Instead of chasing ambulances and reporting violent crime prominently and freely, the station vowed to take a more responsible approach toward covering crime. While other stations were reporting a fatal stabbing and a Saturday night brawl which led to a triple shooting, KVUE declined to cover the crimes. Because neither story met the following criteria, neither made it on their air (Kneeland 1996):

1. Does action need to be taken?
2. Is there an immediate threat to safety?
3. Is there a threat to children?
4. Does the crime have significant community impact?
5. Does the story lend itself to a crime-prevention effort?

Spending less time on violent crime gave journalists more time to develop other stories that had great community impact, such as taxes and cost of living. Their investigations of crime stories were more thorough, with an effort to "air information viewers need on violent crimes, while not deluging them with sensational violence" (Kneeland 1996).

Systems of reporting can also influence frame. Newspapers have used beats to cover their communities for years, as have some broadcasters. Reporters are assigned to specialized areas from which they generate their own stories. These beats may be broad themes such as health, technology, business, or the more traditional beats including cops, courts, city government, and schools. Other newsrooms rely on general assignments (GA) reporters who cover a wider range of stories. The most obvious distinction between beat and GA newsrooms is the way they cultivate sources and generate stories. Beat reporters often generate stories the GA reporter doesn't know about, because beat reporters are talking to court clerks on a daily basis or attending committee meetings where issues are born. The GA reporter is off covering a variety of stories and doesn't have a chance to make regular contact with only one portion of the community. The result—the beat and GA newsrooms frame their news programs, Web sites, and newspapers with different stories. Another difference is in specific story framing. The beat reporter may be able to provide context and greater depth than the GA reporter. His contacts may also lend perspective or direct him to other sources for developing the story. On the other hand, because the beat reporter has regular contact with his sources and must rely on them for future stories, those sources may exert control over his reporting. For example, beat reporters followed a governor to a spur-of-the moment press conference when hecklers at a protest rally wouldn't let him speak. Thousands of people had turned out for the rally to protest budget cuts to a state university. But instead of covering the issue, the beat reporters framed the story around the governor, who complained that he had been mistreated by disrespectful faculty and students. The focus of the story had been taken away from the budget cuts and problems, and moved toward a political figure and his agenda.

News Web sites and organizational influence on frame

Major news organizations such as MSNBC, *The New York Times*, and *The Washington Post* commit the resources necessary to produce interactive, multimedia content for their Web sites. But in many U.S. newsrooms, a bare bones staff edits and manages the online edition of the paper or newscast. As few as one person may staff the site, converting earlier broadcast stories to streaming video or posting stories published in the newspaper. Technology in some television newsrooms grabs scripts and converts them to Web stories without human intervention. Headlines from the Associated Press may appear and automatically update. And in the early evening after the staff goes home, many of these Web sites go on auto pilot until the next morning. The picture of reality presented by these sites may be much different from those staffed 'round-the-clock using less automation.

Web sites using Internet content services may also frame the world differently for their audiences. A national service would likely draw from sources in its network rather than focus locally. Editors 1,000 miles away may select stories and reshape them for the Web site. The television producer whose station uses such a service may have little or no communication with the Web editor about online news coverage and story selection.

Updating procedures can also make a difference in a news Web site's overall frame. If an online producer regularly updates the site at 9 a.m., noon, and 5 p.m., stories that break in the interim periods don't appear until the update. The online user doesn't know about the updating policy, but expects to see news on the Web as it breaks. If a tornado hits overnight, people who visit a site at 8 a.m. wouldn't find anything on the storm if the editor doesn't update until 9 a.m.

Newsroom policy may also dictate the focus of a Web site as local, national, or international. Even though the Internet allows worldwide access to your site, your newspaper or television station may dedicate itself to local news on its Web site. The overall site frame would differ because of this policy.

Audience Impact on Frame

Before the Internet, audiences had limited opportunity to interact with the news media. They could call the newsroom to complain about a story, or to draw attention to issues they deem important. Or they could write letters to the editor. Those calls and mailings might have led to a correction, but contributing to a story as it was being framed was much less likely. Today, the audience can contribute to the story frame in several ways. First, as a potential source; second, by navigating an interactive story.

Audience as Source

As shown in Chapter 4, reporters now seek sources online through devices such as the reporter's query. Audience members then respond to the reporter to provide information or voice opinions. Often the queries focus on those who experienced or were affected by a recent event, such as those who got stuck in traffic, have a relative in Iraq, got hit hard by a storm, and so on. This type of sourcing can have a positive or negative effect on story frame, depending on how the reporter handles the information. Relying on one person to represent an entire group of people who experienced something can be misleading. Keep in mind that a portion of the population does not use the Internet for news, and by seeking and using only Internet sources, reporters may be limiting viewpoints.

The online discussion can also shape a story frame. Moderators drive the direction of the forum through their questions and comments. This effect has been documented on C-SPAN call-in shows. When callers used a conflict frame in discussing political issues, hosts and guests spent more time responding than they did on other frames, such as issues or strategies (Kurpius 2001).

Audience as Navigator

When television reporters produce their news packages, they craft them believing the viewer will watch and listen to the whole story. They realize that the people at home can turn the dial, leave the room, or converse while the story airs. But, if written and reported well, the story should make it into the viewer's head. These stories are linear, with a beginning, middle, and end, to be consumed in their entirety. Likewise, the print journalist writes a story to be read. It's crafted to be thorough and thoughtful, also linear, with a beginning, middle, and end. But the online, interactive journalist shares control over story presentation with the Web user. She offers choices to the user, who decides which path to follow. The story will unfold differently for that user depending on the paths traveled. For example, latimes.com (2002) gives the user many choices in its story on the plight of foster kids after they turn 18. It features three young adults and tells their stories in print, video, and audio slide shows. Stories in all media are organized by the person's name, Janea, Monique, and Jesse. So, you can choose to read Janea's story or see Monique's slide show or Jesse's video—or any combination of person and media. You also choose which story to see first, next, and so on. Each user frames this story differently, depending on the choices made. And those choices may shape perceptions of these young people and the larger story.

Activities for Further Learning

1. Consider the following information and discuss possible influences on these story and Web site frames based on what you've learned in this chapter.

In February 2003, millions of people worldwide took to the streets to protest the then-proposed war with Iraq. In New York City alone, up to one-quarter-million people marched, joined nationwide by thousands more from Seattle to South Florida. But if you went online for news in the early afternoon the day after the protests, you might have seen nothing about the U.S. marches, and in some cases, nothing about the

international protests, either. Thirteen of sixty-seven major metropolitan newspaper Web sites carried no anti-war rally coverage on their
front page, including sites in Norfolk and St. Louis. The *St. Louis Post-
Dispatch* site, STLtoday.com (2003), did include, however, a special
feature called "Postcards from Kuwait: See and hear some of the local
servicemen serving in Kuwait." More than one-fourth of the Web sites
featured stories on the international protests, but mentioned nothing
about those in New York. *The Washington Post's* 11:20 a.m. online
edition focused on the international protests but mentioned nothing of
the U.S. marches. More than half the sites highlighted the international
protests over those in New York. And 40 percent of the sites presented
information on local protests before mentioning the international
rallies.

References

Gans, H. 1979. *Deciding What's News: A Study of CBS Evening News, NBC
    Nightly News, Newsweek, and Time.* New York: Pantheon Books.
Gitlin, T. 1980. *The Whole World is Watching: Mass Media in the Making and
    Unmaking of the New Left.* Berkeley: University of California Press.
Gordon, M. T. and C. G. Artwick 1993. *Urban Images: Portrayals by Local TV
    and Newspapers.* Seattle: University of Washington Graduate School of
    Public Affairs.
Instrument of Justice. June 15, 1992. *Jet.* p. 36.
Iyengar, S. 1991. *Is Anyone Responsible?: How Television Frames Political Is-
    sues.* Chicago: University of Chicago Press.
KING-TV. Aug. 6, 1991. 11 p.m. newscast.
Kneeland, C. 1996. A grueling standard to live by. *Nieman Reports* (online ver-
    sion). Vol. 53 No. 4 Winter 1999 Vol. 54 No. 1 Spring 2000 http://www.
    nieman.harvard.edu/reports/99-4_00-1NR/Kneeland_Grueling.html
Kurpius, D. D. 2001. Changing frames on C-SPAN call-in shows: The framing of
    citizen comments. Paper presented to the Radio-Television Journalism Di-
    vision of the Association for Education in Journalism and Mass Communi-
    cation. Washington, D.C.
latimes.com. 2002. http://www.latimes.com/news/la-foster-special,0,3126049.
    special?coll=la%2Dadelphia%2Dright%2Drail
Price, V., D. Tewksbury, and E. Powers. October 1997. Switching trains of
    thought: The impact of news frames on readers' cognitive responses. *Com-
    munication Research*, Vol. 24, Issue 5, p. 481. Retrieved from ProQuest.

Schramm, W. 1949. The nature of news. In *Mass Communications*, pp. 288-303. Urbana: University of Illinois Press.

Shoemaker, P. L. 1996. Hardwired for News: Using biological and cultural evolution to explain the surveillance function. *Journal of Communication* 46(3), Summer, pp. 32-47.

stltoday.com. Feb. 16, 2003. http://www.stltoday.com

Tobar, H. and R.L. Colvin. March 7, 1991. Witnesses depict relentless beating; Police: Accounts of Rodney Glen King's arrest describe repeated striking and kicking of the suspect. LAPD officers said King's actions justified the treatment. *Los Angeles Times*, Metro Part B, Page 1, Column 2.

WLS-TV. July 12, 1991. 10 p.m. newscast.

CHAPTER 7

Digital Storytelling Tools

Chapter Objectives

As tropical storm Claudette lumbers toward the Texas coast, digital reporters and producers dig deep into their toolboxes to tell the story. MySanAntonio.com (2003) links to a National Weather Service graphic to show Web users the storm's path and expected landfall. The *Houston Chronicle's* Web site teams up with KHOU to stream a live report from Galveston City Hall warning to evacuate (2003). And, at MSNBC.com (2003), an interactive guide includes a map of infamous floods and a quiz on surviving a flood. A fact box defines storm terminology—from cyclone to typhoon—in both interactive and printable versions.

Telling the story on the Web can be an exciting challenge. But searching through the online toolbox and pulling out the biggest bells and loudest whistles won't necessarily serve the users. You've got to know when to ring the bell and blow the whistle for effective online storytelling that gives citizens what they need and want to know. This chapter will introduce you to the tools online journalists can use to tell their stories, which work best under what circumstances, and how to determine when and how to use them.

Online Storytelling Tools

Have you ever been explaining something to a friend and found yourself reaching for a piece of paper and pencil to sketch out what you wanted to convey? Or perhaps you spoke faster, or slower, louder, or more softly, for emphasis? You may have mimicked what your cousin said and how he said it, or picked up a prop for a how-to demonstration. These are all storytelling tools people use in interpersonal communication. With digital communication, journalists also use an array of tools to convey information. That toolbox is expanding as technology continues to develop. Online extras, multimedia, interactives—we see these terms and the features they represent on today's major online news sites. Many are technically complex and involve a high level of production. But digital storytelling tools also include the basics, such as text and photographs. This section introduces today's most common digital tools and their role in online storytelling.

Text

Text is the workhorse of digital journalism. Processed directly into the computer system and used in many other tools, text holds together the digital story. Using it appropriately online, however, is a challenge not all news Web sites have mastered. The dreaded shovelware that's dug right out of television news scripts and newspaper stories continues to be piled high on many online news sites. But it doesn't have to be. We know from Chapter 5 that when working from an existing print or broadcast story, making a few minor changes can result in more user-friendly material that the reader can stick with. Tighter, shorter copy with section heads, boldface type and bulleted presentations can make for easier scanning and ingestion. We can also pull out compelling quotes and highlight them in a larger font in a colored box either outside or within the story. KTRK (2003) in Houston delivered critical storm information to its audience online by using the bulleting strategy. When the rains from Hurricane Claudette started falling, the water on many roads became dangerously high. A link on the Web site's cover page directed users to a list of road conditions and other relevant information. This approach can help producers post the information quickly and give users an easy-to-read report of conditions.

Time and resources dictate text-only stories

Sometimes, in a breaking news situation, a reporter heads out to the field while a producer or writer gets on the phone or the Internet to gather whatever facts are available. Often, this situation can produce enough information for a brief text story that can be posted online quickly. Let's say a tanker truck leak on the interstate has closed down a section of the highway. The state department of transportation tells you where it happened, the name of the trucking company, and how traffic is being rerouted. You find the company's Web site and its phone number, and in a few minutes you know the truck was traveling from Charlotte to Jacksonville, and that it was carrying ammonium, the liquid form of ammonia. A call to the state hazardous materials department answers your questions about safety issues and the clean up. At this point, you know enough to write a short text story, but have nothing from the field. In this case, you should post your text piece on the Web site and add to it as the reporter develops the story.

In addition to working with reporters in the field, online producers and editors continually monitor the wires for news. And while the Associated Press provides multimedia reporting, not every news operation subscribes to that level of service. When that is the case, the producer may have available only straight text for regional, national, and international stories. Sometimes the text can be reworked into other forms of storytelling, such as graphics or fact boxes. But, if a Web site's focus is local, then taking the time to develop the national story may not be a viable choice. The producer's energy will likely be needed elsewhere, so the wire story gets posted directly onto the site, unchanged. When Arnold Schwarzenegger decided to skip the first debate in California's recall election, numerous Web sites outside California ran a short AP story that basically reported his decision to give a speech instead, named those who would debate, and said that he agreed to only one debate in late September. Running this as straight text is justified for several reasons. First, the Web sites are based outside California and wouldn't likely devote many resources to that state's political news. And second, the small amount of information available on the story (125 words) can be read easily in text format. On the other hand, within the state of California, the story would justify multimedia, interactive treatment.

Text and Links

One of the most distinctive features of online news is the hypertext link. Click on it and arrive anywhere on the Web—from the FBI's Web site for crime statistics to a concert venue database at Pollstar. A link can give users access to original documents used in reporting and take them to fun features related to stories. Within your site, links can provide background through archived stories. These digital "clippings," once housed in newspaper libraries and television script file cabinets, were difficult, if not impossible, for the public to access. Now, journalists can place them beside a news piece, making it easy for readers to delve into past stories from your news organization's archive.

Linking outside the news site provides breadth and depth through related material produced by others. From a medical Web site detailing a colonoscopy to a music site with a performer's commentary on her latest release, off-site linking can give users a richer online experience. But careless linking can lead to bias, blur the line between news and advertising, and more.

Avoiding biased links

Let's say you are covering a story on elderly drivers after an 86-year-old man runs his car into a busy street market in California. Imagine the following scenario. One of your sources belongs to a citizen's group pushing to outlaw drivers who are over 75. She gives you the group's Web address and you link to it. There's another group fighting to preserve senior citizen rights, and it, too, has a Web site. But its leader didn't give you the URL, so you don't link to that site. By linking to one and not the other, your coverage is not balanced. In this case, you, the reporter, need to work a little harder. Make an effort to seek balance and fairness in your off-site links. If you're going to link to one form of citizen action, you should actively seek the other side. Ask if they have a Web site, and get the URL. Even if the senior group does not have a Web site, it would be fair to include its contact person's name and phone number in the vicinity of the other group's Web link.

If your story includes information on a product or business, do you include a link to its Web site? That depends. And the circumstance should dictate how it is handled. For example, when advertisers pay for a link to their Web sites, those links should be clearly marked as paid for (Best Practices 1998). Sites such as TBO.com identify this type of link as a sponsored link. And what if a story lends itself to a product link? Should a story about an upcoming sports event offer a nearby link to a shop that sells team t-shirts and hats? Should a book review link to an online bookseller to make it easy for the Web user to buy the book? NYTimes.com linked to BarnesandNoble.com at the bottom of its book reviews for more than three years and received a fee each time a Web user clicked on the link (Finberg and Stone 2002). The Digital Journalism Credibility Study says, "This raised the specter of whether or not BN.com had influence on *The New York Times'* book reviews" (Finberg and Stone 2002, p. 50). Among its strategies to enhance the credibility of online news, the study advises, "When it's an ad, say it's an ad." (p. 72) News consumers deserve to know when links are sponsored so they can make their own decisions about these ads.

Should we create our links within stories or in a section adjacent to the text? Major sites place related material in nearby boxes. This is preferable for several reasons. First, in-text links may distract readers from a fluid story experience. They may feel compelled to link outside the text, and when they return, the fluency is broken. Or, they may choose to move on to another site and leave the story unfinished. Also, the informal protocol of placing links outside stories has predisposed users to expect to find, and to look for, adjacent links.

How many links should we include with our stories? Some merit none while others lend themselves to multiple related stories and extras. If the purpose of the links is to provide depth and background, then arrange them in a chronological list of most recent to oldest story in the archive. If there's a fee for any of the archived stories, this can be noted by including a dollar sign next to the link, as does *The New York Times on the Web*. Remember that the goal is to provide information without overwhelming the user. On a Web site cover page, linking to one or two related stories and a few extras, such as slide shows or video, would be about right.

Fact Boxes

Print and broadcast journalists weave facts throughout their stories. Online, reporters and producers have the option of taking a set of facts and creating a fact box for quick and easy reference. These work well to add information to the story without incorporating it into the text. Focus on quick and substantial facts that can be presented as bullets or in columns. A story on identity theft lends itself well to the text-box approach. A Federal Trade Commission report includes many statistics that can bog down the text piece, but fit nicely into a fact box (Figure 7.1).

Graphics

Reading statistics online can often make the user's eyes glaze over. But a colorful pie chart or bar graph can offer a welcome alternative to numbers embedded in text. When the newspaper or television station art department is available, an artist can use digital tools as well as manual techniques to create attractive graphics. But there are alternatives when you don't have access to these resources. Microsoft Word includes a simple bar chart that you can link

Number of U.S. victims since 1999:   27 million

Number of U.S. victims in last year: 9.9 million

Cost to victims: More than $1,000 each

Type of fraud:
Credit card - 42 percent
Phone or utility - 22 percent
Bank - 17 percent

Source: Federal Trade Commission, U.S. Department of Justice

Figure 7.1 Building a text box that highlights key facts can help the reader sift through information quickly and easily.

to on your Web page. Just go to "insert" and pull down the menu, choosing "picture." Then pull down "chart." A data sheet will pop up. Enter your information in the columns and rows to create the chart. Remember to include a title for the chart, and any notes you feel are necessary. Copy and paste the chart into your Web page, or, if you prefer, you can save it as a Web page and link to it from your story. See Figure 7.2 for a simple bar chart created in Word.

Linkable Directory

When you've got reams of information you'd like to present, organizing it into a linkable directory can make it easy to access and useful to your audience. For example, state departments of education have been tracking individual school progress on standardized tests. If you had 100 schools in your region, you could group them several ways for ease of navigation. One might be by district. You would name all districts on the story's home page, linking from each name to that district's schools. From there you would link to the individual school for the scores and related data.

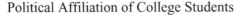

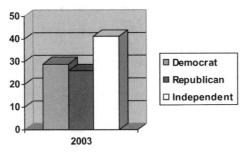

Source: Harvard University Institute of Politics

Figure 7.2 Digital journalists can build simple bar charts in Microsoft Word.

Timelines

What better way to present a story that includes a history, to show change over time or to provide context and background, than through a timeline? These can be static or interactive, depending on the amount of data to present, your deadline, and the resources available to create them. A simple static graphic might mirror what you would find in a history book, using a horizontal line with dates and events noted in chronological order from left to right. No more than, perhaps, five or six dates with a short description for each corresponding date could be treated this way. But exceeding these parameters would clutter the clarity of this tool. Instead, choose an interactive format with a button to drive the user through the information. The *Chicago Tribune Online Edition* (2003) features a timeline in its special report on United Airlines. It presents the company over time, beginning with the 1930s, and features a separate graphic for each decade to the 2000s. The user can move forward by clicking a "next" button. For even more user control, the navigation tool could list each decade and allow the user to click where she chooses. However, the journalist may want the user to see the information in a certain order, and in that case, the "next" button would be preferred.

Online Discussions

The best online discussions have shape and substance, and are guided by a knowledgeable moderator. When reporters become experts in a particular subject, perhaps through years covering a beat, they can serve as discussion leaders. A visiting expert can also do so. MSNBC.com technology editor Jonathan Dube says chats can be a form of interactive storytelling if they're moderated properly. "This can be a very powerful way to convey information because the readers help create and shape the story," says Dube (2003).

Posting reader messages online without any review for language and relevance may risk offending and frustrating readers who seek significant information. And the usefulness of doing so is questionable. So, before producing an online message board or chat, work with an upper-level editor to determine the level of review and/or moderation.

Online Polls

While some people feel comfortable voicing their opinions anytime, anyplace, others would rather keep those thoughts to themselves, unless they can express them anonymously, in an online poll. Critics argue online polls are meaningless, because they mine a select group of people—those who visit a certain site. For a poll to be valid, the people who take it must be representative of the population as a whole. The sample must be random with a minimum number of participants. Questions must be carefully constructed and pre-tested to ensure they measure what they purport to. And answers must be recorded carefully and accurately. But online polls don't meet all these criteria. Nonetheless, they are interactive—you submit your answer and then immediately see the results. And they're popular. So, should we use them in our stories? Yes, but only under certain conditions.

- Avoid controversial issues. If you connect your poll to a controversial issue, it may unfairly sway public opinion. For example, "Do you believe George Bush knew the State of the Union address reference about Iraq seeking to buy nuclear material from Africa was false?" If people are allowed to vote more than once, they may do so. Or, they may e-mail like-minded colleagues to vote. And, the responses don't represent the public at large. So, including such questions may be irresponsible journalistically.
- Avoid serious behavior-related questions. After a government study showed that hormone replacement therapy increased women's risk for heart disease, stroke, and breast cancer, some Web sites targeted the issue in their online polls. Adjacent to their stories, the Web sites

asked readers if they would continue hormone replacement therapy. This is a very personal decision to be made with careful thought and the guidance of a medical professional. The poll's accuracy cannot be guaranteed, and it does not represent the population of women taking the hormones. Just imagine if a pharmaceutical company had its employees vote repeatedly against stopping treatment. Because the potential impact of behavior-related questions is great, avoiding such poll questions is the responsible choice.

- Include light features, sports, and entertainment. These can be fun and often draw heavy reaction. TBO.com asked, "Do you like the USF Bulls' new logo?" (2003) And MSNBC.com synergized with the "Today" show, asking visitors to vote on bridesmaids' dresses for its special program on planning a dream wedding. Light, online poll questions take just a moment to answer and give users a bit of diversion in their day.

Quizzes

A quiz can sometimes be a great way to bring a Web user into a story. Two recent reports about teenagers were perfect candidates for a quiz. The first focused on U.S. teens winning the gold medal in an international geography competition. The other reported high school seniors' dismal financial knowledge. Questions related to either of those stories would engage users and give them a taste of what the students experienced. So, when a story itself focuses on tests and knowledge level, a quiz can bring it to life. Immediate feedback on answers makes the quiz more meaningful, and allowing users to take it repeatedly gives them the opportunity to learn the information. Limit the number of questions to between five and ten so users maintain high interest. And, if feasible, relate quiz questions to the story text.

Visuals

Single photos, slide shows, and streaming video enhance the user experience with many of today's online news sites. When does a story merit a slide show and when will a single photo suffice? And when is it preferable to use streaming video? An online editor might argue that the answer is obvious—to use what you have. Certainly, this is true to a great extent, but it does go deeper than that. The visual content in relation to the event

Figure 7.3 Compelling images such as this one from the Vietnam war can tell an entire story, and should be used alone for best effect. The photo, shot by Eddie Adams in 1968, shows South Vietnamese National Police Chief Brig. Gen. Nguyen Ngoc Loan executing a Viet Cong officer.

should dictate the choice. Is a single photograph so stunning, so compelling, that it alone can tell the story? Many people who lived during the Vietnam era vividly remember the image of Saigon's police chief pointing his pistol at his Viet Cong prisoner a moment before executing him. The prisoner's anguish frozen in time underscores the brutality of war (Figure 7.3). Is motion a key component of the visual, such as a volcano erupting or a bridge collapsing? If so, then the video deserves to run online. Or, does a series of still images contribute to greater understanding of an event? When this is the case, a slide show would be the best route to engage and involve the user. Considering these issues will help you make more informed decisions about your online visuals. See Chapter 9 for an in-depth look at working with images.

Photos

Digital still cameras offer the portability and ease of production that make it possible to include photographs with just about every local story on our Web sites. But just because we can do it, should we? The classic photojournalism textbook, *Pictures on a Page* (Evans 1978), offers guidance that makes sense in print and online. The publishable photograph would have at least one of the following traits: animation, relevant context, or depth of meaning (p. 47). In the animated photo, subjects are doing something of interest—through interaction, expression, or relationship. A photo with context reveals something more than people shaking hands or gathering at a ceremony. The contextual picture will put subjects into the context of the event. For example, instead of seeing someone winning a blue ribbon, feature the teenager who won the prize showing her horse, or the painter who won first place at his easel. The context offers much more than simply the award ceremony. And finally, photos with meaning offer significance. This may be through symbolism or stark realism. An image of starving children with protruding bellies does so through both.

Before going out into the field with a digital still camera, reporters should attend to the three determinants of photo selection, seeking photos that offer animation, context, and meaning. Online producers and editors can commit to quality in their photographs by rejecting those that don't meet one of these three standards.

Slide Shows

Interactive slide shows provide visual access to news events with relative immediacy and minimal production time and effort. And they're one of the most popular features online news sites offer. Using a pre-designed template, journalists can put digital photos into an interactive format and have them up on the site more quickly than an edited video story.

If all your photos are just a variation of the same subject—for example, a wide shot of a speaker on a podium with the audience in the foreground, a slightly tighter composition of the same scene, and a close-up of the speaker's face—a slide show might not be your best choice. But, if you can show many elements of the event, your photographs have more to say and merit building a slide show. For the same event, these might include photos of an enormous crowd waiting to enter the auditorium, the speaker comfortably chatting with the event organizer just before going on stage, a close-up of a young man reacting enthusiastically to the speech, and the speaker at an emotional moment.

Photographs taken by the public can also make excellent slide shows, but care must be taken to ensure fairness and truth. Storm coverage is especially effective because viewers can provide visuals from locations news crews can't get to, or might have missed. Also, because storms are acts of nature, they won't likely involve issues of fairness and truth. On the other hand, users may unknowingly or even purposefully distort reality in the way they photograph organized events such as protests and other potentially controversial happenings. But, wise and careful photo editors can make fair choices, as the BBC has shown. In February 2003, millions of people worldwide took to the streets to protest the impending war with Iraq. Hundreds sent photos to the BBC online edition, which included them in published slide shows. Most of the scenes featured large crowds carrying signs and banners, taken from a raised vantage point. They did not include any physical violence or confrontations with authorities, which did transpire in some locations.

Video

How does one decide on video over a slide show? Cost can be a major factor if the news organization pays a provider for server space. This may limit the number of stories a Web site may stream. Human resources also plays a large role. At a television station, the video will be shot and edited for a news broadcast and its streaming on the Web site will take minimal effort. Creating a slide show from that video would be more labor-intensive. It would require capturing still images from the videotape and then building the slide show.

Concerns about bandwidth and the time it takes users to download video might motivate a preference for the slide show format over video. But, as broadband connections become more common, this concern will subside. At the time of this writing, nearly 30 percent of all home Internet users connected via broadband (Sacramento Business Journal 2003).

Immediate, on-the-scene coverage with moving images and sound lends itself to video streaming. But beware of live-for-the-sake-of-live television reports posted online and left there hours, sometimes days, after an event. A reporter standing in front of a police station talking about a bank robber still at large (he was at the time), even though a suspect is now in custody (24 hours later), will test the online user's patience and erode your credibility. Whereas, a reporter on the scene during a rescue would deliver immediacy and action.

Video and photo quality and quantity must also be considered. There is rarely justification for running video if the shots are dark, out of focus, framed poorly, shaky, or if you have so little video that you have to show the same shot more than once. Amateur video of spot news, such as an accident, tornado, plane crash, or fire, would qualify, but poor quality professional video would rarely be justified. Selected still frames in a slide show are preferable if this is the case.

Size of the image should also be considered. You've witnessed the image degradation when expanding a video window, so expect your user to keep the window small for crispness and clarity. However, with a small window the detail will be difficult to see. If that visual detail is key to the story, you may choose to create a slide show in which larger images can be made and displayed online.

A particularly compelling interview segment, or sound bite, would motivate the video stream. President Clinton's assertion, "I did not have sex with that woman," would rank as a must-stream, as would President Nixon's, "I am not a crook." But even if we're not dealing with the talk of presidents, our sources often say things in a way only they can. Whether it be their emotion, eloquence, or energy, hearing it from the source can have great impact. In a study that examined what people remember from television crime stories, subjects recalled the people interviewed more often than they did the morbid crime images. Specifically, they more often mentioned an interview with a tearful mother of her murdered daughter than they did the morbid scene of the young woman's body bag (Artwick 1996). People, what they say, and the way they say it have an impact and should not be overlooked in our digital stories.

A demonstration in which the action is fluid and synchronously accompanied by narration calls for video streaming. A story on glass blowing comes to mind, in which the glowing glob takes on a shape of beauty before the viewer's eyes. The steps can also be shown in a slide show, but may be conveyed more readily through the fluidity of video.

In many cases, you can use both a slide show and video. But, each should focus on different aspects of the story for the most effective coverage.

Audio

Well-used audio can enhance a story, but this takes more than posting a set of audio clips. Some news Web sites offer audio galleries organized by topic, with a list of links under each broad story category. Users click on the link and the audio begins playing. While this approach appears good from an organizational standpoint, without some context to guide the user, the audio provides little meaning. Alternatives include the Q&A format and text introduction to the clip.

Q&A format

People profiles or stories featuring experts who can give depth to a topic work well in this format. The questions appear in text and link to the answer on audio clip. The producer should be selective and include the clearest and most engaging responses. Remember that you're telling a story, and the sound bites you choose should reveal something about the interviewee (if a profile). The expert bites should lend deeper understanding of an issue or topic without overwhelming the user with excess verbiage. Avoid using the entire interview except for the rare case in which it's so compelling you feel it merits total inclusion.

Text introduction to the clip

Use a brief paragraph to introduce the clip. Through the text you're telling the Web users who they're listening to, and why it's relevant. You're not giving away what the sound bite says. If the clip features a full story, the text should introduce the reporter and what the story is about. A photo may work nicely here, but should follow the guidelines of animation, context, and meaning.

Audio and slide shows

Adding audio to a slide show does not necessarily require field recording. While incorporating sounds of the people and events adds another dimension to the presentation, digital journalists can turn to their own commentary to provide depth and enhance their storytelling. Photojournalist Chang Lee of *The New York Times* told a story of the people in Afghanistan after the war in a narrated slide show called "Beautiful Lives" (2003). This award-winning piece focuses on the courage and spirit of the people while documenting their struggle. Web users can listen to or mute the narration while they click through the photos, and have an option of reading a transcript of the commentary. The narration is not synched with the individual photos, however. For the producer who wants to keep a closer relationship between narration and individual photos, audio for each photo can be programmed to play only with that slide.

Using Storyboards to Organize Digital Material

Some people possess the ability to envision complex story organization in their heads and then make their visions a digital reality. Many do not. And even those who do must often work with others to execute their plans. That's where storyboards come in. The practice originated with film, where it's been used for years to conceptualize movie scenes, and later was adopted by television for commercials and programming. Storyboards are extremely handy for organizing online stories because they help you visualize the material and how it interconnects, as a flow chart would. Let's create a storyboard for online coverage of another famous 2003 storm, Hurricane Isabel. Here's what we have to work with:

- A 90-second video story on flooding in Baltimore
- Photographs from North Carolina, Virginia, and Maryland
- A text story on floods, damage, and power outages throughout the east coast
- A list of damage estimates for ten states

We'll use a large photo and the text piece, include the video, and create a slide show and interactive fact box. Figure 7.4 shows the storyboard for this plan. You can include the headline and caption text right on the storyboard, but for improved clarity, number the elements and then use your computer word processing program to type the information that pertains to each element.

Storytelling Parameters and Digital Tools

Storytelling parameters involve the various elements that contribute to this form of communication: audience, information, story type, newsworthiness, and resources.

Defining the Audience

First, you must know your audience. Theoretically, your Web visitors can come from anywhere in the world. But, are you really writing and producing for that audience? Or, is a local audience your main focus? For most newspaper and broadcast Web sites, the focus is local. They may also

1. Story treatment for the cover page

```
Headline
                Play video
   Photo here
                See
Caption         slideshow
Text------------
----------------    Fact box
----------------
```

2. User links to this page after clicking "play video" from #1

```
              Video plays here


Play    -----summary-------
        ---------------------
Stop    ---------------------
```

3. User links to this page after clicking on "fact box" from #1

```
Title
.  ------------    ----text----
.  ------------    ----goes----
.  ------------    ----here----
.  ------------    ------------
.                  ------------
```

Click on a bullet to get a
full text description.
Bullets remain static--only
the text changes.

4. User links to this page after clicking on "slideshow" from #1

```
         See a slide by
         clicking on a
         number or arrow
      1 2 3 4 5 6 7 8 9 10
            ←      →
         -----caption----
```

Figure 7.4 Storyboards can help journalists organize information and convey ideas to designers.

appeal to niche audiences depending on what their locations have to offer. For example, horse breeding, showing, and racing are a niche market in Kentucky as is aerospace in the Gulf states. Larger market newspapers and broadcast news likely include a broader region and include news in that area—for example, Miami might include news on Latin America. Networks and national sites keep an even broader audience in mind when covering stories.

Once you know with whom you are communicating, you can ask the question that will guide your online decisions: *What does my audience need and want to know?* With the answer at hand, digital journalists can make wise decisions about how to deliver that information. The hurricane story that began this chapter illustrates how defining audiences and targeting what they need and want to know leads to distinct approaches in online news presentation. Let's begin about 24 hours before Hurricane Claudette's landfall. At that point in time, both local and distant audiences needed and wanted to know where and when the storm was expected to hit land. While a journalist can write about this, and include latitude and longitude coordinates, the simplest, clearest way to present this information is graphically. The art department could handle this for you, but why replicate what's already available? Link to a National Weather Service graphic that depicts the storm's path and expected time of landfall. Both local and national sites used some form of this "storm tracker" map in their coverage the day before the storm arrived. (Figure 7.5) A national site might provide some general information on tropical storms and their impact. Interactive fact boxes and quizzes would suit this need. They may also report how people in the storm's path are reacting. Text stories with photographs, slide shows with or without audio, or streaming video packages convey the overall mood.

While this approach would also be useful to the local audience, more pressing questions need to be answered: *Should I evacuate, and if so,*

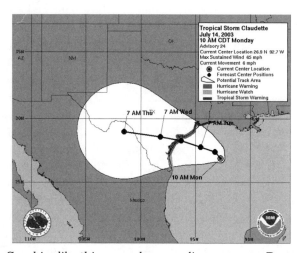

Figure 7.5 Graphics like this can enhance online coverage. Reproduced with permission of NOAA.

when? Where can I go? How do I get there? What should I do before I leave? What if I can't get out in time? Organizing the story elements to address the questions can keep the information clear and accessible. *Should I evacuate?* Answer this question in the main story headline, and stream video from Galveston City Hall, where city officials made the announcement to evacuate. The video lends immediacy and importance to the action. *Where can I go?* Link from the front page to a list of shelters, including their addresses and phone numbers. *How do I get there?* Include a printable map of evacuation routes and shelter locations. *What should I do before I leave?* A text or video story would show how people in the area are preparing for the storm. And a bullet list could be added as a link or an interactive feature within the text. *What if I can't get out in time?* Locate and include links to pre-produced sites that address this.

As time passes and the story progresses, journalists must ask: *How do audience information needs and wants change, and how can I address this in my storytelling?* As the storm approaches and is upgraded to a hurricane, the local audience wants and needs specific information. *Are ferries still running? Are roads flooded? Has it hit land?* Links off the main page to bulleted lists make information delivery quick and easy to access. Many people want to help, or at least participate in some way. The message board on KHOU's Web site gives the user a means to ask or answer questions, or to let others know how high the water is in their neighborhood. They can also send in photos by e-mail to be included on the Web site.

At about noon on Tuesday, Claudette hits land and rips off roofs, sends RVs cartwheeling, and washes the surf into shops and restaurants along a seaside boardwalk. Evacuees, and those near the storm, want to know its impact. *Is my home still standing? How bad is the flooding? What happened in my neighborhood?* Shortly after landfall, KHOU streamed video from its helicopter, bringing the storm to Web users. People in the area sent their photographs to KHOU.com to be used in a slide show online.

The national audience also wants to see the hurricane's impact—the winds, the waves, the damage, the floods. And, they want reassurance that relatives and friends on the Gulf coast are safe. Visual storytelling approaches using video and still photographs communicate the impact.

Again, use the basic question approach to guide you through your decision making when using digital storytelling tools. Thinking about your audience and what it needs and wants to know will help you provide the information in the clearest and most user-friendly ways.

Information Type and Online Tools

A print purist might argue that words alone can always tell the best story. The skilled writer can paint scenes, elicit emotion, and transmit information. Words are indeed powerful. But, as we've learned from television and radio, the medium plays an integral role in effective storytelling. Simply reading newspaper stories over the radio or reporting news for television without visuals were tried and failed in the early days of those media. Moving away from the simple transference of print and broadcast stories to the Web will mark true online communication.

An awareness of information type can help digital journalists choose the most appropriate means of presenting that information. Here's a simple checklist to help identify information type and potential online tool.

Information type and appropriate online tool:

Location: Map
Statistics: Graphic, database, simple linked directory
Sounds: Link to audio, or audio added to photos
Tests or knowledge levels: Quiz
History—tying dates to events: Timeline
Breaking event: Video, audio, photo
Report or recommendations: Bulleted text
Profile interview: Interactive Q&A using text, audio, or video bites

Story Type and Online Tools

At first glance, the casual observer might note that the best story type for online presentation would be the feature. One can easily imagine a piece about a musician that includes recordings and photographs, or a story on a poet with selected poems and audio interviews. Yes, features do make wonderful online reports. But limiting our multimedia/interactive mindset to story type will stifle our digital storytelling. Applying online tools to scheduled events, spot news, and enterprise stories and investigative reports will bring to our audiences a richer news experience.

Newsworthiness and Online Tools

A 5-year-old in Cleveland dies after ramming his grandmother's car into a tree. Should your online news site in Florida run the story, and if so, what online tools should you use to tell it? Questioning its newsworthiness can help guide your decision-making. Tribune Publishing Company president Jack Fuller (1996, p. 7) writes, "Significance and interest provide separate bases for calling an event or piece of information news, and either may be sufficient." With this in mind, we return to the public to guide us, asking: *What does this story mean to my audience?* Let's assume that your users are mostly local and include a range of ages, and professions. You might answer: *Many users have young children or know someone who does. This could be important to them, even though it took place more than 1,000 miles away.* For this audience, the story meets the significance criterion presented by Fuller.

If, instead, the audience consisted of working singles, your answer might be: *It probably doesn't mean much, but it is unusual.* And because of the uncommon nature of the event, you may decide to use the story. It meets Fuller's interest criterion. Of course, the notion of interest is subjective and can lean heavily toward celebrity and crime if journalists are not vigilant. Learning to balance significance and interest can help us better serve our communities with online news.

Significance and interest help determine what stories to include on our Web sites, but they can also guide our use of online tools in storytelling. They may have an impact on the resources we are willing to invest in applying online tools to a particular story. Because the car crash story involving the 5-year-old boy has just moderate significance and interest in the Florida community, a producer there may choose to spend less time on that story than one with greater significance and/or impact. Recalling that another similar story was recently in the news would give the story greater significance, so the producer might decide to spend a few minutes searching the archive to find the story and link to it. About a week earlier, a 6-year-old in another state drove a car 25 miles in search of his mother, and survived. Seeking patterns in news can provide context and greater significance. Also be aware that adding context through links or interactivity can make a story more significant and can also provide higher interest.

Resources and Online Tools

We've seen throughout this chapter that many digital tools can be applied to online storytelling with relative ease and speed. Enhancements such as fact boxes and simple graphics can help an online reader grasp essential details. Bulleted text or Q&A formats offer alternatives to straight copy. Pulling out and highlighting a profound quote or adding links to background stories can improve online storytelling. Even newsrooms with minimal online staffing and technology can do more than push through copy. In those where new technology isn't readily embraced, innovative digital journalists have learned technology such as Flash on their own, through computer and textbook tutorials. Armed with new skills, they've convinced management to make small investments in the software and hardware needed to produce multimedia reports. And as we see a commitment to multimedia, interactive storytelling grow, the digital journalist who knows how to make the most of these tools will best serve the online news consumer.

Activities for Further Learning

1. Consider an issue of local importance (community or campus). Create a storyboard for its online coverage, including the appropriate storytelling tools introduced in this chapter. Explain why you chose each tool.

References

Artwick, C. G. 1996. "Blood, body bags, and tears: Remembering visual images from local television crime news." *Visual Communication Quarterly.* Spring, p. 14-18.

Best Practices for Digital Media. 1998. American Society of Magazine Editors. http://asme.magazine.org/guidelines/new_media.html

Chicago Tribune Online Edition. 2003. United takes flight with the rise of commercial aviation. http://www.chicagotribune.com/news/specials/united/one/chi-030613graphic,1,3034446.photogallery?coll=chi-unitednav-misc

Dube, J. 2003. Online storytelling forms. http://www.cyberjournalist.net/storyforms.htm

Evans, H. 1978. *Pictures on a Page.* Belmont, California: Wadsworth Publishing Company.

Finberg, H. I. and M.L. Stone. 2002. Digital Journalism Credibility Study. http://www.journalists.org/Programs/credibility_study.pdf

Fuller, J. 1996. *News Values: Ideas for an Information Age.* Chicago: The University of Chicago Press.

houstonchronicle.com. July 14, 2003. http://www.chron.com/

khou.com. July 15, 2003. http://www.khou.com

ktrk.com. July 15, 2003. http://www.ktrk.com

Lee, C. 2003. Beautiful lives. http://www.nytimes.com

msnbc.com. July 14, 2003. http://msnbc.com/

mysanantonio.com. July 14, 2003. http://www.mysanantonio.com

Sacramento Business Journal. April 22, 2003. Broadband use increases, but
    speeds vary. http://www.bizjournals.com/sanantonio/

tbo.com. July 17, 2003. http://tbo.com/

The New York Times on the Web. 2003. http://nytimes.com/

CHAPTER 8

The Reporting Process— New Considerations

Chapter Objectives

Ask the top reporters in the business what it takes to excel at their craft, and most will tell you they live by the principles of fairness, truth, and accuracy. Many will add that personal characteristics, such as integrity, curiosity, and persistence, play a big role. A combination of these qualities builds the foundation for good journalism, which is apparent in the best news reporting in print, broadcast, and online. The principles don't waver across media. What does change is the approach to storytelling, and that approach begins during the reporting process. In a multimedia, interactive environment, reporters and producers start thinking about telling the story as soon as they've determined its focus. That requires considering the elements that will best convey the issue or event to the online user and determining how to gather information needed in its appropriate forms.

This chapter will address these considerations, guiding journalists through the reporting process for the digital environment.

Backpack Journalist or Print/ Broadcast/Web Hybrid?

When Jane Stevens (2003) heads out on assignment she packs a digital camera, microphone, tripod, and laptop computer. And with the help of a phone line or satellite phone, she can send stories from anywhere in the world. Her pieces may include any combination of video and audio clips, text, still photos, and graphics information. She's a multimedia backpack journalist—has been ever since she traveled to the Antarctic sea-ice ecosystem where she discovered that "multimedia reporting would be about the closest you could come to being there and exploring the place yourself." (Stevens Bio 2002) While reporters such as Stevens are still somewhat of a rarity, she predicts that in a few years they will be the rule—and that they'll rule (Stevens, Backpack journalism is here to stay 2002). In the meantime, many journalists are making the transition from straight print or broadcast to a hybrid that includes the Web. Others are working in teams and must be conversant in digital storytelling methods. At the heart of this breed of journalism is the multimedia, interactive mindset.

Multimedia, Interactive Mindset

A Disneyland roller coaster derails and news crews quickly take to the air and the theme park to follow the story. The journalists have a common mission—to find out what happened and report the story. But, differences in their reporting mindsets will have an impact on the way they gather information and present it. The newspaper reporter relies on a verbal mindset, using the written word to craft a story the audience will consume through the eye. He must fill his notebook with details from the scene to paint a word picture for the reader. He'll choose quotes to move the story forward, add texture, and convey emotion. The television reporter's audiovisual mindset integrates sound, pictures, and text to produce a story to be consumed through the eye and ear. In the field she must gather sounds, pictures, and notes to weave together as a "package" for the viewer. Her decisions involve what to show, what to say, and what to let others say. The Web reporter engages a multimedia, interactive mindset, seeking combinations of words, sounds, and pictures to craft a story for the Web user to interact with. In the field, she may use a digital video camera, or may prefer a still camera and mini-disc audio recorder. She'll need to think about which parts of the story can best be told through which media, all the while considering how the audience might interact with the information. The process is more complex than print or broadcast, because instead of using words to tell a verbal story, or words, pictures and sound to tell a packaged audiovisual story, the Web journalist uses words, pictures and sounds to tell a multimedia, interactive story.

Table 8.1. Verbal, Audiovisual, and Multimedia/Interactive Mindsets

Big Thunder Mountain Railroad Story

Medium:	Newspaper	TV	Web
Mindset:	Verbal	Audiovisual	Multimedia/ Interactive
Consumed through:	Eye exclusively	Eye/ear simultaneously	Eye/ear simultaneously/ separately
Story gathering:	Notes	Notes Videotape	Notes Videotape
End product:	1,200-word story	2.5-minute print broadcast package	300-word print story Video stream of press conference Slide show from scene Interactive timeline of Disneyland injuries

To do so effectively, the digital journalist must think multimedia and interactive from the outset of the reporting process. It begins with the story focus.

Determining the Story Focus

Reporters who are new to the profession sometimes have a tough time communicating with their editors or producers about their stories. Their descriptions are either too vague or too busy to convey much of anything. Saying that your story is about logging is much too broad. One wonders if you mean legal or illegal logging, logging in the Amazon rain forest or on private U.S. land, logging techniques or job cuts in the industry. Just what *is* the story? On the other hand, detail that's scattered isn't helpful either: Sawmills need timber from national parks to support their business, helicopter logging is becoming more prevalent on steep slopes, and old logging roads provide off-road vehicle riders trails they've been fighting for. Neither the broad, nor the detailed, scattered approach says much of anything. A good story focus must be able to convey in a sentence or two the essence of the story. This not only helps people in the newsroom understand your story, but it can help you write it better.

Frederick Shook (1994, p. 134) says the focus expresses "the heart, the soul, of the story." Michael Roberts, training editor at *The Cincinnati Inquirer*, calls this the "point" of the story, as distinct from what it's "about." (notrain-nogain.org, undated) The point summarizes the main theme or issue in relation to the audience. Roberts calls it the spine or thread that runs through the entire story. "About" shares relevant facts and puts them into context, but doesn't focus the point of the story vis-à-vis the audience.

What's the "point" of the story about logging? Let's say you've pored over documents detailing a plan for the Jefferson National Forest and talked to rangers and a Sierra Club activist. You can now define the point, or story focus, as: *Foresters, the logging industry, and environmentalists are working together to find a suitable plan for logging in the Jefferson National Forest.*

Thinking multimedia and interactive now, at the story focus stage, will help assure you have the proper tools when you go out to the field to report. You think you might like to include a short piece of streaming video showing a logging area, or, perhaps, the process at a sawmill. The digital video camera would be a must for visits to these locations. You would also use it to videotape interviews with key players at these locations. Perhaps you're considering an interactive map with current and proposed logging areas in relation to hiking trails, camping, and fishing sites. Still photographs might suffice for this task. You're also considering a Flash presentation that highlights the many uses of the forest. Still photos with audio might be best for this. However, videotape gives you the option of using sound only, moving pictures, sound and pictures, or making still images from the video. You can also transcribe the interviews for use in text pieces. But in some cases the video camera can get in the way of the story, making people behave differently. Or, they may refuse to go on camera. So, the still camera with audio option may be preferable in these cases. Lighting issues, time to set up the camera, changing the battery, and having a piece of equipment between the subject and reporter can be been minimized by using a mini-disc audio recorder and still camera.

Types of Stories and the Multimedia/ Interactive Mindset

Spot news, scheduled event, or enterprise piece? The type of story may have an impact on your approach to newsgathering.

Spot news

In many television newsrooms, assignment editors hand reporters their stories, and off they go, to a house fire or boating mishap, to cover events as they unfold.

Breaking news may begin and end with just one story, or it may demand continuing coverage. It can also evolve into a larger, issue-based story. When a reporter sets out to cover a spot news event, the story focus doesn't yet exist. The reporting takes place in the field, and in these early stages it would be premature to make final decisions about the online story. If a television station is the "legacy medium" of your journalistic endeavors, then no doubt about it, you must shoot videotape, because you're expected to report for TV. But, what if you're reporting for a newspaper and Web site? Will digital still images captured from the video be acceptable for print? You could bring both cameras and shoot digital still images for the newspaper. Or, settle for the still camera and make a slide show for the Web. If you're going out alone, your mobility may be the determining factor in your choice of gear. Time of day and safety issues also play into your decision. A mini disc recorder and still camera would be less obtrusive and attention-getting than a video recorder. But juggling two pieces of gear might be more difficult. Perhaps the best practice would involve bringing along all the gear you think you might need; the video and still cameras, and the mini disc. Assess the situation when you arrive on the scene, and then choose the gear you'll use.

Planned events

News conferences, speeches, meetings, and even court proceedings fall into this category. Again, if reporting for television and Web, the video camera is a must. But, for the print/Web reporter, still camera and mini disc will likely suffice. For example, consider a story in Lexington, Kentucky, the city with the highest adult smoking rate in the nation. For a year, its Urban County Council has been debating banning smoking in public buildings. The issue is again on the meeting agenda, with a vote expected. You're armed with background information from previous stories, your audio recorder and a still camera. You've captured your quotes on disc and snapped a few photos of the council in action. You've also got a close-up of a man in a haze of smoke. In this case, the gear suited the story. As another example, let's say tennis great Serena Williams faces your city mayor in a friendly game after dedicating a new urban tennis center. Yes, this is a scheduled event, but one that your Web audience would like to see in action. And because still sports photography requires a high level of expertise, it's probably not the best choice unless that's your specialization. The video camera could provide a full-court view for a select point with great action. Choose video for this one and you'll deliver what your audience wants.

Enterprise/issue stories

These stories will likely demand your full arsenal of multimedia gear. And, because you can begin shaping your story focus before going out into the field, you'll have a better opportunity to plan than with breaking news. With these stories you can often involve the audience, and should keep this in mind as you are reporting. Some of the other tools to integrate into these projects include databases and even mapping programs.

Reporting Through the Senses

When would you rely on your nose to report a story? NBC reporter Bob Dotson smelled the heavy scent of pine while on his way to cover a flood. He took a mental note of the sensory experience and when it came time to write the story, drew from that olfactory impression. He wrote that you could smell the flood before you could see it (1999). When a scent strikes you while newsgathering—don't ignore it, focus on it.

Opening ourselves up through the senses can help us tell stories rich in texture. In addition to painting sensory pictures through words, we've got digital cameras and audio recorders to report sight and sound. Learning the basics of these tools will get you started in multimedia storytelling.

Audio recording

Many print reporters already record audio for quote checking and note-taking. But a tiny microcassette recorder placed on a table to help us back up our quotes won't provide the sound quality needed in digital storytelling. Unless it's placed an inch or two from the subject's mouth, a recorder's built-in microphone just won't do. Instead, use an external microphone for the best quality sound. If you're in a one-on-one situation where the interviewee isn't moving around a great deal, choose the lavaliere microphone (Figure 8.1). Attach it to the lapel or shirt collar on the side closest to you (she'll be looking at you during the interview, and with that placement will be talking into the microphone instead of away from it).

Figure 8.1 A lavaliere or lapel microphone works well in a studio or controlled recording environment. Conceal the wire by having the subject run it under her jacket or shirt.

When the person whose voice you want to record is apt to move away quickly, or is surrounded by reporters, a microphone mounted on the camera or held by the reporter would be preferable. Shotgun microphones are ideal for situations in which the reporter can't get close enough to the subject (more than 2 feet away). These are highly directional, meaning they pick up sound directly in their path, and are pointed, like a shotgun, right at their subjects. Many news organizations use this type of microphone for dynamic situations in the field (Figure 8.2).

Another option is the hand-held mike, the rugged workhorse we've all seen television reporters use when they report live from the scene. They also use this mike for interviews, moving it between themselves and their subjects, to ask questions and record responses. Most often, this is a more omnidirectional microphone that picks up sound from its sides and back as well as the front. It works best when placed within six inches to a foot of the subject's mouth (Figure 8.3). You may be tempted to let your subject hold the microphone herself, but don't do it! First, you give away control of the interview when you give away the microphone. Second, people

Figure 8.2 A shotgun microphone is highly directional and can record from a distance.

Figure 8.3 The hand-held microphone is the workhorse of broadcast news. Reporters use them for stand-ups and interviews.

unfamiliar with mike handling will inevitably jiggle the cord, creating crackling sounds throughout the recording. Or, if they gesticulate when they speak, the microphone moves with their hands, again, creating noise and moving the microphone closer to and farther away from the mouth, possibly spoiling the recording. So, hold onto that mike!

There are several other possible threats to your sound quality. Lavaliere and regular hand-held mikes are most likely omni-directional—meaning they pick up sound from every direction. So, if there's a window air conditioner in the room where you're interviewing, its droning may drown out the interviewee's voice. If people are talking in the background, the mike will pick up their chatter. The same goes for music.

Wind can destroy an outdoor interview. A foam cover for the microphone head, called a wind screen, can help. Also watch out for the occasional radio signal. Until recently, our campus radio station transmitter sat atop the journalism building. When standing in certain spots nearby, students would pick up Metallica or Mariah Carey while recording their interviews or stand-ups.

Your best insurance for high-quality recording is using headphones to listen to the audio before, during, and after the recording. Unfortunately, most of us learn this lesson the hard way, when we come back to the newsroom with an unusable audio track.

And poor audio recording technique can spoil the visual content of an interview. A black wire dangling on a person's white shirt looks tacky. Conceal the wire if at all possible by asking the subject to move it behind his suit coat. Or, ask the person to turn around and snake the wire up under his shirt, pulling the lavaliere microphone out at the collar. Another common error is the phantom hand. It's the reporter's hand holding the microphone prominently in the foreground of a shot. This appears in shots that are framed a bit too wide. A more closely framed shot will eliminate the microphone, and the hand. See the phantom hand in Figure 8.4, and how to correct the problem.

Natural sound. While voice recordings serve as the basis for most news audio, natural sound, better known in the business as nat sound, provides texture and even punctuation to multimedia reports. When Tiger Woods swings his driver and connects with the ball, the sound it makes is unmistakable. A story about his career would be incomplete without it. Ice cubes clinking their way into a tall glass followed by a glug-glug bring to life a story about iced tea. Rain on a tin roof, church bells, "come and get it," convey mood and push memory buttons to connect with the audience.

Figure 8.4 The shot in the first frame reveals the reporter's hand, which can distract the viewer. Correct this problem by zooming in slightly.

Reporting the story with your senses will alert you to the sounds you must record. Their effect depends on how they're recorded. Hold your microphone close to a wooden floor and have a friend wearing hard-soled shoes walk toward you from a distance of 10 feet, continue walking past you, and then away and out of the room. Now, stand up and repeat the sequence. Finally, stand outside the room and repeat the sequence once again. When you play back the recordings you'll notice distinct effects in each of the takes. The picture the sound creates in the listener's head will depend on how you recorded it. For example, the bells on the door of a Chinese restaurant jingle as a reporter opens it and enters. His recorder picks up the bells at close range. If he had recorded the jingling bell while seated at his table, the presence would be much weaker, and would serve more as background noise rather than a prominent establishing feature of the story.

You can blend into public areas and record without drawing attention to yourself. While traveling in Brazil and Peru I recorded the sounds of the open-air marketplace by packing my tape recorder into a large canvas bag which I slung over my shoulder. Instead of zipping up the bag all the way, I left a small opening in which I was able to lodge the tip of my small shotgun microphone. I then wandered the market and positioned my body so the microphone faced the action I wanted to record. Let me stress that I would only use this technique to record the generic sounds of the market, and not to covertly record conversations. For interviews, the recorder should be in full view of the interviewee, with the understanding that his/her words are being recorded for use in a news story.

Thinking Visually

Some of us just don't, as general practice, focus on the visual elements of our surroundings or the people in them. Do you remember what your journalism professor wore in class today? What color are the walls in your favorite restaurant? Is the floor in the university library entryway marble or hardwood, tiled or carpeted? For a text-based story, your reporter's notes will include details to paint pictures in your reader's minds. In a visual medium, you must pay attention to and shoot the details that will help tell your story. Chapter 9 offers specifics on shooting visuals, so I won't elaborate here. But I would like to walk you through an example to introduce the concept of thinking visually. You arrive at the scene of a house fire and train the video camera on the flames and the firefighters, as you should. While shooting, you notice a group of people standing on the front lawn holding hands, heads bowed, praying. You turn your attention toward them while continuing to monitor the flames. To respect their privacy, you move back, and shoot wide, with the house in the background. Soon a firefighter joins the group and you continue rolling. You think to yourself that this is unusual, and plan to find out more about the firefighter and why he left his job putting out the fire to join the family in prayer. Later, you approach him and learn that he grew up in the house that the fire gutted. The fire chief insisted they had the fire under control, and told the young man to comfort his parents and younger siblings. Because you opened your visual sense to the entire scene, not just the most sensational flames, you were able to enhance the story by including the human element.

Keep in mind the visuals you may need for certain graphic presentations. A text story for the Web or Flash presentation may require a quick photo of the key people interviewed. Judith Siviglia at newsobserver.com (2002) in Raleigh, North Carolina, asks her photographers to get head shots (a head-and-shoulder close-up) of interview subjects in case they're needed.

Audio for visual stories

In an audiovisual medium, the sounds mustn't be forgotten. When I walked out to my car this morning, I heard something near the rooftops across the street. It sounded like Darth Vader breathing from above. I immediately looked up to spy a hot air balloon. Every Fourth of July a balloon rally in Lexington, Virginia, draws at least a dozen hot air balloons to our fine city. If I had been shooting digital video, I would have kept quiet while rolling, and pointed the shotgun in the direction of that sound, before I even saw the balloon. The sound adds presence and texture, and shouldn't be ignored.

Reporting Using the Internet

What's neuroblastoma? What type of plane is a Jetstream 31? The answers are just a few keystrokes away, and journalists' stories can be much richer using the Internet. When a student reporter covered a fundraising run for neuroblastoma research, she needed information about the disease. A Google search produced more than 100,000 entries, with cancer.gov near the top of the results. In two mouse clicks she learned that neuroblastoma is a disease of early childhood; a solid, cancerous tumor in the nerve tissue of the abdomen and other areas between the neck and pelvis (cancer.gov 2002). In the past, a student reporter might have just named the disease without explaining it, if she didn't get a call back before deadline from a source who could provide the information.

Al Thompkins (2000) of the Poynter Institute used the Internet to help WNEP-TV in Scranton, Pennsylvania, track down information for a story on a plane crash. Using a database on the aviation site landings.com, Thompkins discovered that the plane was a Jetstream 31. He then turned to Google to learn more about the plane. The search led Thompkins to several useful sites, with photos and descriptions of the plane. "We had the first real understanding of the size and vital statistics of the aircraft," said Thompkins. "We learned from that site and a couple of others that the Jetstream had a capacity of 19 people, the same number reported to be onboard the aircraft that called in with engine trouble."

Four out of five U.S. journalists use the Internet to help them do their jobs on a weekly basis (Ten years later: Journalists are older, better educated, better paid, more professional 2003). From e-mail to Google searches, journalists go online to search for story ideas, gather background information, communicate with sources, and more.

Internet Veracity

The ability to judge the credibility of the information we find online is essential to upholding journalistic standards. Information scientists and librarians offer some of the best criteria for evaluating Web sites. Alexander and Tate's *Evaluating Web Resources* (1999) is cited widely, and offers a handy checklist, which I adapt below. My version is called, "Avoid getting duped on the Web." It also includes some advice from Jonathan Dube's "Internet IQ Checklist for Journalists" (2002):

Avoid getting duped on the Web

Who are you? Alexander and Tate, as well as Dube, call this criterion "Authority." Who created the content? Who runs the Web site? Can you contact the author or organization? Is an address and phone number listed? (E-mail may not be enough.) Can you identify qualifications or credentials?

Why are you publishing this on the Web? Is the content unrelated to a product or service? Is the content free from a sponsor's influence? Is it free from bias? The above authors call this category "Objectivity."

Where's the date? When was the information written, published on the Web, updated?

Is it true, correct? Typographical and grammatical errors should raise suspicion. Are facts cited by source, and can sources be verified elsewhere?

The more questions you can answer, the more likely the information quality is high. When in doubt, don't use the information, or find another Web site and repeat the process.

E-Mail Issues

Not long ago, a friend sent me an e-mail in a slightly panicked tone that warned of a Web site that allows users to access driver's license data for free. She had gotten the e-mail from someone who urged her to pass it on to others. It gave no URL, but mentioned something about the state department of motor vehicles. Considering privacy issues, this seemed fishy. Why would the state post this personal information online? Well, it didn't. With a quick visit to the state DMV site, it was easy to confirm that driver's license data were not online. That e-mail was similar to another hoax about (the fictitious) National Driver's License Records Bureau. With that one, the e-mail recipient clicks on a URL and enters a name and related information. Up pops a picture of a laughing chimpanzee with the message, "You didn't really think you could get someone's driver's license over the Internet, did you?" (What you need to know about, 2003) Hoaxes like this that are e-mailed to us can play on our fears and attack our vulnerabilities. In this case, just visiting the site revealed its nature. But others are trickier and can sometimes fool journalists. Check out suspected hoaxes at urbanlegends.about.com, which devotes a large portion of its site to Internet myths and hoaxes.

E-Mail Interviews and Other Technological Issues

Many reporters interview sources via e-mail, touting it as convenient and reliable. No need to get past the secretary who screens calls, no leaving voice mail messages and waiting for call-backs, and no note-taking. You can even cut and paste quotes from e-mail interviews into your story. What's not to like? Well, when technology enters an interview, it can alter communication. Just chatting with a source can be comfortable and informative. It's a good conversation, with real listening and follow-up. The reporter can observe body language, look the subject in the eye, and respond with empathy. But all that can change when the notebook or minicassette tape recorder comes out. The subject may speak more cautiously, or become affected because of the focus on his words. The camera can have an even greater impact due to self-consciousness and the obtrusiveness of the gear. But the face-to-face interaction is still strong and often overrides the technological intrusion.

The convenience of the telephone interview often dictates its use in today's newsrooms. The journalist doesn't have to leave her desk. She can take notes directly on the computer during the conversation. She can still interact, still hear vocal nuances. And she can include sources that are twenty or 2,000 miles away. But the visual element isn't there. Facial expressions can speak volumes, but they can't be seen over the phone. Nor can other body language that can be telling. And the interview subject may be an impersonator. Using telephone sources may miss those with unlisted numbers and, albeit few, those who don't have phones.

Finally, we have e-mail. It can get us directly to our sources and they can respond when convenient. But, again, while providing convenience, the technology creates concerns. E-mail reduces the pool of sources to those who have accounts. If the e-mail is sent to us first, we have to be wary of its authenticity. An imposter may be using the source's e-mail account. The live, interactive flavor of a conversation is lost. And there are no verbal or visual cues. So, digital journalists must assess the pros and cons of e-mail and other technologies to decide which is best in which cases. If you do choose to interview via e-mail, some tips to follow (adapted from Junnarkar 2003).

- Introduce yourself and your story. Link to clips if possible to establish your credibility.
- Offer to conduct the interview via telephone.
- Use proper spelling, grammar, and style (upper and lower case, please).
- Avoid attachments because many of us are suspicious they might contain a virus.
- Note that you're on deadline.
- After receiving a response, follow up for clarification if necessary. Then, thank the source.

Documents, Databases, and Links

Digging through documents can lead to the most remarkable stories, as can examining databases. Many government agencies and other organizations now post these resources on the Internet, making it possible for journalists to report online. Need to find the status of a bill in Congress? The Library of Congress' Web site Thomas (as in Jefferson) lets you search by bill number or word/phrase. Research fatal accidents in your community on the Fatality Analysis Reporting System. Or find quick profiles of major businesses on hoovers.com.

Online data can be linked to directly within our stories, which is a quick and easy way to direct the public to the information. Or, newsroom staff with the expertise can cull the information and create databases to both enrich reporting and to post online. A team at *The Atlanta Journal-Constitution* spent a year researching and developing a searchable database on nursing homes in Georgia. "Editors had the Web in mind from day one," explained database designer, Adrian Holovaty (2003). The process started with special projects reporter Carrie Teegardin, who found some of the information quite readily online at medicare.gov. But she also spent months examining paper documents and entering the data into her own database. Toward the end of the data collection, Holovaty came in to build the online resource. He met with Teegardin to see what she had been doing, and to learn what she and her editor wanted to display on each nursing home's information page. Holovaty ended up creating 3,200 files to accommodate all the possible search patterns. But for the user, the ajc.com Nursing Home Guide is clear and easy to use. The enthusiastic response to this tool confirmed its need and the investment in its creation.

Not every data-rich story requires a year-long investment and programming expertise. For example, student reporters investigating the efficiency of their local fire department learned that response times had soared in just one year. They decided to use Global Positioning System (GPS) to plot fire locations on an area map and relate them to response times. Elizabeth Nelson (2003), who now reports for *The Daily Progress* in Charlottesville, Virginia, says, "The GPS was surprisingly easy to use. It took minutes to learn how to collect the data, and it helped us understand what we were writing so we could better explain it to others." They imported their map into a PowerPoint file, which they then inserted into their Web site (Figure 8.5). The students enhanced their story by considering from the beginning of the project how they might present their data on the Web. You can make your stories richer and more Web-appropriate by approaching the task from the outset with a multimedia/interactive mindset.

The Digital Asset Management System

Managing digital information has been one of the biggest challenges to news organizations in recent years. Some systems serve a legacy medium

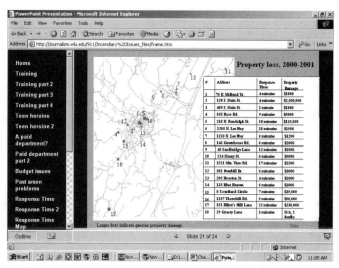

Figure 8.5 Maps can help journalists present data clearly and to see patterns. Student reporters plotted fire locations using GPS technology, and created this map showing location, response time, and damage.

and its Web counterpart, such as a television station and its Web site or a newspaper and its online version. Others, such as Belo Interactive, or Tribune Interactive, serve numerous stations, newspapers, and Web sites nationwide, with the same ownership. Their operations differ widely. This carries over to the way they integrate systems so they will "talk" to one another, store large data files, archive and search digital information, and simply make material accessible to the people who need to use it. While each system is distinct, a familiarity with the overarching similarities and a look at some specifics will prepare you to enter the digital newsroom.

Although digital assets are, essentially, just zeros and ones, they encompass complex media products ranging from text to 360-degree images. But before they reach the point of being a computer-based entity, they make take other forms. For example, Robert E. Lee's letter to Ulysses S. Grant, handwritten on February 18, 1865, is now a digital asset. Using computer hardware and software, archivists scanned the original letter, saved it as a JPEG image, stored it on a server, and made it available on the Internet (Figure 8.6). Fast-forward about 100 years to the movie Mary Poppins. Although it was shot on film in the early 1960s, we can now find digital movie clips from the film on the Web. Again, a combination of hardware and software facilitated the transfer process from an analog to a digital medium.

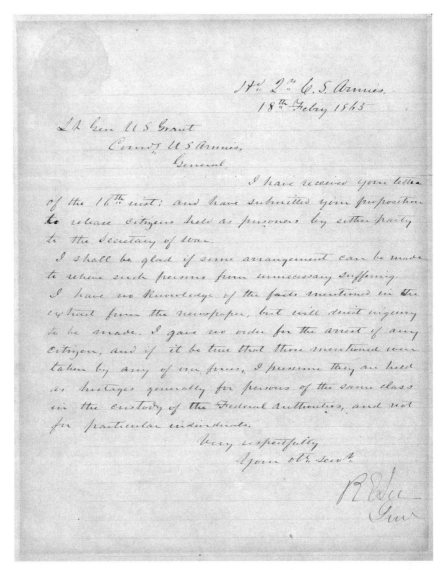

Figure 8.6 This letter written by Robert E. Lee to Ulysses S. Grant in 1865 is now available in cyberspace through digital technology. Courtesy of Lee Papers, Special Collections, Leyburn Library, Washington and Lee University.

Much of today's digital hardware records binary data onto a recording medium, such as tape. Those data are then ingested into a computer system for editing, playback, and storage. With digital videotape, the transfer process is real time, meaning it would take 10 minutes to ingest 10 minutes of recorded video into the system. Some of the newest camcorders record directly onto mini DVD, which can speed the process. But, expect to export the video rather than dragging it from the DVD onto the computer. A Hitachi DVDCAM exports at about one second per one minute of video (Lang 2003).

In any case, the raw material a digital journalist gathers must be ingested into the computer system for editing and production. Once it's ingested, it can be used exclusively by one person or made available to many simultaneously. Let's say President George W. Bush spoke at your university, and a student camera person videotaped the event and reaction to the speech. Your campus radio station wants to run the entire 20 minutes on its 6 p.m. public affairs program, while that evening's television news producer and the Web producer want to use different segments of the speech in their media. The student newspaper reporter has a paper copy of the speech, so doesn't need the recording, but wants to quote some of the reactions. And the reporter who shot the videotape will also use the content in a television news package. With a fully integrated digital asset management and production system, such as DaletPlus, those five people can work with the same material simultaneously to produce content for their respective media. With a stand-alone video editing system, such as AvidXpress DV, the raw material would also be ingested, and a final product for each medium could be created, but only one person at a time could use the system. So, one of the major benefits of the integrated system is the easy and shared access to content. Another is the search capabilities.

Digital journalists can quickly find background information for their stories by searching the asset management system. Text can be opened, printed, and copied into new files. In many cases, the search also produces audio and video related to the key words. If the story is timely, or expected to be needed, that material will likely be available to work with immediately. But, because multimedia files can consume large amounts of space, they are sometimes stored outside the system on DVD. If that is the case, you will need to re-ingest the material to work with it.

The Digital Rundown

Not long ago, only the television producer and technical crew needed access to the rundown—the plan for the television news program, which lists all elements of the newscast and essential related information in order of

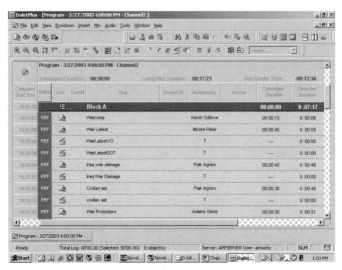

Figure 8.7 In today's fully-integrated digital newsroom, producers create their television news shows in the rundown, including text, graphics, and video. It organizes all the materials for on-air playback.

presentation. Today, television writers and reporters must work within the rundown, and in the converged newsroom, even print journalists must be able to do so. Figure 8.7 presents a typical digital rundown.

In fully automated newsrooms, journalists embed their edited digital video into the rundown for direct on-air play. This obviates the need for stacks of tapes, streamlining the producing and directing process.

Desktop Video Viewing and Editing

Another advantage of the digital asset system is desktop video editing. When videographers return from the field they ingest their sounds and images into the computer system, making them available simultaneously to many users. Let's say this unedited material includes a 20-minute news conference with your city's police chief on a missing student, shots of the park where she was jogging when she disappeared, and an interview with her roommate. A Web writer can listen to the news conference and select quotations for his story while a television reporter edits portions of the news conference into her package. At the same time, the Web producer can create a still photo of the park from the video. Journalists don't change the original video, but instead, copy and transform it into another format (such as

JPEG for a photo), or reference it by section into something called an edit decision list (EDL). That EDL is essentially a computer-driven blueprint for the finished story, a document that tells the computer what images and sounds to put in what order, and how long each should run. Specific details on the technical aspects of desktop editing go beyond the focus of this textbook, but some conceptual editing issues are discussed in Chapter 9.

Integrating the Old and the New

Digital journalists don't always work exclusively with digital media, but must often convert analog to digital. Analog technology basically replicates a signal onto a recording medium, while a digital recording makes a sample of the signal and converts it to ones and zeros. Analog media can also be converted to digital. For example, we can shoot with a film camera and then scan the prints into the computer, or record onto an audio cassette and digitize the sound for computer editing. While the most technologically advanced newsrooms have moved to all-digital operations, many still use some combination of analog and digital. Some major market television Web producers and editors must wait until after their news broadcasts to use video images online. That's because they record the program off air and then ingest it into the computer for digital editing and Web streaming. Using this approach almost guarantees shovelware from the air to the Web. Provided management doesn't proscribe posting stories on the Web before they air, savvy Web producers can pursue the video when it comes in from the field on breaking stories. That way, they can use a sound bite or a visual image along with their text story to serve the public. Audiotapes and photographs can enhance the digital story, and should not be eschewed because they're not digital. A relatively inexpensive audio editing program and scanner can make the transition possible.

Activities for Further Learning

1. Write a story focus for an issue you would like to cover.
2. Gather natural sound for a story on your campus student center or other place students gather. Keep in mind the effects of close-range versus distant recording techniques.
3. Go to your university library and use your senses to report on the building and what takes place there.

4. Use the "Avoid getting duped on the Web" guidelines in this chapter to assess the veracity of the Web site at http://www.mcwhortle.com (Dube 2002).

References

Alexander, J. and M.A. Tate. 1999. Evaluating Web resources. http://www2.widener.edu/Wolfgram-Memorial-Library/webevaluation/webeval.htm

cancer.gov. 2002. Neuroblastoma home page. http://cancer.gov/cancerinfo/types/neuroblastoma

Dotson, B. 1999. Presentation to RTNDA annual convention.

Dube, J. May 31, 2002. Internet IQ checklist for journalists. *Poynteronline*. http://poynter.org/column.asp?id=32&aid=3086

Holovaty, A. 2003. Behind the scenes: The making of ajc.com's nursing home guide. *CyberJournalist.net* Web site. http://www.cyberjournalist.net/features/behindthescenes/ajcnursinghomeguide.htm

Junnarkar, S. Oct. 16, 2003. Step-by-step e-mail interviewing tips. *Poynteronline*. http://www.poynter.org/content/content_view.asp?id=50462

Lang, P. October 2003. Test bench: Hitachi DZ-MV380A DVDCAM RAMcorder reviewed. *Videomaker*, pp. 28-31.

Nelson, E. Aug. 4, 2003. E-mail correspondence.

Roberts, M. Undated. *No Train, No Gain* Web site. http://www.notrain-nogain.org/train/exer/edit/focus.asp

Shook, F. 1994. *Television Newswriting: Captivating an audience.* New York: London.

Siviglia, J. Aug. 26, 2002. Personal interview.

Stevens, J. April 12, 2002. Backpack journalism is here to stay. *Online Journalism Review.* http://www.ojr.org/ojr/workplace/1017771575.php

Stevens, J. April 2002. Bio. http://www.ojr.org/ojr/workplace/1017771575.php

Stevens, J. Sept. 10, 2003. E-mail correspondence.

Ten years later: Journalists are older, better educated, better paid, more professional April 10, 2003. http://www.knightfdn.org

Thompkins, A. May 26, 2000. Get online and get information fast. *Poynteronline*. http://poynter.org/content/content_view.asp?id=4436

What You Need to Know About. 2003. Can people look up my driver's license on the Internet? http://urbanlegends.about.com/library/bldriverslicense.htm

CHAPTER 9

Working with Images

Chapter Objectives

"Does your Web site look as good as your newscast?" This question ran as part of a full-page ad for ready-made Internet content in a recent broadcast industry publication. On first read, the query may seem superficial or irrelevant to good journalism. But, the visual components of any medium consumed through the eye play a key role in user attention and processing. They also convey a site's image as professional or amateurish. But why should reporters and producers concern themselves with visual appeal? Isn't that the job of graphic designers or the art department?

While digital journalists rarely design and program their organizations' Web sites, they do make daily decisions about when and how to incorporate visual elements into their stories. Those choices can affect storytelling and audience interpretation of online news. In some cases, a photograph will draw attention to a story; in others, it will drive readers away. A piece of streaming video may enhance people's understanding of an issue, or may simply frustrate them. How can we make the right choices?

This chapter offers a working knowledge of the nuts and bolts of digital imagery and introduces the research behind the practice to better equip multimedia reporters and producers to make informed decisions when using images in their Internet stories.

Research in Visual Communication

Let's begin by examining the "why" to become familiar with a number of key findings in visual communication research, and save the "how to" for the second half of the chapter. A few studies pertain specifically to imagery on the Internet, but because this line of inquiry is still nascent, much of what you will read here involves print or broadcast media placed into context vis-à-vis the Internet. The evidence from this research should help provide a foundation for decision making when working with visuals on the Web.

Visuals and Attention

Capturing audience attention and keeping it has been a concern of mass media industries since their inception. Conventions guiding newspaper and magazine picture editors and page designers dictate that they use photographs and graphic images to secure reader attention and direct it to news copy. But is the same practice effective on the Web? Investigators have been using physiological measurement tools to determine what commands user attention on the Web. Indiana University's Annie Lang and her colleagues attached sensors to experimental subjects to measure their heart rates in response to information presented via computer, and to learn how people pay attention to and learn from that information (Lang, Borse, Wise, and David 2002). They found that Web users' heart rates decelerated briefly after being exposed to animated banner ads and warnings. A slower-beating heart indicates "orienting" to the stimuli, which is basically the "what is it" response (Lynn 1966). Plain and boxed text did not decrease heart rates, nor did non-animated banner ads. These findings suggest that viewers are reacting to moving images. What they can't tell us is whether what follows the orienting response is positive or negative. Your heart may slow as an animated butterfly wafts across your screen, but are you annoyed or mesmerized by it? Using an animation in conjunction with an online news story must be well motivated, and not simply a gimmick. For example, MSNBC.com effectively uses a small moving hand to guide users to click on a "play" button to begin a multimedia report. If the user orients to this tool, the next logical step is clicking on it to interact with the site.

Another study, conducted by researchers at Stanford University and The Poynter Institute (2000), employed eye-tracking technology to document exactly where readers look when browsing Internet Web sites. Although industry conventions predicted online readers would be drawn to pictures before text, the study found the opposite. But the research methods have come under scrutiny, questioning the validity of the findings. The main concern—a small number of research participants who may not be representative of Internet users.

In their first round, the researchers examined eleven subjects inter-acting with sites containing text and graphics. Four of the online readers went to graphics first, and seven went to text. Even after a second round of analysis examined sixty-seven subjects, graphic designer Alan Jacob-son (2000) found the participants to be a "narrowly focused group," drawn from "the limited universe of 'frequent Internet news readers' rather than the Internet-using public at large." (Poynter posted this crit-icism on its own Web site.) Jacobson also questioned the content of the pages, arguing that certain photographs might garner attention, whereas others would not. Researchers did not control the pages participants read, but instead examined subjects as they interacted with sites of their own choosing. As Jacobson suggests, further research is in order, with a more representative sample of Internet users and "pages designed to de-light the eye in addition to informing the mind." He wagers "dollars to donuts" that using this methodology, the online reader's eyes will track to images first.

What are we to make of this controversy? Those of us who find our-selves in digital newsrooms may encounter managers who embrace text over graphics because that's how they've interpreted the Stanford-Poynter findings. But the research was not intended to be predictive. As its inves-tigators point out, it is "a beginning reality check of the ways regular on-line users view news within and across various sites." (Stanford-Poynter 2000) The eyetrack research is just a start, and should be used as such, opening the doors to further research that continues to examine online user behavior and the effects of online news.

Visuals and Memory

After grabbing online readers' attention, what happens next? Do they remember the photos they see on those sites? Will adding a photograph to a Web story make the prose more memorable to the reader? While schol-ars are just beginning to search for answers to these questions, early re-search on visuals and memory, which began more than a century ago, indicate that memory for visuals is stronger than memory for words. At that time, Kirkpatrick's (1894) research subjects recalled greater numbers of objects than words describing objects. A quarter century later, Moore (1919) found that immediate recall was better for objects than for pictures, and better for pictures than for words. And Shepard (1967) provided fur-ther evidence of higher picture recall when his subjects identified a greater percent of pictures than words they had seen. More contemporary research focuses on the distinctiveness of visuals and their relation to memory.

Recall and picture type

Specific types of visual images also appear to play a role in what people remember. In Graber's (1990) experiments on political news, subjects most often recalled close-ups of people, familiar faces such as the president or the pope, and those of unfamiliar people in exotic circumstances. The author's own research on the recall of compelling crime news visuals confirmed Graber's findings (Artwick 1996). Subjects remembered close-ups of people's faces with greater frequency than macabre scenes, such as a body bag on a stretcher. A robbery suspect recorded on surveillance video, a police sketch of a rape suspect, and a murder victim's mother close to tears were all recalled more often than the body bag. So, while morbid scenes may compel audiences to look at the visual, viewers may not necessarily remember what they saw. Thus, the heavy use of gruesome pictures may not be the most effective approach to visually communicating crime news. The human experience, as conveyed in people's faces, appears more relevant to recall.

Visuals and their relation to text recall

A rich body of research that encompasses cognitive psychology to mass communication has long probed the relation of pictures to memory for text. From book illustrations to graphic visuals in television news stories, researchers have explored a range of questions and potential effects. Among those investigations, a study carried out in the late 1990s offers results relevant to the Internet news journalist. Prabu David's experiments (1998) offer evidence that adding a photograph to a news report increases memory for that story. Subjects who read stories with accompanying photos recalled a greater number of stories than subjects who read the text-only versions. His research is guided by Paivio's (1986) dual-coding theory, which posits that visual and verbal information are stored and processed in two separate, yet interconnected systems in memory. Hence, recall and recognition would be enhanced through a combination of pictures and text.

Visuals and Meaning

Moving beyond whether the audience will remember online news photos and text, we ask what meanings the users glean from the pictures on

Web sites. They may not necessarily mirror the Web editor's perception, sometimes differing in level of abstraction. Consider a photo of a police cruiser parked in front of an old house, for example. To some, it's simply a car and a building. To others, it's a domestic violence call. What might explain the difference? Semantic memory variations among online users may play a role in the meanings they construct from news photographs. This form of memory may be considered a network of interrelated words, concepts, and properties (Quillian 1968, Collins and Loftus 1975), or in other words, pre-existing knowledge. That knowledge may have come from personal experience or through media use, and may be drawn upon to make sense of a visual representation. Three distinct levels of abstraction can be found in the study of semiotics, or the science of signs.

Semiotics

Charles Sanders Peirce (1991) identified three types of signs—the iconic, the indexical, and the symbolic. The iconic is least abstract, and signifies the physical thing it represents. For example, a photo of a Dell Inspiron 8200 would signify a laptop computer at the iconic level. An indexical interpretation would require reliance on cultural knowledge and assumes an existential relationship between the sign and what it represents. That same Dell, displaying a Web page on its screen, could signify Internet connectivity at the indexical level of interpretation. And finally, the symbolic signification of the Dell may be a reflection of its user, as business traveler or student, or perhaps, a more abstract symbolism of computer as knowledge.

What does any of this have to do with visuals and digital journalism? It's a reminder that pictures on a page do not just "pretty up" a site or story. There's a user at the other end of the Web who may make meaning from the visuals on your site. Even if the pictures aren't processed beyond simple recall, they may be stored in the semantic memory for future use.

Visual stereotyping

When journalists use visual stereotypes, they often don't realize what they're doing. Several years ago a television news director presented his station's work at a community relations conference. The videotape he showed was intended to illustrate fair and accurate coverage of the people living in his community. But not all viewers saw the stories the same way. After watching the tape, a man in the audience became somewhat agitated with one of the stories. It had featured a basketball celebrity who took a group of disadvantaged kids to a major city game. The disgruntled man told the news director he was tired of seeing black men on television news who were only associated with sports. Instead, he asked when we were going to see black community leaders—business people, teachers, clergy—who were making a difference. The news director was stunned. He hadn't considered the representation as a stereotype, but the African American male had.

In this case, as in most instances of visual stereotyping, the action was not malicious. Unawareness explains the presence of many such visuals in our media today. Paul Martin Lester (1997) has long been a crusader against pictorial stereotyping in the media. To prevent stereotyping he suggests to: "use your common sense and to be reasonable." He also advises journalists to "show members of diverse cultural groups in everyday life situations." So, before choosing a photograph for a Web site, heighten your sensitivity to its portrayal of individuals and groups, whether social and economic, racial and ethnic, age and gender, religious and sexual orientation, or other characteristics.

Visuals and Social Reality Construction

The day after snipers killed five people in public places around suburban Maryland, MSNBC.com (2002) displayed the story prominently at the top of its cover page. A boxed graphic featured a bullet hole and its spider web-like cracks in the window where the bullet had entered. Above the photo appeared the words, "Random violence—Does it worry you?" Readers could vote and get immediate feedback. And by 10:21 a.m. there were already 1,751 responses; 54 percent voting yes, and 46 percent voting no.

As the story unfolded on the day of the murders, a reporter for Washington, D.C.'s NBC4 used the bullet hole visual to entice viewers to keep watching the station's coverage. "I want you to see something," said reporter Pat Collins. "We have a picture of a bullet hole from one of the incidents. It is a graphic picture but it gives you an idea of what police are dealing with in this case. You'll want to see this picture. It gives you some idea of the force and violence out here in Montgomery County today." (NBC4.com 2002) In closing his report, Collins discussed the cause for concern during the coming rush hour, because the shootings took place during that time frame. NBC4's Web site carried Collins' report as streaming video.

In both cases, the Web sites connected the visual image of the bullet hole with the crimes, linking it to concern for personal safety. A long-standing research tradition called cultivation theory relates media use to people's perception of the world, often regarding their fear of crime.

Its roots reach back to the late 1960s and early '70s, when George Gerbner conducted his first large-scale analyses of television content. The findings revealed an overwhelming level of violence in television programming. Gerbner coupled those data with viewer surveys that measured hours of exposure to television and viewers' perceptions of reality. His findings led to cultivation theory, which asserts that the more one is exposed to television (and its violent content), the more likely one will perceive the world as it is depicted on television (often a mean and dangerous world) (1998). Decades of subsequent research have supported the relationship between heavy television viewing and the increased viewer fear Gerbner pinpointed so many years ago.

What from these findings can we apply to digital reporting and producing? First, that viewing visuals relates to perceptions of social reality, or view of the world. This means the photos or video in your stories can help form the "pictures in our heads" (Lippmann 1922) of life in our neighborhoods, our nation, and our world. A Web journalist's choice of photograph and its juxtaposition with text may contribute to online reader fear, or other constructions of social reality, such as stereotyping. In the case of the D.C. snipers, the fact that perpetrators were at large, shooting and killing apparent random victims, had great fear-inducing potential in and of itself. Did pairing the bullet-hole photo with the notion of worrying about random violence have an impact on reader's fears? We can only speculate that answer. But as the day progressed, MSNBC.com replaced the bullet-hole graphic with a photo related to another story. And by day's end, the survey statistics nearly evened out, with 51 percent of the 6,478 votes worried about random violence, and 49 percent not worried.

Using Visuals in Digital Storytelling

Many organizations now expect their digital journalists to be able to shoot and edit images for the Web, so a familiarity with some basic concepts and mechanics is becoming more and more important. Although many established practices have been carried over from print and broadcast media to the Web, new conventions are also developing for using visuals on Internet news sites. This section combines traditional with emerging approaches while raising red flags where techniques are not Internet-appropriate.

Photos

Although many photographers still swear by film as their medium of choice, digital photojournalism is taking hold in newsrooms worldwide. Those who prefer digital over film tout its immediacy as a major advantage in this medium. "The best thing about digital is the instant gratification of seeing the image as it is made," says *Newsweek* contract photographer Chris Usher (2003). "It's like a never-ending pack of Polaroid film." Seeing what you've shot before leaving an event helps assure that you have the images you need. And digital photographs can quickly be transmitted to the newsroom from the field. Another big plus is not having to set up a darkroom in your hotel bathroom when you're on assignment.

Many newsrooms now rely on reporters to shoot their own digital images, so it's important to have a basic working knowledge of some photographic composition and camera operational features.

Photographic composition

Vertical or horizontal? Check your favorite Web sites, and you'll find both vertical and horizontal photographs on their home pages. Just because the camera's "default" position is horizontal, don't forget to shoot vertically when appropriate. And if you can't decide which is best, shoot both. Pay attention to the flash mechanism when you rotate the camera on its side, making sure you're holding it so the flash is on top rather than on the bottom. This should give you more evenly distributed lighting.

Scale: The speck and the famous landmark. You've seen this photo, or perhaps have even taken it—a person and famous landmark. She's standing near the doorstep of the building and appears so small in the frame she's hardly distinguishable. Avoid this mistake by making the landmark your background, and pulling the person to the foreground. If she stands near the camera, well in front of the building, you can establish the location and at the same time see the subject. Figure 9.1 shows before and after photos of this effect.

An important exception is the use of a human figure to illustrate scale. Let's say a winter of snowstorms led to a pile of snow two-stories high at the edge of the Wal-Mart parking lot. A man walking his dog passes in

Figure 9.1 In the first frame, the subject is so small she is hardly recognizable. Correct this problem by pulling the subject to the foreground, within ten feet of the camera, as the second frame shows.

front of the mountain of snow, looking very small in comparison. His size in relation to the snow pile is key to telling that story visually.

Shooting above, below, and at eye level. In most cases, we'll want to shoot subjects at eye level. This will mean stooping down to photograph a young child, or holding up the camera for a tall person. Shooting down on a subject can make him look small or perhaps weak. The opposite is true when shooting up at someone. Keep in mind these possible psychological effects and fairness when using non eye-level shots.

Framing the subject. Think about the background and foreground when shooting, because those elements play an important role in the framing of your subject. Move in tighter to eliminate distracting background items from the shot. Include foreground items when they can add a pleasing touch to a scenic view.

Also, consider the natural elements of the location to frame your subject. The photograph in Figure 9.2 uses a fence in the foreground and a clothesline in the background to frame the little boy.

Depth. We can enhance interest and add three dimensionality to our photographs through attention to angles and the foreground and background elements in the scene. A sidewalk can run vertically or horizontally through the frame, or can cut through left-front to right-back, or right-front to left-back. Each provides a different effect. The three-dimensional perspective is enhanced with the sidewalk cutting through at an angle. The positioning of the people in the shot also contributes to depth. Those closer to you look larger, and those farther away look smaller. Focusing on the foreground versus the background also changes the effect. Figure 9.3 illustrates the use of angles to create depth.

Subject placement within the frame. Placing your subject slightly off center can make a photograph more pleasing, as can moving in for a closer shot. But moving in too close can cause a soft focus, so beware of this possibility and avoid blurry shots.

Digital camera features

Sometimes we're lucky and the point-and-shoot approach produces an acceptable photograph. But that's more the exception than the rule. A familiarity with digital camera features helps ensure a higher success rate. First, know what storage medium it uses—its capacity and proper insertion. These range from memory cards the size of postage stamps, to the mini CD-RW, with storage ranging from 16 MB up to 1 GB and more.

Next, test out the camera's manual features. Note that fully-automatic cameras do not allow for manual adjustments.

Figure 9.2 Foreground and background elements contribute to subject framing.

White balance. Different lighting conditions influence the way the camera "sees" white. This is important because the camera uses that interpretation of white to determine all colors. Digital cameras can white balance automatically, but the automatic setting works best in bright conditions (megapixel.net 2003). Manual may be preferable when working with indoor lighting or outdoors on an overcast day. If your image has a bluish or reddish tint when using automatic white balance, correct the colors for the next shot by changing the setting manually.

Shutter speed. The higher the shutter speed, the more effectively the camera can freeze motion. When photographing action, set the shutter to at least 1/250 seconds to avoid blur. Note that the speed of the movement

Figure 9.3 Use angles when shooting to create the illusion of depth in your two-dimensional image.

may require an even faster (higher) shutter speed to stop action (megapixel.net 2003).

Focus. Automatic focus doesn't allow for much flexibility and can sometimes prove unreliable, so the option to focus manually is often desirable. For example, let's say you're photographing a crowd of women protesting the marketing of suggestive clothing to pre-teens. Two elderly women in the foreground are burning a pile of V-neck midriff tops and short shorts, while young moms in mid-frame are wearing Britney Spears masks. You want to focus on the bonfire and leave the masks a bit blurry, but the automatic focus won't obey. It makes the masks sharp and the bonfire soft. You'll need to use manual focus to get the shot you want.

Burst mode. You may want to take a fast-moving sequence of shots, but find that your shutter can't keep up. In this case, burst—sometimes called continuous—mode allows you to do so. When in burst mode you can take numerous pictures in succession by depressing and holding down the shutter button. This can quickly fill your memory card, so plan accordingly (megapixel.net 2003).

Camera features and operation vary among companies and models, so refer to your camera's user guide for specifics. Many digital camera company Web sites provide online tutorials with specific operational directions.

Shooting Video for the Web

Looking at life through a lens may feel slightly awkward at first, but reshaping our approach to the gaze should lead to better visual storytelling. The first challenge is being able to think in terms of scenes and shots within scenes. This approach is often referred to as sequence shooting (Hewitt 1992), one of the most valuable concepts for digital videographers to understand and put into practice. But the term itself sometimes confuses students (who equate sequence with sequential, which is NOT the idea), so I prefer to teach students to identify and shoot *scene components*.

Component shots take three basic forms—the wide shot, medium shot, and close-up—and when edited together, make the scene come alive. Take, for example, the scene of a busy computer lab in which students are working at every station. A professor glides through the aisles, stopping regularly to browse the screens over students' shoulders. The wide (establishing) shot for that scene includes as much of the room as possible, and will likely be taped from the entryway or a raised vantage point (such as the top of a desk). Within that scene, the videographer would find numerous components: medium shots of individual students at computers, and the professor lurking over a student's workspace; close-ups of faces, hands on keyboards, a steaming latte, and computer screens; more close-ups—hand grabbing latte, lips preparing to sip, desk's edge as latte is placed down haphazardly, and latte spilling over books and papers. A nervous student shakes his leg while trying to think. A clock ticks away the minutes as students write to deadline. The printer spits out a document. By identifying and shooting individual components of the scene, those pieces can be edited together to tell a much more visually interesting story than a sweeping panorama of the lab.

Most of what you shoot will directly relate to the action. But you will also need shots to use as transitions between subjects in scenes and between scenes. Those transition shots that take the viewer away from the focus of action are called cut-aways. For example, while the clock is tangentially related to what's going on in the computer lab scene, it can be used to move away from the action conveyed in a shot of a student and professor to another shot of that professor alone or with another student. To assure the usability of each shot, hold it steady for about ten seconds.

Figure 9.4 Scene components. Left: Wide shot of beluga whale watching establishes the scene. Center: Close-up of boy serves as a transition from the whale's posterior to its head. Right: Close-up of whale "smiling" moves the scene forward.

Of course, if action is taking place within the shot, for example, a little league player is at bat, let her hit the ball before you stop recording. Figure 9.4 illustrates scene and shot components of a marine mammal show at Chicago's Shedd Aquarium.

Camera movement

One of the toughest temptations for neophyte videographers to resist is camera movement—pans, zooms, and tilts. The pan is a lateral movement across a scene. Zooming takes the shot from tight to wide, or vice versa. And tilting points the camera upward or downward. We use these movements to set up our shots, but rarely need to record shots while panning, zooming, or tilting. Reserve movement for rare cases when it's truly justified. For example, a Seattle videographer tilted up the side of a steep hill to illustrate the path a woman climbed to seek help after she had been severely beaten. In that case, the tilt helped convey the struggle the woman endured in her climb. With tilts, pans, and zooms, begin the shot by holding it steady for at least five seconds, smoothly execute the movement to its end, and hold there for a minimum of five seconds.

Composition

While quirky angles and other unorthodox approaches may capture our attention during television commercials, news videography adheres to more traditional standards of composition. Attending to depth and subject screen placement can add interest to and improve our shots. Let's start with the interview shot. Envision your viewfinder divided into horizontal thirds by imaginary lines. Place the subject's eyes on the top line while filling the screen with a head-and-shoulder shot. Leave just a tiny bit of

Figure 9.5 Dividing your viewfinder into thirds horizontally can help you compose your shots.

space at the top (head room), and some look or lead room on the side the person is facing. Figure 9.5 shows you how this should look.

Just because the audience will view your work on a flat or semi-flat screen doesn't mean your shots have to look flat. Add dimension by finding the angles in the scene that will add depth and interest. Instead of interviewing your subject parallel to a wall, use the room's corner as a background for depth. Or, better yet, use as a background an appropriate environment that adds context to the scene. But beware of objects behind or next to the subject. The juxtaposition of trees, signs, and pictures can make them look like they're growing out of the subject's head (Figure 9.6).

Automatic iris

Most video cameras come equipped with several automatic features, among them an auto iris, which lets in light for proper picture exposure. However, environmental conditions can sometimes "fool" the iris into thinking it's getting too much or too little light, and when this happens, the shot is spoiled. For example, let's say you're shooting outside on a bright, sunny day, and your subject who is wearing a white shirt stands in front of a pale yellow building. Light is bouncing off the shirt and the walls into

Figure 9.6 Be aware of the background elements, or you may find something "growing" out of your subject's head.

the iris, making it sense too much light. So it closes down a bit to allow less light to pass through. Now your subject's face is too dark. When this happens, switch to the manual setting and adjust the iris to allow more light to enter.

A bright background can also cause the same effect. If your subject stands in the shade, he will likely be too dark in the shot, because the camera reads the entire scene and cuts back on the light. You may be able to adjust the iris manually, but that may let in too much light. Instead, adjust the background, which usually takes a slight repositioning of your subject. Figure 9.7 illustrates this effect.

Focus

Watching a tennis tournament on network television gave me a big surprise when a post-match interview was out of focus. I immediately sus-

Figure 9.7 In the first frame the bright background "fools" the camera into "thinking" there's too much light in the shot. It responds by shutting down the iris, making the subject's face too dark. Correct this problem by moving the subject, or repositioning the camera, as shown in the second frame.

Figure 9.8 The first frame shows the camera's choice of focus—the bookcase. Correct this problem by using the manual setting to focus on your subject, as the second frame illustrates.

pected what had happened when I spotted the people in the background because their images were sharp and clear. The camera person must have been using automatic focus, giving the camera authority to choose what it would focus on, rather than manually adjusting the focus on the subject. Avoid this common faux pas by alerting yourself to its potential when using automatic focus. When your subject does not adequately fill the screen, the camera may choose the background to focus on. Check for a soft focus, and correct it. Switch to manual, zoom in on the subject's eyes, focus, and zoom back out to set your shot (see Figure 9.8).

Digital Video Editing Concepts

Before digital editing, analog systems transferred audio and visual signals from a source tape to an edit master. The process was linear—in other words, once you made that transfer to the master tape, you couldn't go back and insert or delete something half-way through. If you wanted to make the change, you had to resume from that mid-point and re-edit from there. Digital video has dramatically changed that process. First, it's nonlinear—audio and visual elements can be inserted, deleted, copied, pasted, moved, and otherwise manipulated in pretty much whatever order desired. In many cases, the editor refers to in- and out-points for shots on an edit decision list (EDL). In other words, she instructs the computer to find the data needed and present it in a particular order. This allows greater freedom and flexibility, increasing speed and efficiency in editing. Each system has its own intricacies and operating instructions, and is best studied with a reference manual and/or help menu. However, understanding and implementing general editing concepts can improve your video stories.

Make sense

Good editing should inform and enlighten viewers. It weaves together pictures, sounds, and narration to tell a story. And it clarifies, rather than confuses. It must be truthful, and should help viewers make sense of the event or issue at hand. We often shoot five, ten, or twenty times as much videotape as we will use in the final story, so our shot selections and editing choices are key to conveying the essence of the story.

Using scene components wisely. Recall the scene components discussed in the section on digital videotaping. You have a wide shot of a computer lab, medium shots of students at their stations, and close ups of faces, screens, and hands on keyboards. You can randomly edit together 30 seconds of these shots and produce "wallpaper" video—kind of a meaningless visual backdrop for the audio story. Or, you can thoughtfully edit together scene components in a relational manner. If your first shot shows a student on screen left, and a professor on screen right, cut to a closer shot of the student. Be aware of the direction the subjects are facing. If the student looks toward the right in the two-shot, then the close-up should also show him looking right. Otherwise, you violate the continuity of the scene.

Avoid jumping from wide shot to wide shot; instead, move among wide, medium, and close shots. Several close-ups can comfortably be used in succession if they make sense together. Cut on action or at rest. For example, if cutting from a medium shot of a tennis player about to make contact with the ball, and a close up of the racquet head, match the shots at the exact spots during the action. Be sure the racquet is moving forward in both shots. To cut at rest, wait until the tennis player hits the ball, and then cut to the close-up of her determined expression. Most shots should run about three or four seconds in length.

Avoid jump cuts. You've taped a great interview with the mayor, but at the beginning she had her glasses on, and then later took them off. You'd like to use two of her statements back-to-back, one from the beginning and one from the end. But cutting the two shots together would create a jump cut. The video would jump from the mayor with glasses to the mayor without glasses. Avoid the jump by using a cut-away. Recall that this is a shot that can take you away from the main action. In this case, cut to the reporter, or something the mayor is referring to in her sound bite. Be aware that in this case the shot should be long enough to represent the amount of time it would take for her to comfortably take off her glasses. Otherwise, it would still be jarring and unrealistic. Again, you are preserving continuity by avoiding jump cuts.

Remember the audio

Reporters who edit sometimes forget to include natural sound in their edits. But doing so eliminates the texture that can bring the story to life. Chanting during a candlelight vigil, the howling wind of a blizzard, squeals of delight on the school playground—all add a sense of being there to the story. Don't let it drown out your narration, though. And if the sound can stand alone to help tell the story, stop talking for a moment and let it happen. For example, when rescuers pull a child out of a well safely after trying for more than 24 hours, let your viewer experience the excitement by hearing the onlookers cheer.

Converting Video to Still Images

Many television news videographers now supply their own stations' Web sites, and sometimes their online newspaper partners, with still frames from their digital videotapes. This can enhance a site if it is well executed, but will detract from its impact if done improperly.

Remember the old saw, garbage in, garbage out? It's good advice to keep in mind when making still frames from video. A videotaped shot that's too light or too dark, that's out of focus, or poorly composed will carry those problems to the Internet. But can't I just fix it in Photoshop, you ask? You may succeed in tweaking it a bit, but starting with a clean piece of video will produce better results. Another guideline is to avoid motion shots when possible. A moving subject within the shot or camera motion, such as pans or zooms, may distort the still image. The conversion from video to photo can produce a jagged, pixelized effect or fuzzy trail following the movement.

How to convert digital video to a digital still image

Some programs, such as Pinnacle Systems' Studio 7, offer point-and-click image grabbing. But such systems do not provide much choice on image size or type. Others, such as Avid Xpress DV, do, and some understanding is in order before jumping in. First, consider the approximate size you would like the image to be. While you can manipulate the image size after it's been converted, you risk distortion if the changes are too great. Also, keep in mind the 4:3 aspect ratio of the video image (the width of the frame in relation to the height). The video image will be least changed by maintaining that ratio. For example, a full-screen image would be 640 x 480 pixels, while a small photo would measure 160 x 120 pixels. Notice how the 4:3 ratio is calculated for the small photo: 40 pixels x 4 = 160; 40 pixels x 3 = 120. Make the photo larger or smaller by choosing a slightly larger or smaller unit of measure. Instead of 40 pixels to yield a 160 x 120 image, choose 50 pixels for a 200 x 150 image, or 30 pixels for a 120 x 90 image.

Now that you're familiar with sizing images, you're ready to begin the conversion. If you're working from a field tape, the video must first be ingested by the video server (fed into the computer). Some digital video editing programs, such as Avid Xpress DV, refer to this as recording. To conserve precious hard drive space, be selective and only ingest the scenes you intend to use. Be sure to save the file(s) you've recorded. Next, open the video file, and mark an in- and out-point on the frame you wish to convert to a digital still image. Now you're ready to export the file out of the video editor. For Avid, go to the pull-down <File> menu and click <Export>. After naming the new file and its location, select options and then specify the image size and type. JPEG is the format of choice for most Internet news photos, because it was built for photographs, providing millions of colors. The acronym stands for "Joint Photographic Experts Group," which created the standard in the early 1990s (Klein 1999). You may use the Photoshop format if you plan to work with the image in that program before posting it to your Web site. Once you've selected the settings, save your image, open the file, and examine it to be sure it's acceptable for the Internet.

Streaming Video

Most of us have viewed streaming video on the Web, but we may not fully understand what it is and how it works. Simply put, streaming video is a digital file delivered and played real-time, over the Internet, from a streaming server to a computer. Instead of downloading the file, saving it to a hard drive, and then playing it, the streaming video plays as it is being sent to your computer. News organizations use real-time servers to store and deliver streaming video to their audiences, such as the Real Broadcast Network. The video file must be encoded in streaming media format, which is a compressed file that can efficiently move over the Internet.

Converting a television news story to streaming video can be as simple as point-and-click, or so technically daunting that you avoid it at all cost. Let's start with easy, and work our way through tough. Digital video editing software that allows users to encode files directly from the program is the most straightforward. The encoding usually begins at the "File" menu, where the pull-down offers a "save as" or "export" option. Choices may be limited to the program's default settings, and the streaming format will likely be a RealMedia (.rm) file. Following the program prompts, you will create the streaming file in a few easy steps.

Now, for the more complicated method. Our very first efforts to stream video for Washington and Lee University's student news Web site required time, planning, and patience. This may still be the case in newsrooms that are not fully integrated digitally, where you are likely to land your first job. So, you may find a familiarity with the process helpful.

First, the completed story has to be moved out of the digital non-linear editing system. Newer software, such as Avid Xpress DV, exports directly for streaming, but the older software doesn't do so. Exporting as an AVI file may be the best choice, which is the format used on Windows Media Players. This can take up to 30 minutes for a two-minute story. Choose at least 15 frames per second (fps) and a minimum of radio-quality sound (22.05 kHz) with moderate motion for acceptable results.

Next, use RealSystem Producer or other encoding software to compress the file for streaming. Choose settings that best match your video content in terms of movement and complexity.

Finally, move the encoded file to your streaming server. Once it's there, you can link to it within your Web site.

But just because you *can* stream a video, doesn't mean you should. With a 56k modem, which many of the folks at home still use, watching streamed video can be a frustrating, if not futile, experience. You've probably had the "pleasure" of watching a tiny window display images for a few seconds, then stop, then start again, all the while scrambling for the audio to catch up to the video, or vice versa. Or, perhaps the audio was so distorted it was barely discernable. With continuing penetration of high-speed DSL and cable Internet access in the home market, these concerns will become less important. But until low-speed transmission is no longer relevant, Web journalists must take extra care in choosing and preparing streaming video. Here are some suggestions for doing so.

Avoiding live for the sake of live

You've seen it on local television news more often than you might like—the reporter standing at a crime scene, reporting live, hours after investigators have gone home. Or perhaps you recall a live report from a long-empty building where a meeting took place earlier in the day. Now you can see these reports on numerous local newspaper and television Web sites, as streaming Realvideo or Quicktime movies. This practice takes one of the biggest TV news content foibles and shovels it onto the Web. Sure it's fast, and it's easy. Just record the program as it's broadcast, convert the story to a streaming media file, and insert it into the Web page. Place a camera icon next to the headline, and voilá, you've got video. Too bad the story was dated when it appeared on the air and may be inexcusably inappropriate online. For example, a Texas online news operation was still streaming a live report at 6 p.m. from the previous day's 10 p.m. newscast. When the station broadcast the story live, the reporter was standing in front of police headquarters a half-day after the victim was shot. Streamed on the Web, at least twenty-four hours had passed.

Instead of choosing to stream those dated pieces, deliver the breaking news you've promised your users. For example, Oklahoma City's NewsOK .com used video from a helicopter sky cam to report a gas line rupture that closed a street. The reporter never appeared in the story, but instead, voiced over the pictures, giving the audience what it needed to know to avoid the area. A television producer might have wanted to see the reporter in the helicopter for drama, but on the Web, that wasn't necessary. What if there is no helicopter in the budget? A map of the intersection or video shot from the ground would suffice, as well.

Updating the live piece for the Web

With a little updating and editing, the old "live" story can serve the community as news. This will keep users coming back, instead of turning away, because the Web site offered no more than the broadcast. Instead of streaming the whole piece, selected video frames could be converted to JPEG still images to accompany the story text. Or, key sound bites could be linked to in the updated presentation.

Flash Presentations

The technical intricacies of programming a Flash presentation go beyond the scope of this book. Instead, this section discusses Flash productions and provides a systematic approach to planning and storytelling with Flash.

What is Flash?

Flash is a Web production program for creating presentations that can include audio, visual, text, animation, and interactivity. It uses vector graphics technology, which offers smaller file size and the ability to adjust the image size without distortion, unlike bitmapped images such as JPEG and GIF (Macromedia Flash 2000). Using Flash for online news offers the journalist more storytelling options and the audience greater interactivity with the presentation. They range from the simple slide show (driven by a "next" button) to multimedia productions including quizzes and animation.

Planning Flash Presentations (Using Key Facts, Photos and Sounds)

Even if you don't have the technical know-how to produce stories in Flash you can always work with someone who does. Many digital journalists conceptualize, report, and plan stories, and will then work with a Flash producer who handles the technical production. The process will go more smoothly if you can envision and communicate your story plans to the producer. Using the key facts approach presented in Chapter 5 and a technique called storyboarding, you can make your Flash ideas a reality.

Let's plan a Flash interactive slide show on major earthquakes worldwide since 1900. You decide to use ten slides, beginning with the 1989 San Francisco quake and ending with 1906 in the same city. Your key facts include statistics for each quake: the location, date, Richter scale measurement, number

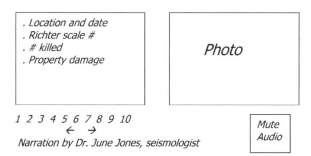

(Note: Each photo represents a different earthquake. The information in the left-hand box corresponds to each individual earthquake, and changes as the user clicks through the photos.)

Figure 9.9 This storyboard sketches out an interactive Flash slide show on earthquakes. Using storyboards can facilitate communication among reporters, producers, and programmers.

of people killed, and property damage. In addition, you have photos from each quake and a video news report from 1989. Audio of a seismologist explains what the Richter scale is and what the measurements represent. The storyboard in Figure 9.9 sketches out how this slide show might look, which information will be included where, and how the user will navigate through this interactive.

While storyboards usually include a series of frames, each representing a separate scene or slide, this slide show storyboard uses only one frame. The title, navigation tool, audio control, text box, and photo box will remain the same for each of the ten slides. Only the content of the photo and text boxes will change for each slide. And for the 1989 quake the producer will add to the text box a small "play video" clickable button to launch the video, which will play in that slide's photo window. Organize your notes so the producer knows which information goes in which slide. Also label the photos and their placement. Working with a clear plan and organized material, the producer should be able to execute your ideas and create the interactive you've envisioned.

Activities for Further Learning

1. Using a digital video camera, shoot five minutes of videotape related to a newsworthy story. Be sure to shoot scene components, including a minimum of five wide, medium, and close-up shots. Also shoot at least two cut-aways.

2. Create several JPEGs of various sizes using a digital video file.

3. Find an outdated live story being streamed on a hometown television station's Web site. Suggest ways you might update that story for the Web site.

4. Plan and storyboard a Flash presentation on college students and plagiarism. Include audiovisual elements in addition to text, and make the production interactive.

References

Artwick, C. G. 1996. Blood, body bags, and tears: Remembering visual images from local television crime news. *Visual Communication Quarterly*. Spring pp. 14-18.

Collins, A. M. and E.F. Loftus. 1975. A spreading-activation theory of semantic processing. *Psychological Review*. 82 pp. 407-428.

David, P. 1998. News concreteness and visual-verbal association. *Human Communication Research*. December p. 180.

Gerbner, G. 1998. Cultivation analysis: an overview. *Mass Communication and Society*. Summer-Fall v.1 i3-4 p. 175(2)

Graber, D. 1990. Seeing is remembering: How visuals contribute to learning from television news. *Journal of Communication*. 40(3) pp. 134-155.

Hewitt, J. 1992. *Sequences: Strategies for Shooting News in the Real World.* Mountain View, California: Mayfield Publishing Company.

Jacobson, A. July 12, 2000. Projects too much from too little. *Poynter.org*. Today in Journalism Today's Centerpiece. http://www.poynter.org

Kirkpatrick, E. A. 1894. An experimental study of memory. *Psychological Review*. 1. pp. 601-609.

Klein, L. R. Oct. 15, 1999. Slicing the image pie. *Library Journal*. pp. 13-14. Retrieved from ProQuest.

Lang, A., J. Borse, K. Wise and P. David, P. 2002. Captured by the World Wide Web: Orienting to structural and content features of computer-presented information. *Communication Research*. June v.29, i3. p215(31).

Lester, P. M. 1997. Images and stereotypes. http://commfaculty.fullerton.edu/lester/writings/mediastereo.html

Lippmann, W. 1922. *Public Opinion*. New York: Harcourt, Brace and Company.

Lynn, R. 1996. Cited in Lang, et. al. Attention arousal, and the orientation reaction. Oxford, UK. Pergamon Press.

Macromedia Flash. 2000. White paper: Flash player for developers and publishers. http://www.macromedia.com/software/flash/survey/whitepaper_jul03.pdf

megapixel.net. 2003 http://www.megapixel.net/html/issueindex.php?lang=en

Moore, T. V. 1919. Image and meaning in memory and perception. *Psychological Monographs*, 27, whole no. 119.

msnbc.com. Oct. 4, 2002. http://www.msnbc.com

nbc4.com. Oct. 4, 2002. http://www.nbc4.com

Paivio, A. 1986. *Mental representations: A dual-coding approach.* New York: Oxford University Press.

Peirce, C. S. 1991. *Peirce on signs: writings on semiotic.* Edited by James Hoopes. Chapel Hill: University of North Carolina Press.

Quillian, M. R. 1968. Semantic memory. In M. L. Minsky (Ed.). *Semantic Information Processing. .* Cambridge: MIT Press. pp. 216-270

Shepard, R. N. 1967. Recognition memory for words, sentences, and pictures. *Journal of Verbal Learning and Verbal Behavior*, 6. pp. 156-163.

Stanford-Poynter Project. 2000. http://www.poynterextra.org/et/i.htm

Usher, C. 2003. Cited in The digital journalists survey on the impact of digital in photojournalism by Dirck Halstead. http://www.digitaljournalist.org/issue0309/editorial.html

CHAPTER 10

Operating within a Convergence Model

Chapter Objectives

When a tractor-trailer jackknifes on heavily-traveled Interstate 81, Gene Adams grabs her digital video gear and hustles out to the field. She's covering the story for the Rockbridge Report, a student broadcast news program and Web site. Meanwhile, a student news intern researches the crash from the newsroom and writes a rough draft for the Web. When Adams returns, the two journalists share information, and each crafts a piece for her respective medium. A still frame from the video accompanies the online version. In addition, a student Web editor fine tunes a related story that focuses on plans to widen the interstate, and ties to the truck crash spot news, providing context. Collaboration makes it possible for these student journalists to turn around this story across media, quickly and efficiently.

But in other newsrooms, the thought of crossing over into another medium's territory terrifies some journalists. Print reporters may fear stammering or freezing on camera, broadcasters may be daunted by writing "long," and resentment may fester when a scoop is shared with a partner. News media convergence—it's still defining itself, taking shape in different forms in newsrooms around the country and the world. This chapter examines working in a converged news media environment and explores how journalists can best serve their audiences while crossing platforms.

Figure 10.1 Journalism students collaborate to produce a Web site, broadcast news program, and newspaper front page in the converged newsroom at Washington and Lee University.

What Is Media Convergence?

Critics of media convergence often equate it with media conglomeration—behemoth corporations swallowing up newspapers, television stations, and online news sites, resulting in streamlined operations through staff cuts and content repurposing. They fear limiting voices in the marketplace of ideas and reducing the caliber of reporting by requiring journalists to develop stories for three forms of media instead of one. While media mergers may contribute to some forms of convergence, they don't necessarily fit this doomsday scenario, and they don't necessarily define it.

So, if convergence isn't strictly conglomeration, what is it? It's largely a matter of cooperation—among organizations, individuals, and their work practices. Today, U.S. media form 62 convergence relationships (API 2004), ranging from news coverage and content to advertising sales and promotion. Here are some specific arrangements:

- A common print/broadcast/Web newsroom
- Print reporters appear on TV
- TV reporter writes for newspaper
- Single management over print, broadcast, and Web

- Share story budgets
- Cross-promotion
- Shared assignment desk
- Team storytelling
- Linked Web sites
- Cross-media ad sales

Any of these elements can affect how you do your job as a digital jour-nalist. In your newsroom it may mean simply posting your print story, un-changed, on the newspaper's Web site. Or it may involve an in-depth cross-media team project that takes a distinct form online, in print, and on air. Relationships vary among and within media organizations and their people. Those who find success embrace cooperation and a spirited com-mitment to convergence. The *Chicago Tribune Online Edition* has show-cased some of the best exclusives, projects, and prize-winning stories from the newspaper and WGN broadcast operations. But, "The equal chal-lenge on a day-to-day basis is developing a culture at the newspaper, at the TV stations, at radio, and at the Internet, where we are sharing information and resources on a routine basis," said Mitchell Locin, *Chicago Tribune* Senior Electronic News Editor (2002). That value of cooperation is re-flected in the definition that guides this chapter's examination of news me-dia convergence (adapted from Castaneda 2003):

> News media convergence involves cooperation among broadcast, print, and online journalists to tell stories effectively in appropriate media to a wide-reaching audience.

While it appears revolutionary, convergence is not new. One of the pre-miere convergence operations in the United States, *The Tampa Tribune*, WFLA-TV, and TBO.com, had its roots in a cooperative relationship many years ago, among WFLA television, radio, and *The Tribune* (Bryan 2003). But when the FCC tightened joint ownership rules in 1975, the cross-pollination waned, even though the Tampa relationship was allowed to continue. Then, the FCC loosened its rules in 1996, allowing corporate owner Media General to operate television, newspaper, and Web out of one facility. Today, the news operation in Tampa serves as one of our na-tion's models for convergence journalism. Another, the Tribune Company, owned newspaper, television, and radio stations in Chicago in 1948, and today runs major convergence operations from coast to coast.

But early convergence efforts weren't limited to large corporate own-ership. Veteran broadcaster Ron MacDonald recalls the joint newsroom in

Roanoke, Virginia, in the 1950s and 1960s, where a partition separated the print from the broadcast journalists. "There was lots of camaraderie," says MacDonald, of the relationships both in and outside the newsroom. WDBJ-TV got much of its content from *Roanoke Times-World* reporters who hung a carbon copy of their stories on a hook near the broadcasters. MacDonald and his staff rewrote those pieces in broadcast style for the television newscast. And journalists from both sides of the partition sometimes conducted joint interviews and shared breaking news coverage (MacDonald, 2003).

Early convergence not only crossed media platforms but traversed international borders. Former *Ms.* magazine editor-in-chief Tracy Wood reported for multiple media in Vietnam during the war in the early 1970s. Although the term "convergence" hadn't been coined yet, Wood and others in Vietnam sometimes worked outside their specializations to report the war. She filed print stories for United Press International (UPI) but also recorded audio and shot photographs.

It was no easy task—the equipment was bulky and her technical training, basic. But, Wood (2003) says, "We did not consider it a hardship because the pressure was not on most of the time. It would come on only when you were the only source." And on critical stories where no UPI photographer or radio reporter was present, Wood took charge. Such was the case in early 1973, when American prisoners of war in Hanoi were being released from captivity. Wood was one of only three journalists who made it to the scene. Her minimal photographic experience kicked into gear as she trained her camera on the POWs. "See if you can get the eyes in focus, and snap it fast," recalls Wood. She succeeded, and captured the emotion of the POWs through their facial expressions. "Pure, dumb, blind luck," says Wood. Between photos, she switched on her tape recorder and dictated descriptions of the scene into the microphone. Her attempts to interview the released prisoners met with silence, as many had suffered brutal torture and feared compromising their freedom. "As a reporter, you keep trying, and hope you have common sense and good judgment. If you don't ask the question, you don't know what the answer is," explains Wood. Because of her persistence and commitment to reporting, Wood's account of the historic moment reached the world through the UPI news wire, photo wire, and radio.

The cross-platform arrangement worked well because Wood did not produce three media products on a daily basis. Her top priority was always the story, to do the story right. So she refused to let shooting photographs or gathering audio get in the way of a fully-reported story. When she did provide audio, UPI paid extra for each piece. But the cash incentive led some journalists to produce more than they could handle. "One reporter got into audio to the detriment of his stories," says Wood. And sacrificing quality for quantity by reporting across media doesn't bode well with Wood: "When it makes sense to cooperate, when it makes the story better, do whatever it takes. If it's not going to make the story better, fight it as hard as you can." Wood's news judgment guided her to cross media platforms when it would enhance telling the story and informing the public. She also willingly took risks to send her audio and visuals to UPI for processing and distribution, as you can see in the sidebar.

Addressing Cultural Issues

Walk into a television newsroom and one of the first things you'll notice is the noise. Police and emergency scanners squawking, reporters reading scripts aloud as they write, producers listening to taped interviews, and the occasional shouting across the newsroom make it hard for the uninitiated to concentrate. Newspaper newsrooms, on the other hand, are more subdued, so when broadcast and print operations come together, the environment can take some getting used to. Web operations may be located in small offices or in a partitioned area set off from the main newsroom. They may even be offsite. But physical workplace is only one facet of many cultural issues facing converged news operations. Identifying potential problem areas can heighten awareness and smooth the way for the converged working relationship.

Perceptions and Misperceptions

A reporter for your local newspaper spends hours in city meetings each week covering her beat. She's done it for years, knows everyone in city hall, and understands how local government works. So when the new television reporter in town rushes into a city council meeting for a rezoning vote, the print reporter may think the coverage will be shallow. She may hold this opinion even if the television reporter has researched the issue and spent time in the community interviewing people who would be affected and those making the decision. That's because she's seen TV crews swing by city hall in the past, arriving late and disrupting the meeting with their lights and cameras, only to videotape heated arguments and put them on the air with little thought to the issues at hand. Her perceptions have been shaped by past observations, and might have an impact on a converged relationship.

Tracy Wood

Tracy Wood reporting the American POW release outside Ly Nam De prison in North Vietnam, March 14, 1973.

When Vietnam War reporter Tracy Wood shot photos and recorded audio for UPI, she had to send them to headquarters for processing and editing. This posed a great challenge in Hanoi, Wood said, because the U.S. government didn't want journalists there to report the POW releases. But she relied on creativity and trust to deliver the film and tape for processing and editing. To get the materials from Hanoi to the Philippines, Wood cultivated a military source for help. "The person sidled up next to me and put a camera bag down near some equipment. As I was walking around, I would surreptitiously drop film into the camera bag. When I finished recording a tape, I'd do the same thing. I hoped like crazy I got the right bag." Wood was right on target, and as a result, the world got to see and hear the POW release story.

Likewise, that television reporter may have seen the print journalist drinking coffee in the mayor's office or joking with the secretaries. The broadcaster may perceive that instead of having to rush back to do a live shot for the noon newscast, the print journalist has "all the time in the world" to write her story, or that she's elitist because she appears to socialize with the government leaders. Because of her own deadlines and work patterns, she does not realize that the newspaper reporter may be researching several stories concurrently, requiring more time with the mayor. Or, that the secretaries are more willing to help the reporter with information because she takes the time to get to know them.

Our misperceptions of journalists who work in media other than our own can impede a positive working relationship when it comes to convergence. Whether they were shaped by stereotypes in film or fiction, learned in college, or based on personal observations, opening our minds can be the first step to a positive cross-media relationship. Let's begin by addressing these common generalizations:

Broadcast journalists

Have thirty-second brains. This assumes that because they write short pieces to be consumed by the ear, they can't write anything longer than thirty seconds. French philosopher and mathematician Blaise Pascal wrote, "I have made this (letter) longer than usual, only because I have not had the time to make it shorter." Writing short isn't easy; it takes skill. Those who do it well deserve respect.

Care more about their hair than the story. You will find some narcissistic people in broadcasting, as you will in many other fields. But good grooming doesn't equal bad journalism. The hair is just another facet of the job that must be attended to.

Are insensitive. How can they stick a microphone into a mother's face after her child drowns, and ask, "How do you feel?" Reporters for print, broadcast, and the Web must interview people in difficult situations. But their approach must be respectful. The motivation for badgering is sensationalism and should not be tolerated in any medium.

Are rude. They barge into meetings late, disrupt proceedings with their lights and cameras, and then leave early. Some do this. But the most professional are unobtrusive and sensitive to their own presence.

Don't write. Because broadcasters write as they speak, the conversational style seems to convince a lot of people that they extemporaneously "tell us" the news. While on-camera reporters and anchor people must sometimes ad-lib, the bulk of television news is scripted.

Print journalists

Are old curmudgeons with green eyeshades. This movie stereotype depicted the proofreader combing over copy in preparation for the hot metal type. Be thankful for the persnickety editor who catches bad grammar, misspellings, and just plain stupid mistakes we can make under times of stress.

Think only they can do serious journalism. This has a lot to do with broadcasting's time limitations and the difficulty of going in depth during a thirty-minute local news broadcast. Many local television news stations have strong investigative teams that expose corruption. And news programs, such as Nightline, and Frontline, that devote their coverage to one issue per program, provide greater depth. Yes, television news runs its share of cute pet stories, but newspapers cover them, too.

Have all the time in the world to write their stories. While their deadlines may not come as early or as frequently as broadcasters', print reporters must race the clock when reporting and writing their stories. Consider that one 2,500-word newspaper story would take fourteen minutes to read aloud. That's the time often allotted to news in an entire half-hour newscast.

Never have to leave the newsroom to report. While print reporters do have the advantage of conducting interviews over the phone, relying on them exclusively would limit the reporting and storytelling process. Good reporters in any medium spend time in the field seeking truth by interacting with people and observing.

Web journalists

Some perceive online news people as mysterious. They're off working in cyberspace with acronyms and code, i.e. HTML, JPEG, GIF, URL. Traditional journalists may assume the Web staff knows little about journalism because of their technical acumen. They may not trust them for their youth and inexperience. However, many Web editors and producers have come up through the ranks and have decades of news experience. These misconceptions should wane as Web staff are more fully integrated into converged news operations.

Laying our preconceptions on the table is the first step to forging a convergence relationship. When *The Tampa Tribune* and WFLA-TV began to explore a converged operation, they spent months in "prenuptial meetings," says Dan Bradley, Vice President of News for Media General Broadcast Division. Bradley was WFLA's news director at the time, and clearly recalls their first meeting in an unattractive back room near the printing presses. "Even the sandwiches we brought in weren't very good," says Bradley. The mediocre food and dreary environment set the stage for the leadership teams to talk about what made them uncomfortable about one another. Comments ranged from thinking television news spent more time promoting itself than it did at covering the news, to the newspaper's overemphasis on its design. Meetings continued a couple of days each month, for three to four months, giving key leaders time to define their core values. "We learned we may use different language," says Bradley (2003), "but if we stop and listen to each other we're actually talking about the same things."

Medium-Specific Approaches to News

The Arizona Republic partners with KPNX-TV in Phoenix and both contribute to the Web site azcentral.com. The newspaper shares its story budgets with the television station, and editors and producers talk with one another about breaking news and enterprise pieces. But, some basic differences in each medium's approach to news sometimes affect what stories the partners share. Tracy Collins, the *Republic's* deputy managing editor of planning and multimedia says, "We're a newspaper, and newspapers pride themselves on thoughtful stories loaded with context and told in narrative form when possible. Highly competitive TV news focuses everything on the headline and the human impact" (2003, Collins, cited in Finberg). As a result, says Collins, the television station often passes on a page-one story for a less prominent piece with a "more readily accessible human element." For example, the station chose to follow a story on a broken gas pipeline over an in-depth look at charter schools in Arizona. Even though the pipeline story had been breaking news a day earlier, says Collins (2003), "they felt it was a hotter-button item than the charter schools investigation."

The charter school story may not have conveyed a sense of urgency or immediacy, but the issue has far-reaching significance, because it affects every taxpayer in the state. The complexity of the story may scare away broadcasters, who must be able to tell their stories in a clear and accessible manner. But, that difficulty can make the storytelling a positive challenge, provided the television reporter isn't expected to turn around the story in one day. But because most broadcast newsrooms require their reporters to produce something for the air on a daily basis, a complex, issue-based story will likely get passed over for something that can be reported easily, such as a gas line break.

In some cases, newspapers may choose to hold a story for further reporting, which can frustrate the broadcasters' sense of urgency. Time sensitivity, in the form of short-term deadlines and story length, has a great impact on television news editorial choices. Take a thirty-minute news program and subtract eight minutes for commercials, five for sports and weather, a minute for teases, and another minute for the show open and close, and you're left with fifteen minutes for news. Some news holes are even shorter. This leaves precious little air time for each news story, running from twenty seconds to a few minutes at most. Consider also that broadcasters must quickly turn around their stories, sometimes rushing out to the field, interviewing, shooting and editing video, and then reporting live from the scene in an hour's time. Contrast this with the newspaper reporter who generally has a full day to report and write a story. Complex issues or investigations may take weeks or months to report. The Web is helping to bridge some of these differences, requiring give and take from each side. The newspaper writer faces earlier, if not continuous, deadlines on the Web, while the television counterpart can go into greater depth online.

Newsroom schedules

The clock by which newspaper, television, and Web journalists work can impede cooperation for convergence. A typical morning newspaper would have two shifts, dayside and nightside, with the staff on both contributing to one product. Television newsrooms may have one, two, or three shifts, depending on market size and number of news shows. Staff may contribute to several shows throughout their shifts, or just one, depending on the station. Web sites may be staffed round-the-clock, or just dayside, going to autopilot in the evening. These operating schedules can have an impact on the coordination among partners. To smooth these differences, some convergence operations have created new positions, which they may call the executive producer of content or multimedia manager. These key people work with partners to facilitate sharing and story development.

The Language of News

If a print editor tells a broadcaster to write a twenty-inch story, will that reporter know that means about 750 words, or two-and-a-half double-spaced
pages? Will a print reporter understand what a broadcast producer wants
when she says, "Get me a SOT?" Will print or broadcast reporters know what
a Web producer means when he asks for an extra or an interactive? Media-
specific language can flummox journalists when they cross platforms. Some
of the more common terminology for each medium follows.

Print terminology[1]

Above the fold: Material that appears on the front page, top half, of
   a broadsheet newspaper, so when folded and inserted into a vend-
   ing machine, appears in the window to catch the eye of
   passersby.
Banner: A headline that goes across the entire width (six columns) of a
   newspaper.
Bright: A light, upbeat story.
Broadsheet versus Tabloid: A broadsheet is the standard-sized U.S.
   newspaper, with a single page measuring about 17 by 22 inches. A
   tabloid's dimensions measure 11 by 17 inches, half the size of a
   broadsheet and twice that of a letter-sized page.
Budget: A list and short description of stories being worked on for the
   next day's paper.
Cuts/cutlines: Another name for a photo is a cut, and the caption underneath it is a cutline.
Deck: The headline that appears underneath the main head (subhead).
Double truck: A center page story that covers both pages with printing
   over the center fold.
Inches: Newspapers measure stories by inches. A broadsheet column
   typically measures 20 or 21 inches from top to bottom. A twenty-
   inch story is a medium-long newspaper story of about 700 words.
Jump: The place where text ends on one page and directs the reader to
   continue the story on another.
Head: Headline.
Nut graph: A paragraph that appears high up in a story that helps explain the significance of the story to the reader.
Set-up, curtain-raiser, or scene-setter: A story that runs the day before
   a big event.

Sidebar: A story that's related to another, longer piece. Sidebars are shorter, yet can stand on their own.

Strip: A story that runs across the full width of a newspaper page.

Weekender, or *think piece*: Newspapers showcase their best work on Sundays, so this type of story would be a longer analytical or interpretive piece to be run in the Sunday paper.

Broadcast terminology

Blocks: These are news program segments between commercial breaks. They're generally labeled the A-block, the B-block, et cetera.

B-roll: This is an old film term, which refers to the pictures shot for a story which were kept on a separate reel for playback. The A-roll, on the other hand, includes the interviews with sound and pictures. While still used in the industry, I advise my students to avoid it, because it tends to discount the importance of the visuals in a story.

CG, lower-third, or super: This is the text that appears on the lower-third of the screen, usually a name and title.

DMA: Designated market area. Nielsen Media Research defines the DMA, which is measured by the number of households in the station's broadcast reach.

Kicker: The light, usually happy piece that ends a newscast.

Ratings: A measurement of audience size. The amount of money a television station can charge for advertisements is based on ratings. Higher ratings equal higher fees, and more money for the station.

Rundown: A list of stories appearing in a television news program.

Story formats: Television stories take many forms, and reporters and producers must be familiar with this language to know what is expected of them. They follow here, from least to most complex.

AOC (ay-oh-SEE): Anchor on camera. This is a copy story that has no accompanying visual except for the anchor person who reads it on air. These stories generally run no longer than twenty or thirty seconds.

VO (VEE-oh): Voice over. This is an AOC with video. The anchor generally reads the story's first sentence on camera, and continues reading while the video appears on the screen.

SOT (ess-oh-TEE or saht): Sound on tape. The SOT is a piece of video that contains sound. It's usually a piece of an interview, or sound bite, that will be played for the audience to see and hear. The anchor person stops reading when a SOT is played.

VO-SOT (VOH-saht): Combination of a VO and an SOT.

Package: A pre-produced reporter story that contains the reporter's recorded narration, visuals, and sound.

Donut: A story that begins in studio with the anchor on camera, tosses to the reporter live in the field, who tosses to her pre-produced package, then goes back to the reporter who concludes the piece and tosses it back to the anchor person.

Sweeps: These are special Nielsen ratings periods. Stations often run series on high-interest topics during these periods to draw viewers.

Talent: News people who appear on the air, such as the anchors, reporters, and weathercasters.

Talking head: An almost painfully long shot of a person talking on camera.

Tease: A short promotion of what's to come in a newscast.

Wallpaper video: Shots that just fill space on air. A story about GPAs of women college students that simply shows wide shots of students walking on campus between classes is using wallpaper video.

Web terminology

Art the story: Adding graphics to the Web story.

Bitmap: Also called a raster image. These images map out the placement and color of each pixel in the file (Rey 2002). File formats for saving bitmap images include GIF, JPEG and TIFF. The image cannot be made larger or smaller without distortion.

Extras: Online content that goes above and beyond the story text. Extras can include graphics, maps, slide shows, video, audio, and more.

Flash: A software program for producing multimedia presentations. Flash can integrate text, audio, video, and graphics into interactive Web content.

Front (cover): The front page of an online news site.

HTML: HyperText Markup Language. The programming language for creating Web pages.

Interactives: Web content that allows the user to interact with it. Quizzes, slide shows, online polls, and clickable maps are examples of interactives.

Streaming video: Video that plays directly from the computer where it is stored, rather than having to be saved to the user's computer and played from it.

Slaying the Three-Headed Monster

The three-headed monster is a derogatory term for the journalist who must report for three media on a daily basis. Proponents, usually media managers, argue that the motivation to do so is story exposure. The say that if your report appears in the newspaper, on television, and on the Web, chances are more people will get to see it. But critics of this approach to news reporting say that the motivation is profit, and that the journalistic quality is going to suffer. "If you spend an hour doing three different things...that's time that you're not filling out your story, says Tracy Wood (2003), who reported cross-platform in Vietnam. "Very few just get whipped out. You can do it, but you'll have a superficial story."

How does a digital journalist deal with this situation? Some, frankly, are fighting it. The Washington-Baltimore Newspaper Guild writes of Web work at *The Washington Post* (2003) in an online bulletin, "the recent demand for more and more work, ever earlier in the day, strikes some of us as shamefully exploitative." Others are finding ways to share and collaborate, drawing from their own specializations. In Lawrence, Kansas, in a new, common newsroom, *The Lawrence Journal-World* and 6News Lawrence cover the issue of homelessness through online, print, and television reports. LJWorld.com streams a series of reports by 6News city hall reporter Jeff Golimowski. It also posts text stories by two *Journal-World* reporters and offers an audio slide show (ljworld.com, 2003). World Company owns all three partners, and offers financial rewards for journalists who contribute to convergence (Gentry 2003).

Journalists can facilitate convergence in many ways. For example, instead of having a print reporter write a thirty-second copy story for television on the three-hour school board meeting she attended, she can share key issues with the broadcast side. That way, they can develop the story properly for television, making a significant story interesting for the viewer through people and visuals. A television reporter may have a lengthy interview on tape that isn't fully exploited on air. Print and Web staff may be able to benefit from the interview in the form of story background or quotes. Video can be grabbed for still images, or still photos for Web slide shows. Contributing pieces of your reporting efforts to a converged pool where journalists can go for material to enhance their work is just as much convergence as is having a newspaper reporter appear on TV. Rather than having to do it all, all of the time, as a three-headed monster, enhance the converged relationship through sharing your specialization. In addition, apply your understanding and basic working knowledge of newspaper, Web, and television journalism to facilitate collaboration on larger projects.

Story Ownership

The Cincinnati Enquirer reporter James Pilcher had been wondering about the safety of the Brent Spence Bridge for some time. He'd seen numerous crashes as he crossed the bridge driving to or from work, and jumped on the story when he got wind that political leaders would be pushing to fund its improvement. Months of reporting and researching 800,000 bridge records led Pilcher to the discovery that the Brent Spence had the seventh-highest accident rate of fifteen bridges of its type nationwide. Pilcher wanted to develop the story for the Web, but hadn't considered including the company's television partner, WCPO. And when management suggested sharing the story with the television station, Pilcher (2003) says, he initially "didn't like the idea." It was his story, and he didn't know how it would be handled by TV. But when management said they were going to do it anyway, Pilcher said, "At that point I knew, why fight city hall? So, let's go for it." In his first meeting with WCPO reporter Tom McKee, Pilcher says, "We really hit it off." McKee assured Pilcher from the start that he and *The Enquirer* would get credit for the story, and, says Pilcher, "that made me feel a lot better about the process."

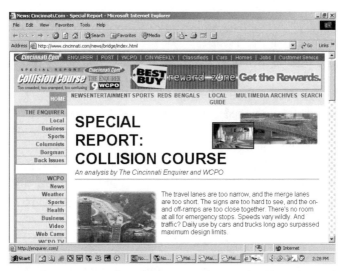

Figure 10.3 *The Cincinnati Enquirer* teamed up with WCPO to produce an in-depth report on bridge dangers. *Enquirer* reporter James Pilcher recommends early collaboration for the best results.

The willingness of a partner to fully credit reporters for their stories can make a difference when it comes to sharing work. Even better—collaborate earlier to assuage the feeling that the partner is copying your material. Working together in the early reporting stages can lead to a richer story. While McKee interviewed the same people Pilcher interviewed, the responses he got from subjects weren't all the same. For example, a police traffic investigator told McKee a compelling story about a man who lost a leg when he was hit by a car after his vehicle broke down on the bridge. Pilcher said he would have liked to include that account in his report, but didn't have it because the television interviews took place separately, and he didn't view their tapes.

Early collaboration can enhance the reporting process. But the willingness to share isn't a common value among journalists, who have traditionally been highly competitive. Media General's Bradley (2003) says story ownership is "one of the paradigms we have been trying to shift." When a WFLA television anchor got an exclusive interview with a man who had been suspected of murdering his wife and children, the company decided to break the story in *The Tampa Tribune* first. When the anchor learned of the plan, says Bradley, "She was beside herself. Quivering jaw, piercing eyes—if she had something in her hand she might have thrown it at me." But management decided it would be best to start the story in the newspaper, then run it on television, and finally, the Web. Bradley says the audience owns the story, and the greater the exposure, the better. In this case the anchorwoman did not get to run her television interview first. But the byline in *The Tampa Tribune* story credited her: "Gayle Sierens, of WFLA Newschannel 8." (Sierens 2000)

An open attitude toward sharing can enhance the converged newsroom working relationship. But while story ownership may be shifting, receiving credit for your work is still paramount. As we saw with the bridge story, the journalists involved got credit for the work they had done. The WFLA anchorwoman was also properly credited for her interview. On the Web, editors sometimes rewrite reporter stories, freshening the lead with an update, or expanding the pieces with further information. Newsroom treatment of the byline varies. Not crediting reporters may simply be an oversight. In our converged newsroom, a student recently rewrote another student's broadcast story for the Web, but did not include the original reporter's name in the byline. After noticing this, we decided to use a dual byline in such cases. Ignoring such details can lead to ill feelings, whereas recognizing and discussing them is the first step to smoothing potential resentment.

Crossing the Line

After you've worked months on an enterprise story and it's about to go up on the Web, you might like to introduce the piece on streaming video, so the Web user will know why you did the story and how you reported it. You may also want to talk about the issue on a partner's television news program. But will you be comfortable doing it? Or as a television reporter, you may have an opportunity to write a longer story for your partner newspaper. Will your sourcing and reporting transfer to the print format? And with either medium, can you find innovative ways to tell the story online, even if you just make a suggestion to a Web producer who will "magically" make it happen?

Understanding some basics about working in television, newspaper, and online news can help you expand your horizons beyond your specialization. In addition to what follows, Chapter 5 offers specifics on differences and similarities among media.

Interviewing for Broadcast

Some newsrooms provide audio recorders to print reporters to take with them into the field for recording interviews. In addition to assisting in note-taking, the recordings can be streamed over the Web when appropriate. But if the interviewee's sound will be used online, certain measures must be taken to ensure the quality of the recording.

1. Don't assume the built-in microphone will give you a usable recording. If the Web user can't hear the speaker because of a bad recording, it's not worth putting the sound on the Web. Test the built-in microphone ahead of time and have the Web producer put the test audio onto the computer system as CD-quality audio for playback. If the internal mike doesn't produce acceptable audio, a hand-held or lavaliere mike will be necessary. See Chapter 8 for specifics on using external microphones.

2. Watch out for your own reactions to the speaker's comments. You may be stepping over the subject's most important words with your, "Oh, really?" or, "That's amazing." Keep quiet until the speaker has finished his thought. And don't finish interviewees' sentences for them!

Going Live On Camera

You may know your story inside and out, but when the red camera light illuminates, signaling that you're on the air, your mind may go blank. Don't let this scare you. Instead, be prepared.

1. Go over in your mind ahead of time the first few things you're going to say. That way, you can look directly into the camera lens and convey confidence and trust. Before you even accept a television assignment, practice in front of a mirror until you feel comfortable with your appearance and delivery.
2. Jot down key facts on a notepad, so they're available if you need them. Under the lights and camera, you may momentarily lapse on a key figure's name—but if it's in your notes, you've got insurance.
3. Keep body movements to a minimum, without making yourself uncomfortable. Even a small swivel could put you out of frame or focus. So keep your chair still.
4. When you're finished talking, keep looking into the camera lens until given the "all clear."

Photojournalism

Photojournalist Roger Richards (2002) of *The Virginian-Pilot* newspaper crosses media boundaries in his daily work. His video essays and still images appear on the newspaper's Web site, requiring him to move between still and video journalism, so he's learned to approach each slightly differently:

> Still photography requires more of an instinct for "the moment." Video, though, demands carefully thought-out sequences. If you miss an element when shooting video it becomes difficult to properly edit a video essay. You also add another crucial element, gathering good sound.

Los Angeles Times senior photo editor Gail Fisher has also moved into the realm of video. Her award-winning multimedia project, "Ready or Not: Crashing Hard Into Adulthood," required more than a year in the field documenting the lives of former foster children. After getting access to her subjects, the next challenge was the videography. "Just because you have photo storytelling skills doesn't mean video is the same as still photography," says Fisher (2002). A Platypus workshop for still photojournalists gave her the foundation for the audiovisual medium. Fisher wanted the flexibility to publish still photos in the paper and also online, so she also shot still photos on film. "It was a balancing act," Fisher says. Carrying the camera gear, including a heavy tripod, added to the difficulties of following one of her subjects to Las Vegas, spending time in shelters and on the street. The time spent logging hours of tape and editing meant that her weekends merged into the work week.

Differences in reporting styles can surface when photographers and reporters work together in the field. For television crews, this is often learned early in careers, but when veterans of one medium begin working in another, they may find the differences startling. "Sometimes reporters want to go in and make small talk," says Fisher. "That's not the way I work. When I have my camera up to my face, you ignore me." Fisher says she's a purist when it comes to documenting someone's life. "If someone is drowning, I will save them, but I'm not going to change people living their lives."

Newsgathering for Print

Jackie Barron (2000) of WFLA-TV in Tampa, Florida, found she needed to adjust her reporting techniques when she covered a murder trial for *The Tampa Tribune*, and TBO.com, in addition to her television station.

I had to approach the story a little differently from the moment I took my seat in the courtroom. I wrote down every facial expression, described in detail who came in, who went out, what they wore, how the jurors reacted, how often the defendant scribbled notes to his attorneys, and when he smiled at his wife. The judge, who was prone to making jokes, became an element in my newspaper story.

Barron says the details that usually don't make it to air "came to life in print." And the extra color eventually carried over to her television stories. Barron found the importance of detail to *show* rather than *tell*. Moving away from reliance on the camera to show the viewer essential elements of the story is key in writing for print. Paint pictures with words. Instead of writing that the tailgate party was wild, show your readers by writing that the Buffalo Bills fans drank shots from a bowling ball.[2]

Also, while a single source may work for some television news stories, it rarely meets newspaper standards. Provide greater depth and meaning by interviewing multiple sources. And while it's often difficult to cite documents on the air, in print they are common, reliable sources of information.

Broadcast reporters discuss story ideas with assignment editors and producers, and before reporting have a general idea of the desired story format and length. Newspaper reporters do so with editors. It's important in both media to clarify the expectation. The television reporter will approach a forty-second VO differently from a three-minute package. A print brief of about five to six inches would require far less reporting than would a twenty-inch story. Calculate story length by using the following formula (Adapted from Carr 2004):

Number of inches $\times$ 32 = total number of words in a newspaper story
Number of words $\div$ 180 words per minute = total time for a
broadcast story

Another difference to expect in print is the level of editing. In some broadcast newsrooms, news managers review reporter scripts, but in many others, the copy is not edited. Print stories go through several levels of editing before running in the newspaper. Working with an editor to make changes is preferable to having the editor independently rework the story, but to meet deadlines, editors sometimes must take control. Making every effort to finish drafts for early review can help this process.

Online News

Keeping in mind that online storytelling involves an interactive, multimedia mindset can help reporters gather the information they need in the formats that will best tell their stories online. Mitchell Locin (2002) of the *Chicago Tribune* summed it up succinctly: "The best online storytelling allows the consumer to make choices, while still making sure that you as a journalist have the chance to tell the main thrust of the story that you think needs to be told." Revisit the preceding chapters in this book for specifics about online storytelling.

Activities for Further Learning

1. Visit a converged Web site and identify a story contributed by a partner (see the convergence tracker at http://americanpressinstitute. org/convergencetracker/search/). Discuss the story presentation, depth of reporting, completeness, and clarity. Does the story work well on the Web or does it belong in its own medium?

2. Meet with a small group of print, broadcast, and Web journalism students to discuss perceptions of one another's media and write a short paper on the discussion.
3. Collaborate on a story with a student journalist outside your media specialty.

References

API. 2004. Convergence tracker search page. http://americanpressinstitute.org/convergencetracker/search/

Barron, J. Winter 2000. Multimedia reporting in a never-ending news cycle. *Nieman Reports.* http://www.nieman.harvard.edu/reports/00-4NRwinter/NRwinter00.pdf

Bradley, D. Oct. 17, 2003. Telephone interview.

Bryan, S. Oct. 14, 2003. Personal interview.

Carr, F. 2004. The brave new world of multimedia convergence. In Tuggle, C. A., F. Carr, and S. Huffman. *Broadcast News Handbook.* Boston: McGraw-Hill.

cincinnati.com. 2003. http://www.cincinnati.com/news/bridge/

Castaneda, L. March 6, 2003. Teaching convergence. *Online Journalism Review.* http://www.ojr.org/ojr/education/p1046983385.php

Collins, T. Oct. 16, 2003. E-mail interview.

Collins, T. July 10, 2003. Cited in Finberg, H. I. How convergence works: Phoenix, Arizona. *Poynteronline.* http://poynter.org/content/content_view.asp?id=39587

Fisher, G. Nov. 6, 2002. Telephone interview.

Gentry, J. April 14, 2003. Convergence case study: LJWorld.com. http://americanpressinstitute.org/content/p777_c979.cfm?print=yes

ljworld.com. 2003. Homeless not hopeless. http://www.ljworld.com/section/homeless/

Locin, M. June 2002. Personal interview.

MacDonald, R. Oct. 13, 2003. Personal interview.

Pilcher, J. Oct. 8 and 9, 2003. Telephone interview.

Rey, C. 2002. *Macromedia Flash MX: Training from the Source.* Berkeley: Macromedia Press.

Richards, R. July 26, 2002. Cited in Tompkins, A. Triple threat: The convergence of Roger Richards. http://www.poynter.org/centerpiece/convergedvideo.htm

Sierens, G. Jan. 3, 2000. Man grieves over slain family. *The Tampa Tribune.* Retrieved from LexisNexis.

Washington Post Guild Unit. July 10, 2003. Bulletin. http://www.wbng.org/post/bulletins/2003/071003.html

Wood, T. Oct. 15, 2003. Telephone interview.

Notes

1. A special thanks to Pam Luecke, Reynolds Professor of Business Journalism at Washington and Lee University, for guidance on developing this list.
2. Colleague Bob de Maria shared this word picture which was sent to him in an e-mail by W&L alum Brendan Harrington, who witnessed the event.

Glossary

3G   Third-generation wireless technology. Mobile communication networks using high-speed data transmission for applications that go beyond voice, including Internet access, video streaming, and video conferencing.

Analog   Technology that transmits information in a continuous electronic signal. An analog recording replicates a signal onto a recording medium, whereas a digital recording makes a sample of the signal and converts it to ones and zeros.

ArcView   Computer mapping software using GIS (Geographic Information System) for visual and special representation.

Aspect ratio   The width-to-height relationship of an image. It's important to maintain an image's aspect ratio to avoid distortion when manipulating its size.

Avid   Digital video editing software and systems.

Bandwidth   The capacity of a communication channel to carry data. The higher the bandwidth, the greater the amount of information that can be sent in a given time. Whereas a dial-up modem can carry about 56 kilobytes of data per second, high bandwidth Internet connections carry 28 times that, at 1,581 kilobytes per second.

Bit   Binary digit. The smallest unit of information in digital technology. Its value of zero or one represents off or on.

Bitmap/BMP   Digital image made up of pixels that form a pattern.

Blog   From "Web log." A journal in the form of a Web site, which is frequently updated, with postings in reverse-chronological order.

Broadband   A data transmission medium capable of carrying multiple high-speed signals.

Byte   A unit of computer code consisting of eight bits.

CD-RW   A compact disc that allows the user to both record and rewrite data. Also refers to the computer drive that facilitates this process.

Convergence   Cooperation among broadcast, print, and online journalists to tell stories effectively in appropriate media to a wide-reaching audience.

Cyberspace   The world of computer networks and the people who use them. Writer William Gibson created the term, using it in his science-fiction novel, *Neuromancer,* in 1984.

Digital   Information encoding using a binary system of zeroes and ones.

DSL   Digital subscriber line. Technology that provides high-speed Internet access through ordinary telephone lines.

EDL   Edit decision list. During digital editing, the user is creating an EDL with each edit, which specifies all the particulars pertaining to each edit—for example, exactly where the video begins and ends, if audio is included, if a graphic is included, etc. This data file can then be used to render the project into a finished video.

Excel   A spreadsheet software program by Microsoft.

Flash   A software program for producing multimedia presentations. Flash can integrate text, audio, video, and graphics into interactive Web content.

GB   Gigabyte. Approximately 1 billion bytes (1,024 MB).

Google   An Internet search engine that allows the user to find Web pages that contain specified words.

HTML   Hypertext markup language. Computer code used to create Web documents.

Image grabbing   Converting a single image frame from a video to a digital image, or copying and saving a digital image off the Web.

Ingest   Transferring digital data from a recording device to a computer. Also, sometimes called recording.

JPEG   Joint photographic experts group. A digital image format that compresses data for smaller file size. Most appropriate for color photos.

LCD   Liquid crystal display. Technology used in digital displays, such as clocks and laptop computer and digital camera monitors.

Legacy media   Traditional forms of media such as newspapers, television networks, magazines, and books.

Link   A word, line of text, image, or area on a Web page that directs the user to another Web location when clicked on. Links are usually highlighted or underlined for easy identification.

MB   Megabyte. Approximately 1 million bytes.

MiniDisc   A digital recording medium that measures 2.5 inches square. This rewritable disc stores 74 minutes of audio.

Photoshop   A popular photo editing software program.

Pixel   Picture element. The smallest graphic unit of a digital image.

Repurposing   Taking content produced for one medium and using it in another.

Screen shot/screen capture   Saving a full-screen image off a computer monitor. To do so, press the "print screen" key, and copy into an image processing program, such as "Paint."

Semantic   Having to do with meaning in language.

Semiotics   The study of symbols and signs, and their meaning.

Sound bite   A portion of a recorded interview used in an electronic news story. Its equivalent in print is a quote.

Storyboard   A series of sketches or frames used to plan multimedia presentations.

Streaming   Technology that allows data to be transmitted continually, in a stream. Streaming video or audio can be played directly from the computer where it is stored, rather than having to be saved to and played from the user's computer.

Technological determinism   The belief that technology is the major force causing historical change.

URL   Uniform resource locator. A Web site address.

Web producer   A journalist who is responsible for choosing and presenting content for a news Web site.

World Wide Web   An Internet-based system for global information sharing, invented by Tim Berners-Lee. The Web is not synonymous with the Internet.

Appendix

Code of Ethics and Professional Conduct

Radio-Television News Directors Association

Reprinted with permission of the Radio-Television News Directors Association, Washington, D.C.

The Radio-Television News Directors Association, wishing to foster the highest professional standards of electronic journalism, promote public understanding of and confidence in electronic journalism, and strengthen principles of journalistic freedom to gather and disseminate information, establishes this Code of Ethics and Professional Conduct.

PREAMBLE
Professional electronic journalists should operate as trustees of the public, seek the truth, report it fairly and with integrity and independence, and stand accountable for their actions.

PUBLIC TRUST: Professional electronic journalists should recognize that their first obligation is to the public.
   Professional electronic journalists should:

- Understand that any commitment other than service to the public undermines trust and credibility.
- Recognize that service in the public interest creates an obligation to reflect the diversity of the community and guard against oversimplification of issues or events.

- Provide a full range of information to enable the public to make enlightened decisions.
- Fight to ensure that the public's business is conducted in public.

TRUTH: Professional electronic journalists should pursue truth aggressively and present the news accurately, in context, and as completely as possible.
Professional electronic journalists should:

- Continuously seek the truth.
- Resist distortions that obscure the importance of events.
- Clearly disclose the origin of information and label all material provided by outsiders.

Professional electronic journalists should not:

- Report anything known to be false.
- Manipulate images or sounds in any way that is misleading.
- Plagiarize.
- Present images or sounds that are reenacted without informing the public.

FAIRNESS: Professional electronic journalists should present the news fairly and impartially, placing primary value on significance and relevance.
Professional electronic journalists should:

- Treat all subjects of news coverage with respect and dignity, showing particular compassion to victims of crime or tragedy.
- Exercise special care when children are involved in a story and give children greater privacy protection than adults.
- Seek to understand the diversity of their community and inform the public without bias or stereotype.
- Present a diversity of expressions, opinions, and ideas in context.
- Present analytical reporting based on professional perspective, not personal bias.
- Respect the right to a fair trial.

INTEGRITY: Professional electronic journalists should present the news with integrity and decency, avoiding real or perceived conflicts of interest, and respect the dignity and intelligence of the audience as well as the subjects of news.

Professional electronic journalists should:

- Identify sources whenever possible. Confidential sources should be used only when it is clearly in the public interest to gather or convey important information or when a person providing information might be harmed. Journalists should keep all commitments to protect a confidential source.
- Clearly label opinion and commentary.
- Guard against extended coverage of events or individuals that fails to significantly advance a story, place the event in context, or add to the public knowledge.
- Refrain from contacting participants in violent situations while the situation is in progress.
- Use technological tools with skill and thoughtfulness, avoiding techniques that skew facts, distort reality, or sensationalize events.
- Use surreptitious newsgathering techniques, including hidden cameras or microphones, only if there is no other way to obtain stories of significant public importance and only if the technique is explained to the audience.
- Disseminate the private transmissions of other news organizations only with permission.

Professional electronic journalists should not:

- Pay news sources who have a vested interest in a story.
- Accept gifts, favors, or compensation from those who might seek to influence coverage.
- Engage in activities that may compromise their integrity or independence.

INDEPENDENCE: Professional electronic journalists should defend the independence of all journalists from those seeking influence or control over news content.

Professional electronic journalists should:

- Gather and report news without fear or favor, and vigorously resist undue influence from any outside forces, including advertisers, sources, story subjects, powerful individuals, and special interest groups.

- Resist those who would seek to buy or politically influence news content or who would seek to intimidate those who gather and disseminate the news.
- Determine news content solely through editorial judgment and not as the result of outside influence.
- Resist any self-interest or peer pressure that might erode journalistic duty and service to the public.
- Recognize that sponsorship of the news will not be used in any way to determine, restrict, or manipulate content.
- Refuse to allow the interests of ownership or management to influence news judgment and content inappropriately.
- Defend the rights of the free press for all journalists, recognizing that any professional or government licensing of journalists is a violation of that freedom.

ACCOUNTABILITY: Professional electronic journalists should recognize that they are accountable for their actions to the public, the profession, and themselves.

Professional electronic journalists should:

- Actively encourage adherence to these standards by all journalists and their employers.
- Respond to public concerns. Investigate complaints and correct errors promptly and with as much prominence as the original report.
- Explain journalistic processes to the public, especially when practices spark questions or controversy.
- Recognize that professional electronic journalists are duty-bound to conduct themselves ethically.
- Refrain from ordering or encouraging courses of action that would force employees to commit an unethical act.
- Carefully listen to employees who raise ethical objections and create environments in which such objections and discussions are encouraged.
- Seek support for and provide opportunities to train employees in ethical decision-making.

In meeting its responsibility to the profession of electronic journalism, RTNDA has created this code to identify important issues, to serve as a guide for its members, to facilitate self-scrutiny, and to shape future debate.

Adopted at RTNDA2000 in Minneapolis September 14, 2000.

Society of Professional Journalists

Reproduced with permission of the Society of Professional Journalists.

Preamble

Members of the Society of Professional Journalists believe that public enlightenment is the forerunner of justice and the foundation of democracy. The duty of the journalist is to further those ends by seeking truth and providing a fair and comprehensive account of events and issues. Conscientious journalists from all media and specialties strive to serve the public with thoroughness and honesty. Professional integrity is the cornerstone of a journalist's credibility. Members of the Society share a dedication to ethical behavior and adopt this code to declare the Society's principles and standards of practice.

Seek Truth and Report It

Journalists should be honest, fair and courageous in gathering, reporting and interpreting information.

Journalists should:

- Test the accuracy of information from all sources and exercise care to avoid inadvertent error. Deliberate distortion is never permissible.
- Diligently seek out subjects of news stories to give them the opportunity to respond to allegations of wrongdoing.
- Identify sources whenever feasible. The public is entitled to as much information as possible on sources' reliability.
- Always question sources' motives before promising anonymity. Clarify conditions attached to any promise made in exchange for information. Keep promises.
- Make certain that headlines, news teases and promotional material, photos, video, audio, graphics, sound bites and quotations do not misrepresent. They should not oversimplify or highlight incidents out of context.
- Never distort the content of news photos or video. Image enhancement for technical clarity is always permissible. Label montages and photo illustrations.
- Avoid misleading re-enactments or staged news events. If re-enactment is necessary to tell a story, label it.
- Avoid undercover or other surreptitious methods of gathering information except when traditional open methods will not yield information vital to the public. Use of such methods should be explained as part of the story.

- Never plagiarize.
- Tell the story of the diversity and magnitude of the human experience boldly, even when it is unpopular to do so.
- Examine their own cultural values and avoid imposing those values on others.
- Avoid stereotyping by race, gender, age, religion, ethnicity, geography, sexual orientation, disability, physical appearance or social status.
- Support the open exchange of views, even views they find repugnant.
- Give voice to the voiceless; official and unofficial sources of information can be equally valid.
- Distinguish between advocacy and news reporting. Analysis and commentary should be labeled and not misrepresent fact or context.
- Distinguish news from advertising and shun hybrids that blur the lines between the two.
- Recognize a special obligation to ensure that the public's business is conducted in the open and that government records are open to inspection.

Minimize Harm

Ethical journalists treat sources, subjects and colleagues as human beings deserving of respect.

Journalists should:

- Show compassion for those who may be affected adversely by news coverage. Use special sensitivity when dealing with children and inexperienced sources or subjects.
- Be sensitive when seeking or using interviews or photographs of those affected by tragedy or grief.
- Recognize that gathering and reporting information may cause harm or discomfort. Pursuit of the news is not a license for arrogance.
- Recognize that private people have a greater right to control information about themselves than do public officials and others who seek power, influence or attention. Only an overriding public need can justify intrusion into anyone's privacy.
- Show good taste. Avoid pandering to lurid curiosity.
- Be cautious about identifying juvenile suspects or victims of sex crimes.

- Be judicious about naming criminal suspects before the formal filing of charges.
- Balance a criminal suspect's fair trial rights with the public's right to be informed.

Act Independently
Journalists should be free of obligation to any interest other than the public's right to know.

Journalists should:

- Avoid conflicts of interest, real or perceived.
- Remain free of associations and activities that may compromise integrity or damage credibility.
- Refuse gifts, favors, fees, free travel and special treatment, and shun secondary employment, political involvement, public office and service in community organizations if they compromise journalistic integrity.
- Disclose unavoidable conflicts.
- Be vigilant and courageous about holding those with power accountable.
- Deny favored treatment to advertisers and special interests and resist their pressure to influence news coverage.
- Be wary of sources offering information for favors or money; avoid bidding for news.

Be Accountable
Journalists are accountable to their readers, listeners, viewers and each other.

Journalists should:

- Clarify and explain news coverage and invite dialogue with the public over journalistic conduct.
- Encourage the public to voice grievances against the news media.
- Admit mistakes and correct them promptly.
- Expose unethical practices of journalists and the news media.
- Abide by the same high standards to which they hold others.

The SPJ Code of Ethics is voluntarily embraced by thousands of writers, editors and other news professionals. The present version of the code was adopted by the 1996 SPJ National Convention, after months of study and debate among the Society's members.

Index